Communications in Computer and Information Science 719

Commenced Publication in 2007
Founding and Former Series Editors:
Alfredo Cuzzocrea, Dominik Ślęzak, and Xiaokang Yang

Editorial Board

More information about this series at http://www.springer.com/series/7899

Lynn Batten · Dong Seong Kim
Xuyun Zhang · Gang Li (Eds.)

Applications and Techniques in Information Security

8th International Conference, ATIS 2017
Auckland, New Zealand, July 6–7, 2017
Proceedings

 Springer

Editors
Lynn Batten ⓘ
School of Information Technology
Deakin University
Geelong, VIC
Australia

Dong Seong Kim ⓘ
University of Canterbury
Christchurch
New Zealand

Xuyun Zhang ⓘ
The University of Auckland
Auckland
New Zealand

Gang Li ⓘ
Deakin University
Geelong, VIC
Australia

ISSN 1865-0929   ISSN 1865-0937 (electronic)
Communications in Computer and Information Science
ISBN 978-981-10-5420-4   ISBN 978-981-10-5421-1 (eBook)
DOI 10.1007/978-981-10-5421-1

Library of Congress Control Number: 2017944321

This Springer imprint is published by Springer Nature
The registered company is Springer Nature Singapore Pte Ltd.
The registered company address is: 152 Beach Road, #21-01/04 Gateway East, Singapore 189721, Singapore

Preface

The present volume contains the proceedings of the 8th International Conference on Applications and Techniques in Information Security (ATIS 2017). ATIS has been held annually since 2010. This year, the eighth in the series was held at Massey University, Auckland, New Zealand, during July 6–7, 2017.

The scope of ATIS includes all the areas of information security from cryptography to system security, network security, and various applications. ATIS provides a valuable connection between the theoretical and the implementation communities attracting participants from industry, academia, and government organizations.

This year, ATIS 2017 received 29 submissions. Each paper was reviewed by at least three reviewers. Following this independent review, there were discussions among reviewers and program co-chairs. A total of 14 papers were selected as full papers, and another four papers were selected as short papers.

We would like to express our appreciation to all the people who participated in the development of the ATIS 2017 program. The general organization of the conference also relied on the efforts of the ATIS 2017 Organizing Committee. We would like to thank Julian Jang-Jaccard for the local arrangements and her kind help in providing such a nice venue at Massey University. We especially thank Judy Chow, Julian Jang-Jaccard, Mehmood Baryalai, and Jodi Bubeck for the general administrative issues, the registration process, and the maintenance of the conference website. We would give special thanks to the Program Committee and external reviewers, for their hard work in reviewing papers and providing their detailed and valuable feedback to the authors. We would like to thank all the participants of this conference. Finally and most importantly, we thank all the authors, who are the primary reason why ATIS 2017 was so exciting, and why it was the premier forum for presentation and discussion of innovative ideas, research results, applications, and experience from around the world as well as for highlighting activities in the related areas. Because of your great work, ATIS 2017 was a great success.

May 2017

Lynn Batten
Dong Seong Kim
Xuyun Zhang
Gang Li

Organization

ATIS 2017 was organized by the School of Information Technology, Deakin University, Australia, and the Institute of Natural and Mathematical Sciences, Massey University, New Zealand.

Steering Committee

Lynn Batten (Chair)	Deakin University, Australia
Heejo Lee	Korea University, South Korea
Gang Li	Secretary, Deakin University, Australia
Jiqiang Liu	Beijing Jiaotong University, China
Tsutomu Matsumoto	Yokohama National University, Japan
Wenjia Niu	Chinese Academy of Sciences, China
Yuliang Zheng	University of Alabama at Birmingham, USA

Organizing Committee

General Chair

Gang Li	Deakin University, Australia

Organizing Committee

Lynn Batten	Deakin University, Australia
Judy Chow	Deakin University, Australia

Program Co-chairs

Dong Seong Kim	University of Canterbury, New Zealand
Xuyun Zhang	University of Auckland, New Zealand

Local Organizing Committee Chair

Julian Jang-Jaccard	Massey University, New Zealand

Web Chair

Mehmood Baryalai	Massey University, New Zealand

Program Committee

Abdulrahman Alarifi	King AbdulAziz City for Science and Technology, Saudi Arabia
Lynn Batten	Deakin University, Australia
Guoyong Cai	Guilin University of Electronic Technology, China

Yanan Cao	Chinese Academy of Science, China
Rohan DeSilva	Central Queensland University, Australia
Jin B. Hong	University of Canterbury, New Zealand
Dong Seong Kim	University of Canterbury, New Zealand
Kwangjo Kim	KAIST, South Korea
Jie Kong	Xi'an Shiyou University, China
Gang Li	Deakin University, Australia
Qingyun Liu	Chinese Academy of Sciences, China
Shaowu Liu	Deakin University, Australia
Wenjia Niu	Chinese Academy of Sciences, China
Eiji Okamoto	University of Tsukuba, Japan
Lei Pan	Deakin University, Australia
Deepak Puthal	University of Technology Sydney, Australia
Lianyong Qi	Qufu Normal University, China
Wei Ren	China University of Geosciences, China
Jinqiao Shi	Chinese Academy of Sciences, China
Zhongzhi Shi	Chinese Academy of Sciences, China
Dirk Thatmann	Technical University Berlin, Germany
Hongtao Wang	Chinese Academy of Sciences, China
Jinlong Wang	Qingdao University of Technology, China
Gang Xiong	Chinese Academy of Sciences, China
Ping Xiong	Zhongnan University of Economics and Law, China
Ziqi Yan	Beijing Jiaotong University, China
Xuyun Zhang	University of Auckland, New Zealand
Yuan Zhang	Nanjing University, China
Sheng Zhong	Nanjing University, China
Yongbin Zhou	Chinese Academy of Sciences, China
Tianqing Zhu	Wuhan University of Technology, China
Tingshao Zhu	Chinese Academy of Sciences, China

Additional Reviewers

Chi Yang
Lefeng Zhang
Matthew Ruffell
Mehmood Baryalai
Mengmeng Ge

Muhan Erza Aminanto
Seongmo An
Simon Enoch Yusuf
Suhan Kim
Tae Hoon Eom

Sponsoring Institutions

Beijing Jiatong University, China
Chinese Academy of Sciences, China
Deakin University, Australia
Massey University, New Zealand

Keynote Speeches

Identity of Things: Nano Artifact Metrics Using Silicon Random Nanostructures

Tsutomu Matsumoto

Yokohama National University, Yokohama, Japan
`tsutomu@ynu.ac.jp`

Abstract. Nano-artifact metrics exploit unique physical attributes of nanostructured matter for authentication and clone resistance, which is vitally important in the age of Internet-of-Things where securing identities is critical. We demonstrate nano-artifact metrics based on silicon nanostructures formed via an array of electron-beam-lithography resist pillars that randomly collapse. There are several ways to utilize such nanostructures. Our first system [1] is based on scanning electron microscopy to capture the nanostructure having extremely fine-scale morphology with a minimum dimension below 10 nm, which is less than the resolution of current lithography capabilities. Although an expensive and huge experimental apparatuses is required, the system has remarkable accuracy with respect to false non-match, false match and clone-match rates.

Our second system [2] adopts an optical approach to characterize the nanoscale-precision signatures of silicon random structures towards realizing low-cost and high-value information security technology. Unique and versatile silicon nanostructures are generated via resist collapse phenomena, which contains dimensions that are well below the diffraction limit of light. We exploit the nanoscale precision ability of confocal laser microscopy in the height dimension; our experimental results demonstrate that the vertical precision of measurement is essential in satisfying the performances required for artifact metrics. Furthermore, by using state-of the-art nanostructuring technology, we experimentally fabricate clones from the genuine devices. We demonstrate that the statistical properties of the genuine and clone devices can be successfully exploited in artificially-constructed solid-state nanostructures. These findings pave the way for reasonable and yet sufficiently secure novel principles for hardware security based on silicon random nanostructures.

References

1. Matsumoto, T., et al.: Nano-artifact metrics based on random collapse of resist. Sci. Rep. **4**, 6142 (2014). doi:10.1038/srep06142
2. Matsumoto, T., et al.: Optical nano artifact metrics using silicon random nanostructures. Sci. Rep. **6**, 32438 (2016). doi:10.1038/srep32438

Five Decades of Software Obfuscation:
A Retrospective

Clark Thomborson

Computer Science Department, University of Auckland,
Auckland, New Zealand
cthombor@cs.auckland.ac.nz

Abstract. We romp through the history of software obfuscation, providing non-technical explanations of key events in each decade. In the 1970s, obfuscation was an elite sport played by overly-clever programmers who hid undocumented features in system software. In the 1980s, obfuscation was a competitive sport in The International Obfuscated C Code Contest, and white-hat analyst Fred Cohen designed self-obfuscating viruses which would evade detection. In the 1990s, obfuscation was a dark-side tool for malware designers, and white-hat inventors produced patentable art for use in the commercial sector. The 2000s was a decade of consolidation: some potent obfuscation methods were released in an open-source software suite, the first commercial vendor of obfuscation services became profitable, and Boaz Barak received a Turing Award for proving that a general-purpose software obfuscator cannot exist. In this decade, most smartphone apps are lightly obfuscated, and obfuscation theorists are hoping to construct a provably-secure restricted-purpose obfuscation method.

Contents

Malware and Malicious Events Detection

System and Network Security

Crypto Algorithms and Applications

Defeating Plausible Deniability of VeraCrypt Hidden Operating Systems

Michal Kedziora[1]([✉]), Yang-Wai Chow[2], and Willy Susilo[2]

[1] Faculty of Computer Science and Management,
Wroclaw University of Science and Technology, Wroclaw, Poland
michal.kedziora@pwr.edu.pl
[2] School of Computing and Information Technology,
Institute of Cybersecurity and Cryptology, University of Wollongong,
Wollongong, Australia
{caseyc,wsusilo}@uow.edu.au

Abstract. This paper analyzes the security of VeraCrypt hidden operating systems. We present attacks on the plausible deniability attribute of hidden Operating Systems (OSs) created using VeraCrypt. We demonstrate that the encrypted outer volume can contain information that compromises the existence of a hidden OS, and the fact that it was running, even if only one copy of the encrypted drive is examined. To further investigate this, we show that cross drive analysis, previously used to analyze deniable file systems, can also be applied to prove the presence of a hidden OS volume and to estimate its size. In addition, we discuss other attack vectors that can be exploited in relation to cloud and network information leaks. This paper also examines the security requirements of a threat model in which the attacker has direct access to a running hidden OS.

Keywords: Deniable file system · Hidden operation system · Plausible deniability · TrueCrypt · VeraCrypt

1 Introduction

A hidden Operating System (OS) is an operating system installed in an encrypted hidden volume, using software such as VeraCrypt. The assumption is that it should be impossible to prove that a hidden volume exists, and therefore impossible to prove that a hidden operating system exists. This concept is known as plausible deniability, as the existence of the hidden volume cannot be proven. This feature was implemented in TrueCrypt/VeraCrypt software as an extension of Deniable File Systems (DFSs) [10], and is based on deniable encryption which was introduced by Canetti [2,11].

One notion of deniable encryption is the ability to decrypt a ciphertext into two different plaintexts depending on the key that is provided. An additional property is to ensure that the adversary cannot detect that a hidden message is present in the ciphertext. The purpose of this is to protect against adversaries

© Springer Nature Singapore Pte Ltd. 2017
L. Batten et al. (Eds.): ATIS 2017, CCIS 719, pp. 3–13, 2017.
DOI: 10.1007/978-981-10-5421-1_1

who are able to force the user to provide a password to decrypt the content, as the password that is provided will only reveal the decoy message/data while keeping the true message/data hidden.

Plausible deniability is implemented in TrueCrypt/VeraCrypt via its ability to create hidden volumes and hidden operating systems. VeraCrypt was developed based on the original TrueCrypt project. VeraCrypt uses XTS mode for encrypting partitions, drives and virtual volumes [11]. This mode of operation is described by Eq. 1; where $\otimes$ denotes multiplication of two polynomials over the binary field $GF(2)$ modulo $x^{128} + x^7 + x^2 + 1$; $K1$ is the encryption key; $K2$ is the secondary encryption key; i is the cipher block index within a data unit; n is the data unit index within the scope of $K1$; and a is the primitive element of Galois Field (2^{128}) that corresponds to polynomial x [11]. This implies that a change in one bit of the plaintext will result in a change to the entire 8-bytes (128 bits) data block of the encrypted volume.

$$C_i = E_{K1}(P_i \char`^(E_{K2}(n) \otimes a^i))\char`^(E_{K2}(n) \otimes a^i) \tag{1}$$

The VeraCrypt documentation provides a guide on how to encrypt a hidden OS [11]. A practical implementation consists of two partitions and a boot loader residing in the first track of a system drive (or a VeraCrypt RescueDisk). However, this is not a smart solution as the unencrypted boot loader will indicate that the drive is encrypted by VeraCrypt. To overcome this issue there is an option to create a VeraCrypt rescue disk containing the boot loader, as depicted in Fig. 1. This will provide plausible deniability as a decoy OS can be created. Obviously, the system installed on the first partition must not contain any sensitive files.

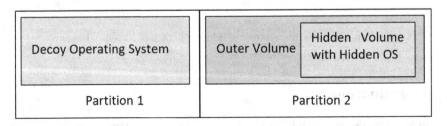

Fig. 1. Layout of a drive containing a hidden operating system.

The second partition is also encrypted and can be mounted by the user upon supplying the second password. The outer volume contains an integrated hidden volume within which the hidden OS is installed. Existence of the hidden volume, which is a DFS, cannot be proven via One-Time Access methods (described in Sect. 2). To access the hidden OS, the user must provide the valid password that is different from the decoy OS volume's password. The boot loader will first try to decrypt the decoy OS's header, and after it is unsuccessful, it will then attempt to decrypt the hidden OS's header. What is important is that when running, the hidden OS will appear to be installed on the same partition as the decoy OS. All read/write operations will be transparently redirected from the system partition to the hidden volume inside the outer volume. The VeraCrypt documentation asserts that neither the OS nor any application programs will know that all data is essentially written to and read from the hidden volume [11]. In this paper, we demonstrate that the above statement is not entirely true, as the presence of the hidden OS can in fact be revealed.

Our Contribution. In this paper, we analyze the security of VeraCrypt hidden OSs. While this software allow for plausible deniability via the creation of hidden OSs, we demonstrate that the encrypted outer volume can contain information that compromises the existence of a hidden OS. Our results are presented from the point of view of a new threat model incorporating One-Time Access, Multiple Access and Live Response Access scenarios. This paper presents experiment results showing that the VeraCrypt hidden OS implementation has faults that can be exploited to compromise the hidden OS even if an attacker only possess one binary copy of the drive. In addition, we show that it is vulnerable to cross drive analysis, which can be used to estimate the size of the hidden OS. Furthermore, this paper discusses other types of attacks that can be conducted to reveal the existence of a hidden OS on a device based on the Live Response Access scenario.

2 Threat Model

This work is based on our previously improved threat model for the security analysis of Deniable File Systems (DFSs) and hidden Operating Systems (OSs) [9]. This new model is an improvement on the model proposed by Czeskis et al. [3], as it addresses the flaws and inconsistencies in the previous model. The improved threat model is depicted in Fig. 2, in which the attack vectors are defined by One-Time Access, Multiple Access and Live Response Access scenarios. Compare with the previous model, this new model is much more practical and suitable for assessing the security of hidden OSs.

The One-Time Access scenario is a situation where an investigator has managed to obtain one or more copies of a device containing only a single copy of the drive containing a hidden OS [3]. Attack vectors based on this model have been presented in related work [4,6,7]. However, most of these findings are based on detecting DFSs, but cannot be applied to detecting hidden OSs. This is because in the case of hidden OSs, the entire drive is encrypted, thus, reducing the potential sources of information leaks that can compromise the hidden volume.

In a Multiple Access scenario, an investigator has access to multiple device images containing multiple hidden encrypted containers. The main threat to DFSs in this scenario lies in possibility of differential analysis for detecting hidden volumes, as this results in the ability to attack the plausible deniability attribute. This issue was raised in Czeskis et al. [3], where they highlighted that if disk snapshots could be obtained at close enough intervals, then the existence of any

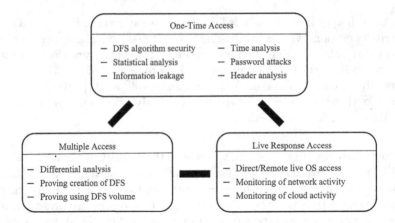

Fig. 2. Threat model and attack vectors on deniable file systems and hidden operating systems.

deniable files would become obvious. This is due to the fact that examination using differential analysis can reveal that seemingly random bytes on the hard drive will change in a non-random fashion. This was practically demonstrated by Hargreaves and Chivers [6], and research on detecting the creation of DFSs inside an encrypted container have been presented in Jozwiak [8].

The Live Response Access model is the model that is most suitable for detecting a hidden OS. Examples of such a scenario is when an investigator has direct live access to a DFS based hidden OS, or has access to the network environment within which a hidden OS is operating, or has access to cloud applications in which a hidden OS is connected to. A typically situation will involve an investigator remotely logging into a system containing a hidden OS using live response tools or just using standard remote access software like Team Viewer or VNC. Live response and memory analysis tools have the capabilities of collecting information from network connections, open ports and sockets, running processes, terminated processes, loaded DLLs, open files, OS kernel modules, process dumps, strings or user logs [12].

3   Defeating Deniability of Hidden Operating Systems

In this section, we present practical attacks on the deniability of hidden Operating Systems (OSs). For this, a test environment was created using Oracle Virtual Box version 5.1.12. A hard drive image size of 50GB was created. However, since the virtual box operates using the vdi file format with included metadata, its image had to be converted to a binary RAW format before analysis using computer forensic tools. Both the decoy and hidden OS (MS Windows 10) where installed using VeraCrypt 1.19. The designed layout of partitions is depicted in Table 1.

Table 1. Layout of the test environment.

Partition	Starting sector	Last sector	Size (MB)
/dev/sda1	2048	1026047	500
/dev/sda2	1026047	43530239	20270
/dev/sda3	43532225	104855551	29240
/dev/sda5	43532288	1048553551	29240
Unallocated	104855552	104857599	1

The first partition, /dev/sda1, was for the Windows Recovery Environment (WinRE) and was unencrypted. The second partition, /dev/sda2, was the one on which the decoy operating system was installed; the whole partition was encrypted. /dev/sda3 was the extended partition that hosts the /dev/sda5/ partition, which was the completely encrypted outer volume; the hidden OS was installed within this partition. As the hidden OS was contained within the encrypted hidden volume, which was located inside the encrypted outer volume, plausible deniability necessitates that it should be impossible to prove the existence of this hidden OS. However, in the next section, we show that plausible deniability of the VeraCrypt hidden OS is not met even in the simplest threat model scenario.

3.1 Encrypted Drive Analysis

First, we investigated the possibility of defeating plausible deniability of a VeraCrypt hidden OS under the most basic thread scenario, i.e. the One-Time Access scenario. An example of such a scenario is when Alice's computer is seized by police, who force Alice to reveal the password of the encrypted partitions. Alice reveals the password for the decoy OS and for the outer volume. According to the plausible deniability attribute of the VeraCrypt hidden OS, the police should not be able to prove that Alice has a hidden OS installed on the computer, as it is stored in an encrypted hidden volume inside the encrypted outer volume.

A VeraCrypt hidden OS requires a special uncommon disk layout consisting of at least two partitions that are both completely encrypted. This information, in conjunction with the fact that VeraCrypt is installed on the computer under investigation, can potentially raise the suspicion of the police to the presence of a hidden OS. Nevertheless, this can reasonably be explained by Alice as the need to separate the system and documents into separate partitions. However, any solid indication that a hidden OS is installed on the computer under investigation is sufficient to defeat plausible deniability.

We conducted randomness testing to check for artifacts in the outer volume. The reason for this is because if a hidden OS is running inside a completely encrypted hidden volume that is located within an outer volume, which is also completely encrypted, no pseudo-random anomalies should be found.

When we performed entropy analysis on the outer volume, it showed that most of the examined data had values between 7.9978 and 7.9986, which represent expected values from correctly encrypted cipher text data. However, we were able to observe some unexpected values in specific sectors that were occupied by the outer volume. In particular, there were two areas which clearly showed significantly lower entropy values of 7.9966 and 7.997, as can be seen in the plot provided in Fig. 3.

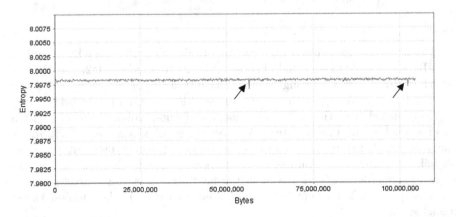

Fig. 3. Areas with significantly lower entropy inside the outer encrypted volume.

The first of these observed areas was located in sector number 61345696, and the second was located 45928448 bytes later in sector number 61435400. Both of these sectors are located within the /dev/sda5 partition, which was within the completely encrypted outer volume. The hidden volume hosting the hidden OS had a size of 42504191 sectors. This could infer that the lower entropy areas indicate the beginning and end of the hidden volume hosting the hidden OS. Presence of these areas violates the plausible deniability of the existence of a VeraCrypt hidden OS.

Both areas are exactly 512 bytes in length and consist of "00" bytes and strings, and the path to the "\windows\system32\winload.exe" file, refer to Fig. 4. Cross drive analysis showed that the second area correlates to running the hidden OS. Three bytes at offset 61435400 are altered every time the hidden OS is started. This is highlighted in Fig. 4, the bytes 90 90 00 change to CD 1E 01 whenever the hidden OS is started. A VeraCrypt ciphertext block size is 16 bytes (128 bits), this indicates that this area is not overwritten by the VeraCrypt encryption algorithm.

In summary, an investigator can easily find these areas in a One-Time Access threat model scenario. The presence of these areas is correlated with the existence of a hidden OS, and thus violates the plausible deniability attribute of a VeraCrypt hidden OS. Furthermore, if an investigator is able to compare this

```
3E5C0FF8 AC 9E E9 D2 3D 5E 89 F4  03 00 00 00 10 00 00 00  00 00 01 00 40 01 00 00  ¬žéÒ=^‰ô..........@...
3E5C1010 A7 D5 00 00 00 00 00 00  00 00 00 00 00 00 00 00  00 00 00 00 00 00 00 00  §Õ......................
3E5C1028 40 00 00 00 01 00 00 00  02 00 00 00 01 00 00 00  E1 07 01 00 1F 00 0F 00  @...............á.......
3E5C1040 0B 00 10 00 00 00 07 00  01 00 00 00 00 00 00 00  A7 D5 00 00 00 00 00 00  ................§Õ......
3E5C1058 00 00 00 00 00 00 00 00  00 00 00 00 00 00 00 00  78 00 00 00 01 00 00 00  ................x.......
3E5C1070 02 00 00 00 11 00 00 00  46 C8 8A D7 BB E1 E6 11  82 E9 C7 85 AF 96 8B 25  ........FÈŠ×»áæ.‚éÇ…¯–‹%
3E5C1088 00 00 00 00 5C 00 57 00  69 00 6E 00 64 00 6F 00  77 00 73 00 5C 00 73 00  ....\.W.i.n.d.o.w.s.\.s.
3E5C10A0 79 00 73 00 74 00 65 00  6D 00 33 00 32 00 5C 00  77 00 69 00 6E 00 6C 00  y.s.t.e.m.3.2.\.w.i.n.l.
3E5C10B8 6F 00 61 00 64 00 2E 00  65 00 78 00 65 00 00 00  90 90 00 00 00 00 00 00  o.a.d...e.x.e...........
3E5C10D0 00 00 00 00 00 00 00 00  00 00 00 00 00 00 00 00  78 00 00 00 01 00 00 00  ................x.......
3E5C10E8 02 00 00 00 11 00 00 00  46 C8 8A D7 BB E1 E6 11  82 E9 C7 85 AF 96 8B 25  ........FÈŠ×»áæ.‚éÇ…¯–‹%
3E5C1100 00 00 00 00 5C 00 57 00  69 00 6E 00 64 00 6F 00  77 00 73 00 5C 00 73 00  ....\.W.i.n.d.o.w.s.\.s.
3E5C1118 79 00 73 00 74 00 65 00  6D 00 33 00 32 00 5C 00  77 00 69 00 6E 00 6C 00  y.s.t.e.m.3.2.\.w.i.n.l.
3E5C1130 6F 00 61 00 64 00 2E 00  65 00 78 00 65 00 00 00  00 00 00 00 00 00 00 00  o.a.d...e.x.e...........
3E5C1148 00 00 00 00 00 00 00 00  00 00 00 00 00 00 00 00  00 00 00 00 00 00 00 00  ....................
3E5C1160 00 00 00 00 00 00 00 00  00 00 00 00 00 00 00 00  00 00 00 00 00 00 00 00  ....................
3E5C1178 00 00 00 00 00 00 00 00  00 00 00 00 00 00 00 00  00 00 00 00 00 00 00 00  ....................
3E5C1190 00 00 00 00 00 00 00 00  00 00 00 00 00 00 00 00  00 00 00 00 00 00 00 00  ....................
3E5C11A8 00 00 00 00 00 00 00 00  00 00 00 00 00 00 00 00  00 00 00 00 00 00 00 00  ....................
3E5C11C0 00 00 00 00 00 00 00 00  00 00 00 00 00 00 00 00  00 00 00 00 00 00 00 00  ....................
3E5C11D8 00 00 00 00 00 00 00 00  00 00 00 00 00 00 00 00  00 00 00 00 00 00 00 00  ....................
3E5C11F0 00 00 00 00 00 00 00 00  00 00 00 00 00 00 00 00  AF 08 40 D8 66 3A 37 E5  ..............¯.@Øf:7å
```

Fig. 4. Lower entropy areas.

area with binary snapshots taken over an interval of time (i.e. in the case of a Multiple Access model), this can provide strong evidence as to the running of a hidden OS on the computer.

3.2 Cross Drive Analysis

In this section, we demonstrate a method of defeating plausible deniability of a VeraCrypt hidden OS in the case of a Multiple Access threat model. This scenario assumes that an investigator is in possession of multiple binary copies of Alice's computer hard drive that were taken over several time intervals during which Alice was using either the decoy OS or the hidden OS. This method has previously been used in DFSs for detecting the existence of TrueCrypt hidden volumes on a drive under investigation [6]. Our research adopts this method for detecting the presence of a VeraCrypt hidden OS.

First, we split the binary images of the investigated drives into 1000 MB blocks. Then the SHA1 of each block was computed. This was done under the assumption that this will help narrow down the analysis from a 50 GB image to smaller parts of the drive where data actually changes, which was true in the case of analyzing TrueCrypt hidden volumes [6]. It turns out that running a VeraCrypt OS's "on the fly" encryption (even when the OS is idle) writes large amounts of data, which distributes changes over the whole system partition. VeraCrypt statistics estimate that 17, 33, and 520 MBs of data written on an encrypted volume correspond to 1 min, 2 min and 5 min intervals [11]. Analysis of the cryptographic hash function values clearly showed that mismatched blocks in the case of running the decoy OS are placed in the first half of the investigated drive image. This is in contrast to running the hidden OS, which changes only the second half of the drive image. We performed a detailed comparison of changes in each corresponding data block, and a visual depiction of this is presented in

Fig. 5. In Fig. 5, every rectangle represents a 1000 MB block of the binary image from the investigated drive (except for the last block which is 200 MB in size). The first block is on the upper left, while the last block is on the lower right. The data that changed during the running of the decoy and hidden OSs are depicted as the horizontal gray lines.

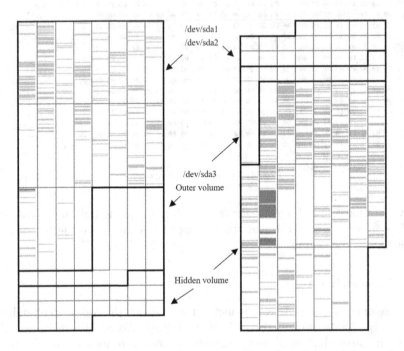

Fig. 5. A visual depiction of changes that were made to the volume while running the decoy OS (left) and hidden OS (right).

The experiment started with the creation of the binary images of the investigated drive containing both the installed decoy and hidden OSs. Then, virtual machines were cloned, switched on and immediately turned off for the decoy OS and a second clone for the hidden OS. While running the decoy OS, only data on the second portion changed. Whereas, running the hidden OS only resulted in changes in the outer volume, located in the third partition. Analyzing the first change sector offset (62351360) and the last sector (103601344) allows for an estimation of the hidden OS partition size. In the case of the experiment, it was estimated as 19.7 GB, which compares favorably with the actual hidden OS partition size of 20.26 GB. It is assumed that a more accurate estimation can be made if we didn't just turn the OSs on and off, but allowed the OSs to operate for some time.

In summary, this demonstrates that cross drive analysis can uncover evidence that a hidden OS is running on an investigated drive based on analysis of changes in the encrypted drive.

3.3   Other Attack Vectors

Hidden OS by design are intended to ensure plausible deniability, especially in the case of a One-Time Access model. In the previous section, we demonstrated that they are vulnerable to Multiple Access attacks. In this section, we discuss attack vectors based on the Live Response Access scenario. This is based on the situation where an investigator has live access to the running hidden OS or to the network/cloud environment within which the hidden OS is operating. Our purpose is to reveal any information that can lead to proving that either a decoy or a hidden OS is running. Despite information provided in the VeraCrypt documentation that asserts that neither the OS nor any application programs will know that all data is essentially written to and read from the hidden volume [11], we discovered that even non-privilege level applications can reveal some information that can be used to detect a hidden OS.

Right after logging into the hidden OS, a pop-up message informing the user that "for security reasons, when a hidden operating system is running, local unencrypted file systems and non-hidden VeraCrypt volumes are mounted as read-only", which gives away the fact that the system is running a hidden OS. In addition, when configuration files located in the %APP-DATA%\VeraCrypt\folder from both the decoy and hidden OSs are compared, there is a configuration key named "HiddenSystemLeakProtNotifStatus" that is initially set to "1", while no such key exists in the decoy OS's configuration file. There is an option to disable the pop-up message, however, upon disabling this message, the configuration key will change to "2". This is simple proof that the hidden OS is running. Moreover, when comparing the configurations files, there are clear differences. The hidden OS's configuration file has 58 lines, whereas by default, the decoy OS's configuration file only has 10. While this by itself cannot be treated as hard evidence, it potentially leaks information.

Another indication that a hidden OS is running can be obtained from mounted volume information that the user can retrieve from the VeraCrypt GUI. By default, a decoy OS runs from an encrypted volume named "System partition" with type "System", whereas a hidden OS runs from a volume mounted with the name "Hidden system partition" with type "Hidden". This is shown in Fig. 6. Even a standard user account is able to obtain this information. If an investigator has administrative rights, it is highly likely that additional information can be obtained by analyzing processes and drives on the kernel.

Another class of attack is based on network/cloud environment information leaks. Modern operating systems are enhanced by default in cloud based

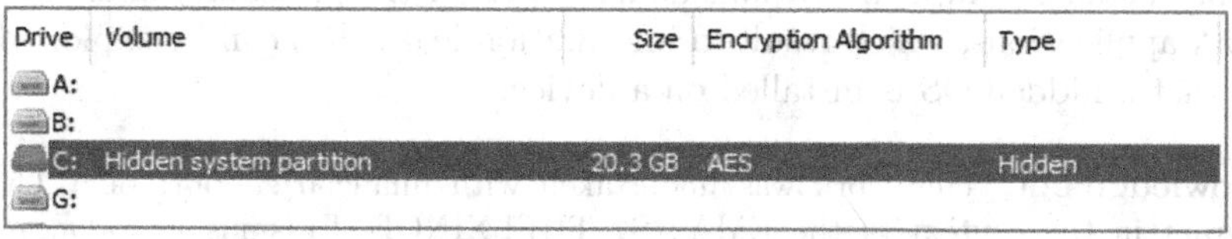

Drive	Volume		Size	Encryption Algorithm	Type
A:					
B:					
C:	Hidden system partition		20.3 GB	AES	Hidden
G:					

Fig. 6. VeraCrypt GUI while running a hidden OS.

mechanisms to make work easier for the user. An example of this is the Microsoft account that involves signing into one account for all devices. This information and the number of login attempts are recorded and stored on user account information which can easily be accessed. In our tests we also checked the Apple ID, which is used to log into Apple's iCloud as well as Google's single sign on account.

The use of both the decoy and hidden OSs is visible in the account logs and this can be an easy way to prove that another OS is installed on the device by simply observing that two OSs are registered and used concurrently on the same device. Combining this information with forensic analysis indicating that only one OS is present on the device and that the drive structure is capable of running a DFS hidden OS, can be used to prove the existence of a hidden OS. Similar attacks can be performed by comparing browser fingerprints. These types of web tracking techniques are described in [1,5]. We conducted a series of tests which confirm that this method can indeed be used to reveal the presence of a hidden OS.

Information that can compromise the existence of a hidden OS can also be obtained from monitoring device network traffic. An attacker can use both passive and active OS identification techniques. As with cloud based information leaks, these techniques can easily reveal the existence of a hidden OS if the user runs different OS types. Techniques for detecting hidden OSs can also include forensic analysis of decoy OSs by indexing application versions and network services and comparing these with intercepted network traffic. Any unusual traffic from the same IP and MAC, but with applications and services not present in the decoy OS can lead to the conclusion that a hidden OS must be installed on the device.

4   Conclusion

This paper demonstrates that the implementation of the VeraCrypt hidden operating system has faults that can be exploited to compromise the plausible deniability attribute of the hidden OS even if an attacker only possess one binary copy of the drive. This paper also presents experiment results showing that the VeraCrypt hidden OS is vulnerable to cross drive analysis. This is because even if the OS is idle, it still performs large amounts of read/write operations that distribute changes to the entire partition area. Simply turning the hidden OS on and off generates enough changes in the binary image to estimate the size of the hidden OS. In addition, we discuss other types of attacks based on the Live Response Access model that can be used to reveal the existence of a hidden OS. Current hidden OS implementations do not cater for the possibility of cloud and network applications, which result in information leaks that can be exploited to prove that a hidden OS is installed on a device.

Acknowledgment. This work was undertaken with financial support of a Thelxinoe grant in the context of the EMA2/S2 THELXINOE: Erasmus Euro-Oceanian Smart City Network project, grant reference number: 545783-EM-1-2013-1-ES-ERA MUNDUS-EMA22.

References

1. Acar, G., Eubank, C., Englehardt, S., Juarez, M., Narayanan, A., Diaz, C.: The web never forgets: persistent tracking mechanisms in the wild. In: Proceedings of the 2014 ACM SIGSAC Conference on Computer and Communications Security, CCS 2014, pp. 674–689. ACM, New York (2014)
2. Canetti, R., Dwork, C., Naor, M., Ostrovsky, R.: Deniable encryption. In: Kaliski, B.S. (ed.) CRYPTO 1997. LNCS, vol. 1294, pp. 90–104. Springer, Heidelberg (1997). doi:10.1007/BFb0052229
3. Czeskis, A., Hilaire, D.J.S., Koscher, K., Gribble, S.D., Kohno, T., Schneier, B.: Defeating encrypted and deniable file systems: TrueCrypt v5.1a and the case of the tattling OS and applications. In: Provos, N. (ed.) 3rd USENIX Workshop on Hot Topics in Security, HotSec 2008, San Jose, CA, USA, 29 July 2008, Proceedings. USENIX Association (2008)
4. Davies, A.: A security analysis of TrueCrypt: detecting hidden volumes and operating systems a security analysis of TrueCrypt. Detecting hidden volumes and operating systems (2014)
5. Fifield, D., Egelman, S.: Fingerprinting web users through font metrics. In: Böhme, R., Okamoto, T. (eds.) FC 2015. LNCS, vol. 8975, pp. 107–124. Springer, Heidelberg (2015). doi:10.1007/978-3-662-47854-7_7
6. Hargreaves, C., Chivers, H.: Detecting hidden encrypted volumes. In: Decker, B., Schaumüller-Bichl, I. (eds.) CMS 2010. LNCS, vol. 6109, pp. 233–244. Springer, Heidelberg (2010). doi:10.1007/978-3-642-13241-4_21
7. Jozwiak, I., Kedziora, M., Melinska, A.: Theoretical and practical aspects of encrypted containers detection - digital forensics approach. In: Zamojski, W., Kacprzyk, J., Mazurkiewicz, J., Sugier, J., Walkowiak, T. (eds.) Dependable Computer Systems. AISC, vol. 97, pp. 75–85. Springer, Heidelberg (2011). doi:10.1007/978-3-642-21393-9_6
8. Jozwiak, I., Kedziora, M., Melinska, A.: Methods for detecting and analyzing hidden FAT32 volumes created with the use of cryptographic tools. In: Zamojski, W., Mazurkiewicz, J., Sugier, J., Walkowiak, T., Kacprzyk, J. (eds.) New Results in Dependability and Computer Systems. AISC, vol. 224, pp. 237–244. Springer, Heidelberg (2013). doi:10.1007/978-3-319-00945-2_21
9. Kedziora, M., Chow, Y.-W., Susilo, W.: Improved threat models for the security of encrypted and deniable file systems. In: Kim, K., Joukov, N. (eds.) The 4th iCatse International Conference on Mobile and Wireless Technology, ICMWT 2017. LNEE, vol. 425, pp. 223–230, Kuala Lumpur, Malaysia, 26–29 June 2017. Springer (2017). doi:10.1007/978-981-10-5281-1_24
10. Loginova, N., Trofimenko, E., Zadereyko, O., Chanyshev, R.: Program-technical aspects of encryption protection of users' data. In: 2016 13th International Conference on Modern Problems of Radio Engineering, Telecommunications and Computer Science (TCSET), pp. 443–445, February 2016
11. VeraCrypt. VeraCrypt Documentation. http://veracrypt.codeplex.com/documentation
12. Waits, C., Akinyele, J., Nolan, R., Rogers, L.: Computer forensics: results of live response inquiry vs. memory image analysis. Technical report CMU/SEI-2008-TN-017, Software Engineering Institute, Carnegie Mellon University, Pittsburgh, PA (2008)

Security Analysis of a Design Variant of Randomized Hashing

Praveen Gauravaram[1], Shoichi Hirose[2(✉)], and Douglas Stebila[3]

[1] Tata Consultancy Services, Brisbane, Australia
p.gauravaram@tcs.com
[2] University of Fukui, Fukui, Japan
hrs_shch@u-fukui.ac.jp
[3] McMaster University, Hamilton, Canada

Abstract. At EUROCRYPT 2009, Gauravaram and Knudsen presented an online birthday attack on the randomized hashing scheme standardized in NIST SP800-106. This attack uses a fact that it is easy to find fixed points for the Davies-Meyer-type compression functions of standardized hash functions such as those in the SHA-2 family. This attack is significant in that it is an attack on the target collision resistance (TCR) of the randomized hashing scheme which is claimed to be enhanced TCR (eTCR). TCR is a property weaker than eTCR. In this paper, we will present a randomized hashing scheme called RMC. We will also prove that RMC satisfies both TCR and eTCR in the random oracle model and in the ideal cipher model. In particular, the proof for the TCR security in the ideal cipher model implies that the attack by Gauravaram and Knudsen is not effective against RMC.

Keywords: Iterated hash function · Randomized hashing · Target collision resistance · Davies-Meyer compression function · Provable security

1 Introduction

Background. At EUROCRYPT 2009, Gauravaram and Knudsen [11] showed an online existential birthday forgery attack on the digital signatures based on a randomized hashing scheme that are enhanced Target-Collision-Resistant (eTCR) secure designed by Halevi and Krawczyk [13]. The randomized hashing was also standardized by U.S. National Institute of Standards and Technology in the SP 800-106 [22]. An interesting aspect of this attack is that it is an attack on the TCR property of the randomized hashing scheme. TCR is a property weaker than eTCR. Namely, an attack on the TCR property implies an attack on the eTCR property. In addition, the attack has a practical impact as it is applicable in the scenarios where a random value used as part of the signature computation is also used for randomized hashing, which is a recommended practice to save on the communication bandwidth from transmitting an additional random value used for randomized hashing.

© Springer Nature Singapore Pte Ltd. 2017
L. Batten et al. (Eds.): ATIS 2017, CCIS 719, pp. 14–22, 2017.
DOI: 10.1007/978-981-10-5421-1_2

Although digital signatures based on a randomized hashing scheme with the eTCR property have a practical advantage of not requiring to sign a random value along with the hash value, in some scenarios such as above, an attack on the eTCR property is not useful to forge randomize-hash-and-sign digital signatures [11] whereas an attack on the TCR property is. This argument is valid for both online and offline attacks on the eTCR property.

Our contribution. We will present a randomized hash function family which we call RMC. It simply feeds concatenation of the randomization input and a message block to each compression function in the iterated hash function. Similar to the randomized hash function family by Halevi and Krawczyk, RMC can be implemented without any modifications to iterated hash functions such as SHA-2 hash functions [7]. We will specify a preprocessing scheme for message input and randomization input to instantiate RMC with the use of iterated hash functions such as SHA-2 hash functions.

Actually, RMC is essentially equivalent to the strengthened Merkle-Damgård domain extension in the dedicated key setting [1] if instantiated with compression functions of SHA-2 hash functions. In the dedicated key setting, the underlying compression function takes as a part of input a key which is not secret but chosen uniformly at random. For compression functions of SHA-2 hash functions, it is natural to feed the key as a part of the message-block input.

Additionally, a negative result is shown for TCR and eTCR properties of RMC. It is shown that neither TCR nor eTCR are preserved by strengthened Merkle-Damgård in the dedicated key setting by Bellare and Ristenpart [1] and by Reyhanitabar, Susilo and Mu [24]. This also applies to RMC. Namely, RMC does not necessarily satisfy TCR and eTCR even if the underlying compression function satisfies TCR and eTCR, respectively.

In this paper, we will give a positive result on TCR and eTCR properties of RMC on a different assumption on the underlying compression function. More precisely, we will show that RMC satisfies both TCR and eTCR if the underlying compression function is an ideal primitive. The result implies that RMC provides better security with respect to TCR than the Halevi-Krawczyk randomized hash function family. In particular, it implies that RMC is secure against the online TCR attack by Gauravaram and Knudsen [11].

We remark that the idea for our RMC design has originated from the randomized hash function variant [8] wherein inputs to the RMX hash function were randomized at both prefix and suffix ends. Although the Gauravaram-Knudsen attack is not applicable to this variant due to suffix randomization, this attack can be combined with the herding-style attack [14] to mount an online birthday forgery attack which does not apply to RMC.

Organization. Some basic notions are introduced and the RMX randomized hash function family is reviewed in Sect. 2. The security notions of TCR and eTCR are formally defined for randomized hash function family in Sect. 3. The RMC randomized hash function family is presented in Sect. 4. It is also shown in the same section that the RMC hash function family satisfies TCR and eTCR in the random oracle model and in the ideal cipher model. In Sect. 5, a preprocessing scheme for message input and randomization input is described, which is used for instantiating the RMC randomized hash function family with widely deployed iterated hash functions such as SHA-2 hash functions.

2 Definitions

Let $\{0,1\}^*$ be the set of the binary sequences of arbitrary length including the empty sequence. The length of $x \in \{0,1\}^*$ is denoted by $|x|$. For x and y in $\{0,1\}^*$, $x\|y$ is their concatenation. $a \leftarrow A$ means that an element is chosen uniformly at random from a finite set A and assigned to a.

2.1 Deterministic Hash Function

A hash function takes as input an arbitrary-length message and outputs a fixed-length digest. A hash function is usually constructed by iterating a compression function, which takes as input a fixed-length message and outputs a fixed-length digest, by applying a mode of operation or domain extension transform such as Merkle-Damgård (MD) [5,19]. In this paper, we consider MD as the hash function mode of operation albeit the extension of our analysis to other modes.

Let $f : \{0,1\}^n \times \{0,1\}^b \rightarrow \{0,1\}^n$ be a compression function which takes as input a b-bit message block and an n-bit chaining value and outputs a new n-bit chaining value. The MD mode of operation iterated over f takes as input a message M of length a multiple of b. M is divided into b-bit message blocks $M[1], M[2], \ldots, M[m]$, and is processed with MD to obtain the digest. The MD mode of operation iterated over f with an initialization vector IV, denoted by MD^f, is formally defined as follows: $\mathrm{MD}^f(IV, M) = V[m]$, where $V[0] \leftarrow IV$, $M[1]\|M[2]\| \cdots \|M[m] \leftarrow M$ and $V[i] \leftarrow f(V[i-1], M[i])$ for $i = 1$ to m.

Let $H^f : \{0,1\}^n \times \{0,1\}^* \rightarrow \{0,1\}^n$ be a deterministic hash function constructed by using the MD mode of operation iterated over f. H^f takes as input a message M of arbitrary length. With the application of a padding procedure, M is extended as $M\|pad$, which is processed by MD^f. The length of $M\|pad$ is a multiple of b. pad usually depends only on the length of M. A hash function H^f with an initialization vector IV is formally defined as $H^f(IV, M) = \mathrm{MD}^f(IV, M\|pad)$.

For deterministic hash functions such as SHA-256 and SHA-512, their initialization vectors are fixed and public. Thus, we will use the notations $\mathrm{MD}^f(M)$ and $H^f(M)$.

2.2 Randomized Hash Function Family and RMX

A randomized hash function family is defined by a deterministic hash function with an auxiliary randomization input. Randomized hash function families were first introduced by Naor and Yung in the name of universal one-way hash functions (UOWHFs) [21]. The UOWHFs were called target-collision-resistant

(TCR) hash functions by Bellare and Rogaway [2] and they satisfy TCR property which is *weaker* than collision resistance. Bellare and Rogaway [2] and later Shoup [25] proposed and analyzed composition constructions to build TCR iterated hash functions from TCR compression functions. Halevi and Krawczyk [13] designed randomized hash functions with TCR and *stronger* property of enhanced Target Collision Resistance (eTCR) by using properties related to second preimage resistance of the compression function. One of their eTCR designs is called RMX.

The scope of this paper is in proposing design improvements for RMX hash function family, and we limit our design description to RMX. An RMX hash function family over H^f is defined by $\bar{\mathcal{H}} = \{\bar{H}_r^f \mid r \in \{0,1\}^c\}$, where $\bar{H}_r^f(M) = H^f(r\|(r \oplus M[1])\|(r \oplus M[2])\| \cdots \|(r \oplus M[m]))$. For simplicity, it is assumed that the length c of r equals the message-block length of f. It is also assumed that $M = M[1]\|M[2]\| \cdots \|M[m]$ and $|M[i]|$ equals the message-block length of f. The detailed specification for the general cases is given in NIST SP 800-106 [22].

2.3 Fixed Points in Block-Cipher-Based Compression Functions

Several practical block-cipher-based compression functions [23] such as Davies-Meyer [20], Matyas-Meyer-Oseas [18] and Miyaguchi-Preneel [23], that are provably collision resistant and (second) preimage resistant in the ideal cipher model [3,4,26], are easily differentiable from a fixed-input-length random oracle [17]. For example, it is easy to find *fixed points* for the Davies-Meyer compression function [20]. This weakness was exploited in several attacks on popular hash function frameworks [6,9–12,15,16]. These attacks make use of *fixed points* in compression functions to generate birthday collision attacks that are used to find second preimages in much less than generic second preimage attack complexity.

3 TCR and eTCR of Randomized Hash Function Family

Let $\mathcal{H}$ be a randomized hash function family using a deterministic iterated hash function H^f randomized with an auxiliary random input. We formalize multi-target (enhanced) target-collision-resistance using the experiments given below:

$\underline{\mathrm{Exp}_{\mathcal{H}}^{\mathsf{TCR}\text{-}t}}$: 1. $st \leftarrow \bot; r_0 \leftarrow \bot$
         2. For $i = 1$ to t: $(M_i, st) \leftarrow \mathcal{A}^f(r_{i-1}, st)$; $r_i \xleftarrow{} \{0,1\}^c$
         3. $(M^*, r^*) \leftarrow \mathcal{A}^f(\mathbf{r}, st)$
         4. WIN iff $\exists i : (M_i \neq M^*) \wedge (r_i = r^*) \wedge (H_{r_i}^f(M_i) = H_{r^*}^f(M^*))$

$\underline{\mathrm{Exp}_{\mathcal{H}}^{\mathsf{eTCR}\text{-}t}}$: 1. $st \leftarrow \bot; r_0 \leftarrow \bot$
         2. For $i = 1$ to t: $(M_i, st) \leftarrow \mathcal{A}^f(r_{i-1}, st)$; $r_i \xleftarrow{} \{0,1\}^c$
         3. $(M^*, r^*) \leftarrow \mathcal{A}^f(\mathbf{r}, st)$
         4. WIN iff $\exists i : (r_i, M_i) \neq (r^*, M^*) \wedge (H_{r_i}^f(M_i) = H_{r^*}^f(M^*))$

An experiment is a game played by an adversary $\mathcal{A}$. $\mathcal{A}$ is given t first preimages. For each first preimage (M_i, r_i), message M_i is chosen by $\mathcal{A}$ adaptively, and the corresponding randomization input r_i is chosen uniformly at random after M_i. $\mathcal{A}$ wins in the experiment if $\mathcal{A}$ finds a second preimage for one of the given t first preimages. The experiment for TCR requires that the randomization input of the second preimage is equal to that of the first preimage.

The TCR advantage of $\mathcal{A}$ is defined as follows:

$$\mathrm{Adv}_{\mathcal{H}}^{\mathsf{TCR}\text{-}t}(\mathcal{A}) = \Pr[\mathcal{A} \text{ wins in } \mathrm{Exp}_{\mathcal{H}}^{\mathsf{TCR}\text{-}t}] \ .$$

The eTCR advantage $\mathrm{Adv}_{\mathcal{H}}^{\mathsf{eTCR}\text{-}t}$ is defined analogously.

4   RMC Hash Function Family

We propose RMC as a randomized hash function family which offers better security bounds against TCR attacks than the RMX hash function family. Let $\tilde{\mathcal{H}}$ be an RMC hash function family which uses MD mode as the underlying domain extension. A hash function $\tilde{H}_r^f$ in this family is formally defined as follows: $\tilde{H}_r^f(M) = H^f(r\|M[1]\|(r\|M[2])\|\cdots\|(r\|M[m])$, where $M[1]\|M[2]\|\cdots\|M[m] \leftarrow M$. Here, $r \in \{0,1\}^c$, and it is assumed that $b > c$, $|M| \equiv 0 \pmod{b-c}$ and $|M[i]| = b - c$ for $1 \leq i \leq m$. For arbitrary-length messages, a preprocessing function producing inputs to the deterministic hash function H^f is specified in the next section.

4.1   Rationale for the Design Choice of RMC

The key criterion is to choose a design so that an RMC randomized hash function family is not vulnerable to length-extended *fixed-point*-based birthday collision attacks used to find *online* TCR collision attacks on RMX hash functions [11,12]. In a length-extended *fixed-point*-based birthday collision attack on an iterated hash function H^f, an adversary develops a colliding pair $(M, M\|M[\ell+1])$ such that $H(M) = H(M\|M[\ell+1])$, where M is an arbitrary ℓ-block message and $M[\ell+1]$ is a *fixed-point* message block for f such that $f(H(M), M[\ell+1]) = H(M)$. As demonstrated in [11,12], this attack is also applicable on RMX randomized hash function families in the following way:

1. Adversary $\mathcal{A}$ is given t preimages $(M_1, r_1), (M_2, r_2), \ldots, (M_t, r_t)$.
2. $\mathcal{A}$ produces s random fixed points for f such that $f(V_j, N_j) = V_j$ for $1 \leq j \leq s$.
3. If $\mathcal{A}$ finds some i and j such that $\tilde{H}_{r_i}^f(M_i) = V_j$, then $\mathcal{A}$ outputs $(M_i\|(r_i \oplus N_j), r_i)$ as the second preimage for (M_i, r_i).

This attack is a TCR collision attack in birthday complexity since it is successful with some significant probability if $ts = O(2^n)$.

This attack cannot be applied to RMC randomized hash function families as the compression function always takes a randomization input.

4.2   Security Analysis

The TCR and eTCR security of the RMC randomized hash function family $\tilde{\mathcal{H}} = \{\tilde{H}_r^f \mid f : \{0,1\}^n \times \{0,1\}^b \rightarrow \{0,1\}^n \wedge r \in \{0,1\}^c\}$ are analyzed in the random oracle model and in the ideal cipher model. In the random oracle model, the compression function f is assumed to be a fixed-input-length random oracle. In the ideal cipher model, it is assumed to be a Davies-Meyer compression function, that is, $f(v, x) = E_x(v) \oplus v$, where the block cipher E with block size n and key size b is chosen uniformly at random. In these ideal models, the advantage of an adversary is evaluated based on the number of calls to the ideal primitive. Let

$$\mathrm{Adv}_{\mathcal{H}}^{\mathrm{TCR}\text{-}t}(\ell, q) = \max_{\mathcal{A}} \Pr\left[\mathcal{A} \text{ wins in } \mathrm{Exp}_{\mathcal{H}}^{\mathrm{TCR}\text{-}t}\right] ,$$

where each preimage given to $\mathcal{A}$ has at most ℓ message blocks and $\mathcal{A}$ calls f at most q times, which exclude the number of calls required to compute the outputs for the t first preimages. $\mathrm{Adv}_{\mathcal{H}}^{\mathrm{eTCR}\text{-}t}(\ell, q)$ is defined similarly. Notice that a call to f in the ideal cipher model is a call to encryption E or decryption E^{-1}.

Theorem 1 given below quantifies the TCR security of the RMC hash function family. The proof is omitted due to the page limit.

Theorem 1. *Let q, t and ℓ be positive integers. Let $\alpha = \min\{t, \lfloor (e \ln 2)c/(\ln c + \ln \ln 2)\rfloor\}$. Suppose that $t \leq 2^c$.*

1. If f is a random oracle, then $\mathrm{Adv}_{\tilde{\mathcal{H}}}^{\mathrm{TCR}\text{-}t}(\ell, q) \leq (\alpha\ell + 1)(t\ell + q)/2^n + 1/2^c$.
2. If f is a Davies-Meyer compression function with an ideal cipher, then

$$\mathrm{Adv}_{\tilde{\mathcal{H}}}^{\mathrm{TCR}\text{-}t}(\ell, q) \leq \frac{(\alpha\ell + 1)(t\ell + q)}{2^n - (\alpha\ell + q)} + \frac{1}{2^c}.$$

It is implied by the result for the ideal cipher model shown in Theorem 1 that the collision attack on the RMX hash function family is not effective against the RMC hash function family.

Theorem 2 gives upper bounds on the eTCR advantage both in the random oracle model and in the ideal cipher model. The proof is also omitted.

Theorem 2. *Let q, t and ℓ be positive integers.*

1. If f is a random oracle, then $\mathrm{Adv}_{\tilde{\mathcal{H}}}^{\mathrm{eTCR}\text{-}t}(\ell, q) \leq (t\ell + 1)(t\ell + q)/2^n$.
2. If f is a Davies-Meyer compression function with an ideal cipher, then

$$\mathrm{Adv}_{\tilde{\mathcal{H}}}^{\mathrm{eTCR}\text{-}t}(\ell, q) \leq \frac{(t\ell + 1)(t\ell + q)}{2^n - (t\ell + q)}.$$

5   Randomized Message Preprocessing for Hash Functions

A randomized message preprocessing algorithm for an iterated hash function is specified for instantiation of the RMC randomized hash function family with widely deployed iterated hash functions such as SHA-256 and SHA-512. It is assumed that the iterated hash function uses a compression function $f : \{0,1\}^n \times \{0,1\}^b \rightarrow \{0,1\}^n$ and the Merkle-Damgård strengthening. For the iterated hash function, let l be the length of the binary representation of the input length. For example, $n = 256$, $b = 512$ and $l = 64$ for SHA-256, and $n = 512$, $b = 1024$ and $l = 128$ for SHA-512.

The message preprocessing algorithm takes as input $r \in \{0,1\}^c$ chosen uniformly at random and a message $M \in \{0,1\}^*$. It is assumed that $l + 1 \leq b - c$.

The algorithm first pads the message M with 10^k, where k is the minimum non-negative integer such that $|M| + k + 1 \equiv (b - c) - (l + 1) \pmod{b - c}$. Then, it divides $M\|10^k$ into the blocks $M[1], M[2], \ldots, M[m]$ such that $|M[i]| = b - c$ for $1 \leq i \leq m - 1$ and $|M[m]| = (b - c) - (l + 1)$. Finally, it produces $(r\|M[1])\|(r\|M[2])\| \cdots \|(r\|M[m])$.

From the TCR security analysis in Sect. 4, since it is assumed that $t \leq 2^c$, where t is the number of the first preimages, it is recommended that $c \geq 128$ for SHA-256 and SHA-512. In addition, it is reasonable to assume that $c \leq n$, where n is the output length and $n < b - l - 1$ for SHA-256 and SHA-512. If $c = 128$, the number of calls of RMC to the compression function is about $4/3$ and $8/7$ times larger than that of RMX for SHA-256 and SHA-512, respectively. Table 1 summarizes the comparison for some other values of c.

Table 1. Performance comparison between RMC and RMX

c	128	256	384	512
SHA-256	4/3	2	n/a	n/a
SHA-512	8/7	4/3	8/5	2

Acknowledgements. A part of this work was done when Dr. Praveen Gauravaram was at QUT supported by Australian Research Council (ARC) Discovery Project grant DP130104304. The second author was supported in part by JSPS KAKENHI Grant Number JP16H02828.

References

1. Bellare, M., Ristenpart, T.: Hash functions in the dedicated-key setting: design choices and MPP transforms. In: Arge, L., Cachin, C., Jurdziński, T., Tarlecki, A. (eds.) ICALP 2007. LNCS, vol. 4596, pp. 399–410. Springer, Heidelberg (2007). doi:10.1007/978-3-540-73420-8_36
2. Bellare, M., Rogaway, P.: Collision-resistant hashing: towards making UOWHFs practical. In: Kaliski, B.S. (ed.) CRYPTO 1997. LNCS, vol. 1294, pp. 470–484. Springer, Heidelberg (1997). doi:10.1007/BFb0052256
3. Black, J., Rogaway, P., Shrimpton, T.: Black-box analysis of the block-cipher-based hash-function constructions from PGV. In: Yung, M. (ed.) CRYPTO 2002. LNCS, vol. 2442, pp. 320–335. Springer, Heidelberg (2002). doi:10.1007/3-540-45708-9_21
4. Black, J., Rogaway, P., Shrimpton, T., Stam, M.: An analysis of the blockcipher-based hash functions from PGV. J. Cryptology **23**(4), 519–545 (2010)

5. Damgård, I.B.: A design principle for hash functions. In: Brassard, G. (ed.) CRYPTO 1989. LNCS, vol. 435, pp. 416–427. Springer, New York (1990). doi:10. 1007/0-387-34805-0_39
6. Dean, R.D.: Formal aspects of mobile code security. Ph.D. thesis, Princeton University (1999)
7. FIPS PUB 180-4: Secure Hash Standard (SHS) (2015)
8. Gauravaram, P.: Generation of randomized messages for cryptographic hash functions, US Patent 9444619 B2 (2016)
9. Gauravaram, P., Kelsey, J.: Linear-XOR and additive checksums don't protect Damgård-Merkle hashes from generic attacks. In: Malkin, T. (ed.) CT-RSA 2008. LNCS, vol. 4964, pp. 36–51. Springer, Heidelberg (2008). doi:10.1007/978-3-540-79263-5_3
10. Gauravaram, P., Kelsey, J., Knudsen, L.R., Thomsen, S.S.: On hash functions using checksums. Int. J. Inf. Sec $9(2)$, 137–151 (2010)
11. Gauravaram, P., Knudsen, L.R.: On randomizing hash functions to strengthen the security of digital signatures. In: Joux, A. (ed.) EUROCRYPT 2009. LNCS, vol. 5479, pp. 88–105. Springer, Heidelberg (2009). doi:10.1007/978-3-642-01001-9_5
12. Gauravaram, P., Knudsen, L.R.: Security analysis of randomize-hash-then-sign digital signatures. J. Cryptology $25(4)$, 748–779 (2012)
13. Halevi, S., Krawczyk, H.: Strengthening digital signatures via randomized hashing. In: Dwork, C. (ed.) CRYPTO 2006. LNCS, vol. 4117, pp. 41–59. Springer, Heidelberg (2006). doi:10.1007/11818175_3
14. Kelsey, J., Kohno, T.: Herding hash functions and the Nostradamus attack. In: Vaudenay, S. (ed.) EUROCRYPT 2006. LNCS, vol. 4004, pp. 183–200. Springer, Heidelberg (2006). doi:10.1007/11761679_12
15. Kelsey, J., Lucks, S.: Collisions and near-collisions for reduced-round Tiger. In: Robshaw, M. (ed.) FSE 2006. LNCS, vol. 4047, pp. 111–125. Springer, Heidelberg (2006). doi:10.1007/11799313_8
16. Kelsey, J., Schneier, B.: Second preimages on n-bit hash functions for much less than 2^n work. In: Cramer, R. (ed.) EUROCRYPT 2005. LNCS, vol. 3494, pp. 474–490. Springer, Heidelberg (2005). doi:10.1007/11426639_28
17. Kuwakado, H., Morii, M.: Indifferentiability of single-block-length and rate-1 compression functions. IEICE Fundam. $90-A(10)$, 2301–2308 (2007)
18. Matyas, S.M., Meyer, C.H., Oseas, J.: Generating strong one-way functions with cryptographic algorithm. IBM Techn. Discl. Bull. 27, 5658–5659 (1985)
19. Merkle, R.C.: One way hash functions and DES. In: Brassard, G. (ed.) CRYPTO 1989. LNCS, vol. 435, pp. 428–446. Springer, New York (1990). doi:10.1007/0-387-34805-0_40
20. Miyaguchi, S., Ohta, K., Iwata, M.: Confirmation that some hash functions are not collision free. In: Damgård, I.B. (ed.) EUROCRYPT 1990. LNCS, vol. 473, pp. 326–343. Springer, Heidelberg (1991). doi:10.1007/3-540-46877-3_30
21. Naor, M., Yung, M.: Universal one-way hash functions and their cryptographic applications. In: Proceedings of the 21st Annual ACM Symposium on Theory of Computing, pp. 33–43 (1989)
22. NIST SP 800-106: Randomized Hashing for Digital Signatures (2009)
23. Preneel, B., Govaerts, R., Vandewalle, J.: Hash functions based on block ciphers: a synthetic approach. In: Stinson, D.R. (ed.) CRYPTO 1993. LNCS, vol. 773, pp. 368–378. Springer, Heidelberg (1994). doi:10.1007/3-540-48329-2_31
24. Reyhanitabar, M.R., Susilo, W., Mu, Y.: Enhanced target collision resistant hash functions revisited. In: Dunkelman, O. (ed.) FSE 2009. LNCS, vol. 5665, pp. 327–344. Springer, Heidelberg (2009). doi:10.1007/978-3-642-03317-9_20

25. Shoup, V.: A composition theorem for universal one-way hash functions. In: Preneel, B. (ed.) EUROCRYPT 2000. LNCS, vol. 1807, pp. 445–452. Springer, Heidelberg (2000). doi:10.1007/3-540-45539-6_32
26. Stam, M.: Blockcipher-based hashing revisited. In: Dunkelman, O. (ed.) FSE 2009. LNCS, vol. 5665, pp. 67–83. Springer, Heidelberg (2009). doi:10.1007/978-3-642-03317-9_5

Secure Two-Party Computation Using an Efficient Garbled Circuit by Reducing Data Transfer

Mohammad Hossein Yalame, Mohammad Hossein Farzam, and Siavash Bayat-Sarmadi[(✉)]

Sharif University of Technology, Tehran, Iran
{yalame,mfarzam}@ce.sharif.edu, sbayat@sharif.edu

Abstract. Secure computation has obtained significant attention in the literature recently. Classic architectures usually use either the Garbled Circuit (GC) or the Goldreich-Micali-Wigderson (GMW) protocols. So far, to reduce the complexity of communications in these protocols, various methods have been proposed. The best known work in both methods reduces the communication up to almost $2k$-bits (k is the symmetric security parameter) for each AND gate, and using XOR gate is free. In this paper, by combining GC and GMW, we propose a scheme in the semi-honest adversary model. This scheme requires an Oblivious Transfer (OT) and a 2-bit data transfer for each AND gate, keeping XOR gates free. The analytical results on different applications, including AES, DES, SHA-1, SHA-256, MD5, multiplier, adder, and comparator show that the data transfer size can be reduced up to 52% and 41% when compared to the best known GC and GMW based methods, respectively.

Keywords: Secure computation · Secure function evaluation · Garbled circuit protocol · GMW protocol · Oblivious transfer protocol

1 Introduction

Secure computation has received significant attention in the literature recently. Applications include secure computation of biometric identification [1], user authentication [2], privacy-preserving ElectroCardioGram (ECG)[3], privacy-preserving remote diagnostics [4], and so on. In two-party secure computation, both parties can perform or evaluate a function together and realize the result; while no party can know about the private inputs of the other party. Such computations usually are performed in two approaches, including Garbled Circuit protocol (GC) [5–7] and the Goldreich-Micali-Wigderson protocol (GMW) [8], [9,10]. In GC, inputs and outputs of the circuit gates are masked so that the intermediate values and input values of one party cannot be determined by the other party in the course of the function evaluation. In GMW, the two parties share all inputs and intermediate values using an XOR-based sharing scheme. Each party evaluates the function with his/her own secret shares to find out one

© Springer Nature Singapore Pte Ltd. 2017
L. Batten et al. (Eds.): ATIS 2017, CCIS 719, pp. 23–34, 2017.
DOI: 10.1007/978-981-10-5421-1_3

share of the final output of the circuit. These two shares are then XORed to make the final output.

In [11–14] some techniques are presented to minimize the GC construction algorithms in terms of computation and communication complexity for secure evaluating of functions. Round complexity in GC is constant [15]. However, in GMW it significantly lies on the depth of the circuit representation of the function [16]. That is why a number of the previous work have tried to reduce boolean circuits depth [10]. The other main direction of improving GMW is reducing communication or computation overhead in the Oblivious Transfer (OT) protocol [9,10]. That is due to the fact that OT is a main component of the GMW protocols.

In this paper, by combining GC and GMW, we have proposed a scheme for the semi-honest adversary model that reduces the communication overhead. This adversary model is widely used in previous work such as [6,9–11]. The contributions of the paper are as follows:

- When compared to GMW which uses OT as one of its main components, the proposed method requires one OT_1^2 instead of one OT_1^4 for most AND gates. We should note that any optimization on the OT protocol improves GMW and the proposed scheme to the same extent. Neither the security nor the computation of the scheme is negatively affected by this optimization.
- In GC-based protocols, wire label size is usually large and determines the level of security. In the proposed work, the security level is independent from the size of the label. This enables reducing label size to 2 bits. Furthermore, in GC, XOR gates are said to be free. However, in fact, the local evaluation of each XOR gate costs k XOR operations (k is the symmetric security parameter). For instance, for the case of $k = 128$, applying an XOR operation on k-bit labels costs 128 XORs. Reducing label size to 2 bits reduces the computation of XOR gate evaluation accordingly.

For evaluating the proposed scheme, we have performed our experiments for different sizes of circuits, including 32-bit multiplier, 32-bit comparator, 32-bit adder, 64-bit adder, AES, DES, SHA-1, SHA-256 and MD5. The results show that overall data transfer size mostly decreases up to 52% and 41% when compared to the best known GC and GMW based methods.

This paper is organized as follows. In Sect. 2, the preliminaries and related work regarding GC and GMW are presented. Section 3 presents the proposed scheme. In Sect. 4, the analytical and experimental results are reported. Finally, we conclude the paper in Sect. 5.

2   Preliminaries and Previous Work

In this section, main components of SFE and its best known previous works are reviewed.

Oblivious Transfer (OT) [17]: This cryptographic protocol runs between a sender and a receiver. Generally, in 1-out-of-n OT the sender has n secret values

$(s_1, ..., s_n)$. The receiver should prepare a selection number r $(1 \leq r \leq n)$. Then, after performing the protocol, receiver learns s_r, but nothing about other secret values of the sender. Additionally, the sender does not learn about r, i.e., does not know which secret has been selected.

Garbled Circuit (GC) Protocol [5]: Yao introduced two-party secure function evaluation (GC protocol)[5]. Each wire of the circuit in GC protocol carries a bit-string (label) instead of one single bit. There are two main phases in GC protocol. In the first phase, the garbler garbles the circuit. In other words, it garbles the relation between gate inputs and output (also known as truth table). The resulting table of ciphertexts, generated for each gate by the garbler, is called Garbled Table (GT). In the second phase, the evaluator computes (evaluates) circuit outputs using GT and garbled value of each wire. In other words, the evaluator and the garbler compute the values of the function outputs without revealing their inputs to each other.

Free XOR Method [11]: The main idea of this method is to evaluate an XOR gate without sending any ciphertexts. In Free XOR, the labels on a wire are chosen in the form of $(W^0, W^0 \oplus R)$; where R is random and common to all wires; however, it is only known to the garbler. "W^0" is also chosen to be a random number and is the label on the wire corresponding to "0" value. This way when the evaluator observes an XOR gate, it XORs the labels of the input wires to compute the label of the output wire (in form of either W_g or $W_g \oplus R$). Therefore, XOR gates do not need GT for evaluation. Each AND gate needs to send three ciphertexts, according to row reduction technique [14], from the garbler to the evaluator.

Garbled Row Reduction [14]: In this method, the required number of ciphertexts for each gate is further reduced. Instead of choosing a random label for each output wire of a gate, it is chosen as a function of W_a and W_b, where W_a and W_b are the labels of input wires of the gate. Using this method, the first row of GT is always zero; hence, it does not need to be sent. So, each gate needs three ciphertexts. This technique is compatible with the Free XOR method; i.e., XOR gates are free.

Half Gate Method [13]: This work enables evaluating AND gates with only two ciphertext while keeping XORs free. To this end, each AND gate is divided into two half gates, i.e., an AND gate for which one party knows one input. Since half gates can be garbled with only one ciphertext, AND gates' garbling will need only two.

Improved OT Extension [15] **and LUT based OT** [9]: As mentioned earlier, OT is a core building block of GMW. In these works, the communication of OT is reduced to make a more efficient GMW protocol. In [15], they achieved this end by reducing a $log_2 N$-bit OT_1^N to $log_2 N$ 1-bit OT_1^2 compared to [18]. This reduction resulted in communication improvements up to 1.6x per each two 1-bit OT_1^2. Continuing this path, in [9], a $log_4 N$-bit OT_1^N is reduced to $log_4 N$ 1-bit OT_1^4 and improvements up to 1.9x per each two 1-bit OT_1^2 is achieved compared to [18].

3   Proposed Scheme for SFE

In this work, the idea is to reduce the cost of data transfer by reducing the size of the labels without compromising the security. In contrast to the previous work [5,11,13], in our scheme, wire labels W^0 and W^1, are of length two. Each AND gate is assigned a ternary $(\alpha_a, \alpha_b, \alpha_c)$, which can be computed using the labels on each input. We have defined A and B to be two functions to identify the first and the second incoming wires of gates, respectively. G is a function that identifies the functionality of gates. Additionally, we refer to the garbled values of the first and the second input of each gate as W_a and W_b, respectively. The garbled output is referred to as W_g. We have also made use of XOR Connected Components (XCCs) in the proposed scheme. To this end, we define $xcc()$ as a function to identify the XCC of each XOR gate and n_{xcc} to represent the number of XCCs in the circuit. Figure 1 illustrates how a sample circuit is partitioned into three XCCs. The XOR gates surrounded by a curve are in the same XCC.

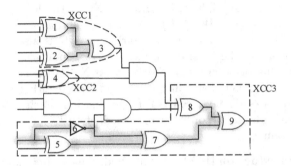

Fig. 1. Partitioning XOR gates in a sample circuit into XCCs.

To clarify how we reached the proposed scheme, our approach is provided in Subsect. 3.1. Also, we describe the details of the scheme in Subsects. 3.2 and 3.3.

3.1   The Approach of the Proposed Scheme

The main idea in this work is to reduce label size without compromising the security. Reducing label size in GC-based works, e.g., [11,13], leads to a security degradation. That is because such work provide the evaluator with a chance to check the correctness of his/her guesses for the garbled output of an AND gate. This problem has been resolved by increasing the state space of garbled values, which in turn needs to increase label size to k-bit, i.e., 128-bit. In this work, we have proposed another solution to this problem not by increasing state space but by changing the protocol in a way that the evaluator cannot check the correctness of his/her guesses anymore. To achieve this end, we have made use of OT for each AND gate.

The simplest way to achieve this goal is to assign a unique index to each row in the truth table of the AND gate. To do so, similar to other work [11, 13], each row of the truth table is indexed by its most significant bit (MSB) of its input labels. Thus, the two labels of each AND gate input wire must have opposite MSBs. The relation between MSBs and actual values is random and secret. In this way, the evaluator can obtain the required garbled value of an output wire by execution of an OT_1^4. In this OT, the garbler provides the garbled outputs of each row of the truth table and the evaluator receives the garbled output by providing the index of the corresponding row.

Table 1. All possible garbling groups for AND gates

A[a]	Garbling group	Garbled inputs			
		$W_a^0\ W_b^0$	$W_a^0\ W_b^1$	$W_a^1\ W_b^0$	$W_a^1\ W_b^1$
0000	G0	$\alpha = 0$	$\alpha = 0$	$\alpha = 0$	$\alpha = 0^*$
0001	G1	$\alpha = 0$	$\alpha = 1^*$	$\alpha = 0$	$\alpha = 1$
0010	G2	$\alpha = 1$	$\alpha = 0^*$	$\alpha = 1$	$\alpha = 0$
0011	G3	$\alpha = 1$	$\alpha = 1$	$\alpha = 1$	$\alpha = 1^*$
0100	G4	$\alpha = 0$	$\alpha = 0$	$\alpha = 1^*$	$\alpha = 1$
0101	G5	$\alpha = 0^*$	$\alpha = 1$	$\alpha = 1$	$\alpha = 0$
0110	G6	$\alpha = 1^*$	$\alpha = 0$	$\alpha = 0$	$\alpha = 1$
0111	G7	$\alpha = 1$	$\alpha = 1$	$\alpha = 0^*$	$\alpha = 0$
1000	G8	$\alpha = 1$	$\alpha = 1$	$\alpha = 0^*$	$\alpha = 0$
1001	G9	$\alpha = 1^*$	$\alpha = 0$	$\alpha = 0$	$\alpha = 1$
1010	G10	$\alpha = 0^*$	$\alpha = 1$	$\alpha = 1$	$\alpha = 0$
1011	G11	$\alpha = 0$	$\alpha = 0$	$\alpha = 1^*$	$\alpha = 1$
1100	G12	$\alpha = 1$	$\alpha = 1$	$\alpha = 1$	$\alpha = 1^*$
1101	G13	$\alpha = 1$	$\alpha = 0^*$	$\alpha = 1$	$\alpha = 0$
1110	G14	$\alpha = 0$	$\alpha = 1^*$	$\alpha = 0$	$\alpha = 1$
1111	G15	$\alpha = 0$	$\alpha = 0$	$\alpha = 0$	$\alpha = 0^*$
actual output		0	0	0	1

[a] $LSB(W_a^0)|LSB(W_a^1)|LSB(W_b^0)|LSB(W_b^1)$.

The data transfer overhead in this scheme is still more than the half gate scheme [13]. The fact that the garbled output of the AND gate has only two different possible values suggests that it may be possible to achieve the same level of security with only one OT_1^2. For using an OT_1^2, we need to use another bit in the labels to classify all the possible garblings. The least significant bit (LSB) of the labels are selected for this purpose. So, label size can be reduced to two bits.

A garbling determines the value of four two-bit labels, i.e., W_a^0, W_a^1, W_b^0 and W_b^1. Although there are eight bits to be determined, there are only 64 different

Table 2. A sample garbling for an AND gate

Input		Output	Garbled input		Garbled output	Index
a	b	g	W_a	W_b	W_g	
0	0	0	11	01	W_g^0	10
0	1	0	11	10	W_g^0	11
1	0	0	01	01	W_g^0	00
1	1	1	01	10	W_g^1	01

valid garblings. This is because the MSBs of the labels on each wire are opposite. The garblings can be classified based on the LSBs of the labels into 16 different groups, namely G0 to G15. These groups are shown in Table 1. Each row of the table is representative of a garbling group. For each garbling, three identifiers, i.e., α_a, α_b and α_c are calculated as follows:

$$\alpha_a = LSB(W_b^0 \oplus W_b^1), \alpha_b = LSB(W_a^0 \oplus W_a^1), \alpha_c = LSB(W_a^1 \oplus W_b^1). \quad (1)$$

It should be noted that the value of each identifier is the same for all the garblings in a group. Table 1 and the newly defined identifiers will be used in the evaluation process of AND gates.

Each AND gate in the circuit is corresponding to one cell in Table 1. To identify this cell, one needs to know the garbling group used for the gate, which identifies the corresponding row. Moreover, he/she needs to know the garbled value on the inputs of the gate, which identify the corresponding column. Neither the garbler nor the evaluator have this information completely. During the function evaluation, when the evaluator reaches an AND gate with two garbled inputs W_a and W_b, he/she computes $\alpha = LSB(W_a \oplus W_b)$. Ideally, we would like to use the value of this identifier as the select signal of the OT_1^2, but it is not possible. That is because the value of this signal is the same in some cells with different actual outputs in each row of Table 1. For instance, consider the first row of the table. The value of α is the same for all the cells in it. In other words, if the garbling group of an AND gate is G0, then the evaluator will get $\alpha = 0$ no matter what the garbled inputs are. Thus, some other condition $Cond$ must be checked for each AND gate. The holding of $Cond$ along with the value of α must be enough for the garbler to assign W_g^0 and W_g^1 to OT_1^2 inputs correctly.

To do so, we mark a cell in each row of Table 1 with an asterisk. Knowing the garbling group of an AND gate, we define $Cond$ holds for it if it is corresponding to the marked cell in that garbling group. This can be checked by comparing the MSBs of the garbled inputs of the AND gate against the MSBs of the garbled inputs in the marked cell for that garbling group. For instance, consider the AND gates shown in Fig. 2. The garbling has been previously described in Table 2. As mentioned earlier, it is clear that this garbling is classified in G14 ($LSB(W_a^0) = LSB(11) = 1$, $LSB(W_a^1) = LSB(01) = 1$, $LSB(W_b^0) = LSB(01) = 1$, $LSB(W_b^1) = LSB(10) = 0$ and $(1110)_2 = 14$).

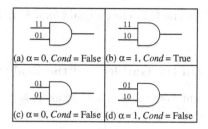

Fig. 2. Determining α and *Cond* for four AND gates as an example. Table 2 presents the corresponding garbling.

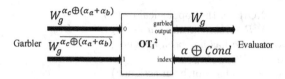

Fig. 3. AND gate evaluation in the proposed scheme using OT_1^2.

Now, only consider the gate shown in Fig. 2(b). According to Table 2, the garbled inputs are W_a^0 and W_b^1. So, the corresponding column of the gate would be the second column in Table 1. Since the identified cell is a marked cell, *Cond* holds for this AND gate.

We proceed with the details of AND gates evaluation. We initially suppose that the used garbling is not in the groups in which the value of α is the same across different cells, i.e., G0, G3, G12 and G15. In this case, a careful examination of all cells in each row of Table 1 shows that the actual output is "0" in marked cells. Among the other cells with no asterisk, the ones with the actual output value equal to "1" and "0" can be distinguished based on the value of α. More specifically, the garbled output of the AND gate would be $W_g^{\overline{Cond \oplus \alpha \oplus \alpha_c}}$. In the other case, when the used garbling is from groups G0, G3, G12 or G15, it can similarly be shown that the garbled output of the AND gate is W_g^{Cond}.

The OT select signal equation must be the same in all garbling groups. Otherwise, the evaluator may find about the garbling group chosen by the garbler. To make the equations identical, we make use of the don't care situations in groups G0, G3, G12 and G15. As it can be seen in Table 1 and Eq. 1, the value of α and α_c are always equal in G0, G3, G12 and G15 and it follows that $\alpha \oplus \alpha_c = 0$. So, W_g^{Cond} can be re-written as $W_g^{Cond \oplus \alpha \oplus \alpha_c}$. The final step to unify both equations is to add a term to differentiate between G0, G3, G12 and G15 with others. This makes the final equation of the garbled output to be $W_g^{(\alpha \oplus Cond) \oplus (\alpha_c \oplus (\alpha_a + \alpha_b))}$.

This is so promising that none of the scheme sides can evaluate this equation, as the garbler and the evaluator do not know the value of $\alpha \oplus Cond$ and $\alpha_c \oplus (\alpha_a + \alpha_b)$, respectively. However, it can be evaluated obliviously if the garbler puts $W_g^{\alpha_c \oplus (\alpha_a + \alpha_b)}$ and $W_g^{\overline{\alpha_c \oplus (\alpha_a + \alpha_b)}}$ on the first and second input of the OT, and the evaluator provides the OT select signal $Cond \oplus \alpha$. This configuration is shown in Fig. 3.

3.2   The Algorithms of the Garbler and the Evaluator Side

Algorithms 1 and 2 present how the garbled circuit is generated and evaluated.

Algorithm 1. Construction of Garbled Circuit Algorithm

1: **Procedure** GARBLE
2: $S \in_R \{0,1\}^{n x cc}$
3: **for** each $G_g ==$ XOR (in the topological order)
4:     $index \leftarrow xcc(g)$, $R \leftarrow \{1\}|S[index]$, $a \leftarrow A(g)$, $b \leftarrow B(g)$
5:     **if** (garbled value of a has not been assigned)
6:         $W_a^0 \in_R \{0,1\}^2$, $W_a^1 \leftarrow W_a^0 \oplus R$
7:     **if** (garbled value of b has not been assigned)
8:         $W_b^0 \in_R \{0,1\}^2$, $W_b^1 \leftarrow W_b^0 \oplus R$
9:     $W_g^0 \leftarrow W_a^0 \oplus W_b^0$, $W_g^1 \leftarrow W_g^0 \oplus R$
10: **for** each wire i that garbled values have not been assigned
11:     $W_i^0 \in_R \{0,1\}^2$, $tmp \in_R \{0,1\}$, $W_i^1 \leftarrow \overline{MSB(W_i^0)}|tmp$
12: **for** each input wire of circuit send the garbled value
13: **for** each $G_g ==$ AND
14:     $a \leftarrow A(g)$, $b \leftarrow B(g)$
15:     $\alpha_a \leftarrow LSB(W_b^1 \oplus W_b^0)$, $\alpha_b \leftarrow LSB(W_a^1 \oplus W_a^0)$, $\alpha_c \leftarrow LSB(W_a^1 \oplus W_b^1)$
16:     $\rho_g \leftarrow [MSB(W_a^{\bar{\alpha}_a})|MSB(W_b^{\bar{\alpha}_b})]$
17:     provide the inputs of OT_1^2: $(W_g^{\alpha_c \oplus (\alpha_a + \alpha_b)}, W_g^{\overline{\alpha_c \oplus (\alpha_a + \alpha_b)}})$
18: **for** each output wire i of circuit
19:     $d_i \leftarrow MSB(W_i^0)$

Algorithm 2. Evaluation of Garbled Circuit Algorithm

1: **Procedure** EVALUATE
2: **for** each input wire i of circuit receive corresponding garbled value
3: **for** each gate g (in the topological order)
4:     $a \leftarrow A(g)$, $b \leftarrow B(g)$
5:     **if** ($G_g ==$ XOR)
6:         $W_g \leftarrow W_a \oplus W_b$
7:     **if** ($G_g ==$ AND)
8:         $\alpha \leftarrow LSB(W_a \oplus W_b)$
9:         **if** $(MSB(W_a)|MSB(W_b) == \rho_g)$
10:             $OT_{in} \leftarrow \bar{\alpha}$
11:         **else**
12:             $OT_{in} \leftarrow \alpha$
13:         provide the select input of OT_1^2 (OT_{in}) and receive its output W_g
14: **for** each primary output wire i
15:     $y_i \leftarrow d_i \oplus MSB(W_i)$

3.3 An Exception in the Proposed Scheme

The algorithms in Subsect. 3.2 present how the scheme works in general. There is a special case in which this general form of the scheme is not applicable due to a security issue. This case occurs when both inputs of an AND gate come from one XCC. Due to page limit, we only discuss the solution but not more details. In these cases the garbler provides the gate's garbled output without sending ρ_g by conducting an OT_1^4. The evaluator uses $MSB(W_a)|MSB(W_b)$ as the select signal, which can uniquely identify a row of AND gate's truth table, and the garbler provides the corresponding garbled outputs. Different benchmarks have been analyzed to see how common this case is and the results are reported in Table 4.

4   Analytical and Experimental Results

In this section, the communication complexity of the proposed scheme has been compared against the schemes proposed in [9,13]. In the next subsection, the communication overhead of each method is investigated when applied to some common SFE applications [19]. The results show significant improvement in communication overheads for most cases. The overheads are stated using the following parameters:

- n_{eval}: the number of the evaluator's inputs,
- k: the symmetric security parameter,
- n_A: the total number of AND gates,
- n_{A_D}: the number of AND gates whose inputs are from two different XCCs,
- n_{A_S}: the number of AND gates with both inputs coming from the same XCC.

The communication of the proposed SFE scheme in this paper depends on the complexity of the OT protocol. To estimate the overhead of the proposed scheme, we need to select one of the proposed OT protocols in the literature. The OT protocols presented in [9,18] are among the best previous work in this field. Although, the communication overhead of the OT protocol in [9] is less than the other work, we consider both to show the efficiency of our work even using OT protocols with more communication overhead. Hereafter, we refer to the protocols presented in [9,13,18] as ExtendedOT, HalfGate, and LutBasedOT, respectively.

4.1 Results

The bit-length of the data transfer (n_{tran}) in different schemes are presented in Table 3. We have considered a number of applications given in [19]. The number of gates in each function, n_{A_D}, n_{A_S}, and n_{xcc} are presented in Table 4. Tables 5 and 6 compare the size of data transfer for HalfGate, GMW and the proposed scheme. The results show improvements in the data transfer size.

Table 3. Data transfer of different schemes

Scheme	n_{tran}(bits)
HalfGate	$2n_A k + nk + n_{eval}k$
Proposed using ExtendedOT	$n_{eval}(k+4) + 2n_{gen} + n_{A_D}(k+6) + n_{A_S}(2k+10)$
GMW using LutBasedOT	$n_{gen} + n_{eval} + 138n_A$
Proposed using LutBasedOT	$75n_{eval} + 2n_{gen} + 78n_{A_D} + 154n_{A_S}$

Table 4. Circuits of basic functions useful for SFE [19]

Function	No. ANDs	No. XORs	No. INVs	n_{A_D}	n_{A_S}	n_{xcc}
AES	6800	25124	1692	400	6400	1
Expanded AES[a]	5440	20325	1927	320	5120	68
DES	18124	1340	10849	16597	1527	10076
Expanded DES[a]	18175	1351	10875	17466	709	10132
MD5	29084	14150	34627	14220	14864	19162
SHA-1	37300	24166	45135	21043	16257	25635
SHA-256	90825	42029	103258	60306	30519	63067
32-bit comparator	150	0	162	150	0	162
32-bit adder	127	61	187	68	59	130
64-bit adder	265	115	379	162	103	278
32 × 32-bit multiplier	5926	1069	5379	4907	1019	3883

[a] Key expanded version of symmetric encryption.

Table 5. The size of data transfer in the proposed scheme and HalfGate using ExtendedOT for several functions

Function	Proposed scheme	HalfGate scheme	Improvement ($\downarrow$%)
AES	1760352	1789952	2
Expanded AES[a]	1414272	1605632	12
DES	2635702	4664320	43
Expanded DES[a]	2537604	4767488	47
MD5	5897160	7576576	22
SHA-1	7179194	9679872	26
SHA-256	16205604	23382272	31
32-bit comparator	24388	50688	52
32-bit adder	28976	44800	35
64-bit adder	57476	92416	38
32 × 32-bit multiplier	930842	1529344	39

[a] Key expanded version of symmetric encryption.

Table 6. The size of data transfer in the proposed scheme and GMW using LutBase-dOT for several functions

Function	Proposed scheme	GMW scheme	Improvement ($\downarrow$%)
AES	1026656	938656	−9
Expanded AES[a]	825856	752256	−9
DES	1534652	2501240	39
Expanded DES[a]	1477870	2508982	41
MD5	3399240	4014104	15
SHA-1	4145956	5147912	19
SHA-256	9404818	12534362	25
32-bit comparator	14164	20764	32
32-bit adder	16854	17590	4
64-bit adder	33426	36698	9
32 × 32-bit multiplier	542136	817852	34

[a] Key expanded version of symmetric encryption.

5   Conclusion

Majority of implementations of semi-honest secure two-party computation schemes still suffer from large communication overhead. The security of the GC-based schemes proposed in previous work mainly depends on the labels of each gate. Hence, the length of the labels has to be larger than a certain value (e.g., 128 bits). In this work, a semi-honest secure two-party computation is proposed whose security is independent of the label size. To this end, we have made use of an oblivious transfer (OT) for each AND gate evaluation. The resulting scheme is similar to GMW; However, it has less communication overhead due to the replacement of OT_1^4 with OT_1^2 in most AND gate evaluation. The results of our experiments on different applications show that the data transfer size of the scheme reduces up to 52% and 41% against GC and GMW based schemes, respectively. We note that any optimization on OT implementation will result in further optimization of the proposed scheme accordingly.

References

1. Bringer, J., Chabanne, H., Patey, A.: Privacy-preserving biometric identification using secure multiparty computation: an overview and recent trends. IEEE Signal Process. Mag. **30**(2), 42–52 (2013)
2. Sui, Y., Zou, X., Du, E.Y., Li, F.: Secure and privacy-preserving biometrics based active authentication. In: IEEE International Conference on Systems, Man, and Cybernetics, pp. 1291–1296 (2012)
3. Barni, M., Failla, P., Lazzeretti, R., Paus, A., Sadeghi, A.R., Schneider, T., Kolesnikov, V.: Efficient privacy-preserving classification of ECG signals. In: First IEEE International Workshop on Information Forensics and Security, pp. 91–95 (2009)

4. Brickell, J., Porter, D.E., Shmatikov, V., Witchel, E.: Privacy-preserving remote diagnostics. In: ACM Conference on Computer and Communications Security, pp. 498–507 (2007)
5. Yao, A.C.C.: How to generate and exchange secrets. In: 27th Annual Symposium on Foundations of Computer Science, pp. 162–167 (1986)
6. Yao, A.C.: Protocols for secure computations. In: 23th Annual Symposium on Foundations of Computer Science, pp. 160–164 (1982)
7. Lindell, Y., Pinkas, B.: A proof of security of Yao's protocol for two-party computation. J. Cryptology **22**(2), 161–188 (2009)
8. Goldreich, O., Micali, S., Wigderson, A.: How to play any mental game. In: Proceedings of the Nineteenth Annual ACM Symposium on Theory of Computing, pp. 218–229 (1987)
9. Dessouky, G., Koushanfar, F., Sadeghi, A.-R., Schneider, T., Zeitouni, S., Zohner, M.: Pushing the communication barrier in secure computation using lookup tables. In: 24th Annual Network and Distributed System Security Symposium (2017)
10. Schneider, T., Zohner, M.: GMW vs. Yao? Efficient secure two-party computation with low depth circuits. In: Sadeghi, A.-R. (ed.) FC 2013. LNCS, vol. 7859, pp. 275–292. Springer, Heidelberg (2013). doi:10.1007/978-3-642-39884-1_23
11. Kolesnikov, V., Schneider, T.: Improved garbled circuit: free XOR gates and applications. In: Aceto, L., Damgård, I., Goldberg, L.A., Halldórsson, M.M., Ingólfsdóttir, A., Walukiewicz, I. (eds.) ICALP 2008. LNCS, vol. 5126, pp. 486–498. Springer, Heidelberg (2008). doi:10.1007/978-3-540-70583-3_40
12. Beaver, D., Micali, S., Rogaway, P.: The round complexity of secure protocols. In: ACM Symposium on Theory of Computing, pp. 503–513 (1990)
13. Zahur, S., Rosulek, M., Evans, D.: Two halves make a whole. In: Oswald, E., Fischlin, M. (eds.) EUROCRYPT 2015. LNCS, vol. 9057, pp. 220–250. Springer, Heidelberg (2015). doi:10.1007/978-3-662-46803-6_8
14. Naor, M., Pinkas, B., Sumner, R.: Privacy preserving auctions and mechanism design. In: ACM Conference on Electronic Commerce, pp. 129–139 (1999)
15. Kolesnikov, V., Kumaresan, R.: Improved OT extension for transferring short secrets. In: Canetti, R., Garay, J.A. (eds.) CRYPTO 2013. LNCS, vol. 8043, pp. 54–70. Springer, Heidelberg (2013). doi:10.1007/978-3-642-40084-1_4
16. Demmler, D., Dessouky, G., Koushanfar, F., Sadeghi, A.-R., Schneider, T., Zeitouni, S.: Automated synthesis of optimized circuits for secure computation. In: ACM Conference on Computer and Communications Security, pp. 1504–1517 (2015)
17. Naor, M., Pinkas, B.: Computationally secure oblivious transfer. J. Cryptology **18**(1), 1–35 (2005)
18. Asharov, G., Lindell, Y., Schneider, T., Zohner, M.: More efficient oblivious transfer and extensions for faster secure computation. In: ACM Conference on Computer and Communications Security, pp. 535–548 (2013)
19. Circuits of basic functions suitable for MPC and FHE. http://www.cs.bris.ac.uk/research/cryptographysecurity/mpc

An Efficient Non-transferable Proxy Re-encryption Scheme

S. Sharmila Deva Selvi, Arinjita Paul[(✉)], and C. Pandu Rangan

Theoretical Computer Science Lab,
Department of Computer Science and Engineering,
Indian Institute of Technology Madras, Chennai, India
{sharmila,arinjita,prangan}@cse.iitm.ac.in

Abstract. Proxy re-encryption (PRE) allows re-encryption of a ciphertext for Alice (delegator) into a ciphertext for Bob (delegatee) via a semi-trusted proxy, who should not obtain the underlying plaintext. Alice generates a re-encryption key (re-key) for the proxy using which, the proxy transforms the ciphertexts. The basic notion of PRE provides security against the proxy from learning anything about the encrypted message given the re-encryption key. However, this is not sufficient in all situations as the proxy can collude with Bob and re-delegate Alice's decryption rights. Hence, non-transferability is a desirable property in real-time scenarios wherein an illegal attempt to transfer Alice's decryption rights exposes Bob's private key as a penalty. In Pairing 2010, Wang et al. presented a CPA secure non-transferable Identity Based PRE scheme in the random oracle model. However, we show that the scheme violates the non-transferable property. Also, we present the first construction of a non-transferable unidirectional PRE scheme in the PKI setting using bilinear maps which meets CCA security under a variant of the decisional Diffie-Hellman hardness assumption in the random oracle model.

Keywords: Proxy re-encryption · Bilinear maps · Public key · Unidirectional · Non-transferable

1 Introduction

Blaze et al. [2] in 1998 first proposed the concept of proxy re-encryption, which allows a proxy with specific information (re-encryption key) to translate a ciphertext for Alice into another ciphertext for Bob, without knowing the underlying plaintext. PRE has many useful applications, such as ensuring security of shared data in the cloud computing setting, enabling a data owner to encrypt shared

---

S. Sharmila Deva Selvi—Postdoctoral researcher supported by Project No. CCE/CEP/22/VK&CP/CSE/14-15 on Information Security & Awareness(ISEA) Phase-II by Ministry of Electronics & Information Technology, Government of India
A. Paul and C. Pandu Rangan—Work supported by Project No. CCE/CEP/22/VK&CP/CSE/14-15 on ISEA-Phase II.

L. Batten et al. (Eds.): ATIS 2017, CCIS 719, pp. 35–47, 2017.
DOI: 10.1007/978-981-10-5421-1_4

data in the cloud in his public key and store them, which can be transformed by a proxy-server into a ciphertext for a legitimate recipient. This consigns the costly burden of secure data sharing to the resource-abundant semi-trusted proxy. PRE offers promising solutions to encrypted email forwarding, digital rights management, outsourced encrypted spam filtering among others [1,3,14].

PRE schemes are classified into bidirectional and unidirectional schemes based on the direction of delegation. They are also classified into single-hop and multihop schemes. In this paper, we focus on unidirectional single-hop PRE schemes.

The existing PRE schemes assume that the proxy is semi-trusted and does not collude with Bob to acquire Alice's private key or re-delegate Alice's decryption rights to a malicious user Carol, failing to provide the non-transferable property which was first proposed by Ateniese et al. [1]. A PRE scheme is said to be non-transferable when the colluding proxy and delegatees should not be able to re-delegate decryption rights to other parties without compromising the private keys of the delegatees or the privacy of the delegatees. Note that Bob can always decrypt and forward the message to the malicious user Carol, but this would require Bob to be online. The notion of non-transferability is to prevent the colluding proxy and Bob to provide Carol with a secret value that can be used to decrypt Alice's ciphertexts when Bob is offline. Hence, the only way for Bob to transfer decryption capabilities to Carol is to reveal his own private key.

1.1 Related Work

While several protocols achieving PRE in various models are available, only a few provides the non-transferable property as well. In this section, we focus on PRE schemes supporting non-transferability. Illegal delegation of decryption rights would cause unauthorised sharing of data and financial losses which marks non-transferability as an important property in practice, such as the cloud service security scenario. Libert et al. [9] stated the difficulty in preventing such collusions and proposed a CPA secure scheme to trace the malicious proxies after a collusion. Even though penalising the colluders after an unauthorised transference is a possible strategy to attain non-transferability, it is more desirable to prevent collusion than discouraging it. In the ID-based PRE scheme given by Wang et al. [13] in the random oracle model, a PKG generates the re-encryption keys and this is undesirable as it requires the PKG to be online for the re-encryption keys generation and introduces the *key-escrow problem* and *key-despotism problem*. He et al. [7] proposes a non-transferable ID-based PRE scheme in the random oracle model that addresses the previous problems but involves multiple rounds of interactions for partial-key generations and key-validations which makes their scheme less practical. Hayashi et al. [6] introduces a partial solution to non-transferability as their schemes are shown to achieve unforgeability of re-encryption keys against collusion attack (UFReKey-CA), assuming the hardness of the variants of the Diffie-Hellman inversion problem in the standard model, which was later shown vulnerable to forgeability attack on the re-encryption keys by Isshiki et al. [8]. Guo et al. [5] uses indistinguishability obfuscation ($i\mathcal{O}$), a highly complex primitive, to resolve the problem of non-transferability in PRE.

1.2 Our Contributions

In 2005, Ateniese et al. [1] stated that "*achieving a proxy scheme that is non-transferable, in the sense that the only way for Bob to transfer offline decryption capabilities to Carol is to expose his own secret key, seems to be the main open problem left for proxy re-encryption*". Guo et al. [5] achieves non-transferability using indistinguishability obfuscation ($i\mathcal{O}$), a highly complex and impractical primitive. Our major contribution lies in providing a non-transferable unidirectional single-hop PRE scheme in the random oracle model that uses bilinear maps and group operations, and is much more practical. To the best of our knowledge, there are no known PRE schemes satisfying non-transferability in the PKI setting based on group theoretic operations. Wang et al. [13] proposed an uni-directional non-transferable PRE scheme in the random oracle model in the identity-based setting, in which the fully trusted PKG generates the re-encryption keys. We present an attack on their scheme, by showing that the colluders can indeed construct an illegal decryption function that can be used by any malicious third party to decrypt the delegator's second level ciphertexts, without any compromise of the delegatees private keys.

2 Preliminaries

2.1 Bilinear Pairings

Our PRE scheme is based on bilinear pairings. Let G_1 and G_2 be an additive and multiplicative cyclic groups respectively of prime order q. G_1 is generated by P. $\mathbb{G}_1$ has an admissible bilinear mapping into $\mathbb{G}_2$, $\hat{e} : \mathbb{G}_1 \times \mathbb{G}_1 \to \mathbb{G}_2$, if the following three conditions hold:

1. *Bilinear*: $\forall P, Q, R \in G_1$, $\forall a, b \in \mathbb{Z}_q^*$
   (a) $\hat{e}(P + Q, R) = \hat{e}(P, R) \cdot \hat{e}(Q, R)$
   (b) $\hat{e}(P, Q + R) = \hat{e}(P, Q) \cdot \hat{e}(P, R)$
   (c) $\hat{e}(aP, bQ) = \hat{e}(P, Q)^{ab}$
2. *Non-degenerate*: $\exists P, Q \in \mathbb{G}_1$ such that, $\hat{e}(P, Q) \neq 1_{\mathbb{G}_2}$.
3. *Computable*: $\forall P, Q \in \mathbb{G}_1$, there is an efficient algorithm to compute $\hat{e}(P, Q)$.

2.2 Hardness Assumptions

In this section, we state the computational hardness assumptions used to establish the security of the schemes.

Modified Decisional Bilinear Diffie-Hellman (m-DBDH) Assumption [12]: The m-DBDH assumption is said to hold if, given the elements $\{P, aP, bP, cP, a^{-1}P\} \in \mathbb{G}_1$ and $T \in \mathbb{G}_2$, there exists no probabilistic polynomial-time adversary which can determine whether $T = \hat{e}(P, P)^{abc}$ or a random element from $\mathbb{G}_2$ with a non-negligible advantage, where P is a generator of $\mathbb{G}_1$ and $a, b, c \in_R \mathbb{Z}_q^*$.

1-Weak Decisional Bilinear Diffie-Hellman Inversion (1-WDBDHI) Assumption [10]: The 1-wDBDHI assumption is said to hold if, given the elements $\{P, \frac{1}{a}P, bP\} \in \mathbb{G}_1$ and $T \in \mathbb{G}_2$, there exists no probabilistic polynomial-time adversary which can determine whether $T = \hat{e}(P, P)^{ab}$ or a random element from $\mathbb{G}_2$ with a non-negligible advantage, where P is a generator of $\mathbb{G}_1$ and $a, b \in_R \mathbb{Z}_q^*$.

3 Definition and Security Model

3.1 Definition

We describe the syntactical definition of unidirectional proxy re-encryption [13] and its security notion. A PRE scheme consists of the following seven algorithms:

- Global setup(λ): returns a set of public parameters *params*, which is shared by all the users in the system.
- KeyGen(*params*): returns the public key and private key pair (pk_i, sk_i) of a user i.
- ReKeyGen($sk_i, pk_i, pk_j, params$): returns a re-encryption key $RK_{i \rightarrow j}$.
- Encrypt($m, pk_i, params$): returns the ciphertext C_i corresponding to m which is allowed to be re-encrypted for another user. The ciphertext C_i generated is called as the second level ciphertext.
- Re-Encrypt($C_i, RK_{i \rightarrow j}, params$): returns a ciphertext C_j', re-encryption of C_i, now encrypted under the public key pk_j. The re-encrypted ciphertext C_j' is called as the first level ciphertext.
- Decrypt($C_i, sk_i, params$): returns a plaintext m or the error symbol $\perp$ if the ciphertext is invalid.
- Re-Decrypt($C_j', sk_j, params$): returns a plaintext m or the error symbol $\perp$ if the ciphertext is invalid.

The consistency of a PRE scheme for any given public parameters *params* and a public-private key pair $\{(pk_i, sk_i), (pk_j, sk_j)\}$ is defined as follows:

1. Consistency between encryption and decryption; i.e.,

$$Decrypt(Encrypt(m, pk_i), sk_i) = m, \forall m \in \mathcal{M}$$

2. Consistency between encryption, proxy re-encryption and decryption; i.e.,

$$Re - Decrypt(Re - Encrypt(RK_{i \rightarrow j}, Encrypt(m, pk_i)), sk_j) = m, \forall m \in \mathcal{M}$$

3.2 Security Model

Since there exists two types of ciphertexts namely first level and second level ciphertexts in PRE, it is necessary to prove the security of each of these two levels as defined in [9]. As in [4], in our model, the adversary $\mathcal{A}$ can only obtain the uncorrupted public keys $pk_{i:i \in HU}$ and corrupted public-private key pairs $\{pk_i, sk_i\}_{i:i \in CU}$ from the challenger $\mathcal{C}$ and cannot determine which parties will be compromised adaptively. $\mathcal{A}$ is provided with re-encryption keys he is entitled to know but can adaptively query the re-encryption and decryption oracles which $\mathcal{C}$ answers as below and simulates an environment running PRE for $\mathcal{A}$.

- Re-encryption oracle $\mathcal{O}_{ReEnc}(C_i, pk_i, pk_j)$: $\mathcal{C}$ runs $C_j' \leftarrow ReEnc(C_i, RK_{i \rightarrow j})$, where $RK_{i \rightarrow j} = ReKeyGen(sk_i, pk_i, pk_j)$ and returns C_j' to $\mathcal{A}$.
- Second level decryption oracle $\mathcal{O}_{Dec}(C_i, pk_i)$: $\mathcal{C}$ runs $Decrypt(C_i, sk_i)$ and returns the result to $\mathcal{A}$.
- First level decryption oracle $\mathcal{O}_{ReDec}(C_j', pk_j)$: $\mathcal{C}$ runs $ReDecrypt(C_j', sk_j)$ and returns the result to $\mathcal{A}$.

Second Level Ciphertext Security. It models the scenario that the adversary $\mathcal{A}$ is challenged with a second level ciphertext C^*, where C^* is the challenge ciphertext under the targeted public key pk_{i^*} where we use the index i^* to denote the targeted user. $\mathcal{C}$ responds to the queries issued by $\mathcal{A}$ to the above defined oracles considering that they do not allow $\mathcal{A}$ to decrypt the challenge ciphertext trivially. For example, $\mathcal{A}$ is not allowed to obtain a re-encryption key $RK_{i^* \rightarrow j}$ where sk_j was already compromised. In such a case, $\mathcal{A}$ can trivially decrypt the challenge ciphertext by first re-encrypting it into a first level ciphertext and then decrypting it with sk_j. Also, for a first level ciphertext $C_j' = Re\text{-}Encrypt(C_i^*, RK_{i^* \rightarrow j})$, querying on $\mathcal{O}_{ReDec}(C_j', pk_j)$ by $\mathcal{A}$ is not permitted.

Below is given the formal definition for second level ciphertext's semantic security under chosen ciphertext attack (IND-PRE-CCA).

Definition 1. *Given a single-hop unidirectional PRE scheme, the advantage of any PPT adversary $\mathcal{A}$ denoted by $Adv_{\mathcal{A}}$ in the game shown below is defined by the probability:*

$$Pr[\{(pk_i, sk_i) \leftarrow KeyGen(\lambda)\}_{i \in CU \cup HU}, (pk_i^*, sk_i^*) \leftarrow KeyGen(\lambda);$$
$$\{RK_{i^* \rightarrow j} \leftarrow ReKeyGen(sk_i^*, pk_j)\}_{j \in HU};$$
$$\{RK_{i \rightarrow j} \leftarrow ReKeyGen(sk_i, pk_j)\}_{i \in HU, j \in CU \cup HU \cup \{i^*\}},$$
$$(m_0, m_1, St) \leftarrow \mathcal{A}^{\mathcal{O}_{ReEnc}, \mathcal{O}_{ReDec}}(pk_i^*, \{pk_j, sk_j\}_{j \in CU},$$
$$\{pk_j\}_{j \in HU}, \{RK_{i^* \rightarrow j}\}_{j \in HU}; \{RK_{i \rightarrow j}\}_{i \in HU, j \in CU \cup HU \cup \{i^*\}});$$
$$b \in_R \{0, 1\}, C^* \leftarrow Encrypt(pk_i^*, m_b); b' \leftarrow \mathcal{A}^{\mathcal{O}_{ReEnc}, \mathcal{O}_{ReDec}}(C^*, St) : b' = b]$$

Note that $|m_0| = |m_1|$. St is the state information maintained by $\mathcal{A}$. A single hop unidirectional PRE scheme is IND-PRE-CCA secure for second level ciphertext if for any IND-PRE-CCA adversary $\mathcal{A}$, $|Adv_{\mathcal{A}} - \frac{1}{2}|$ is negligibly small.

First level ciphertext security. In the first-level ciphertext security, $\mathcal{A}$ is allowed to obtain the re-encryption keys for *any* user, since the first level ciphertext cannot be further re-encrypted in a given single hop PRE scheme. This also justifies the fact that there is no need for any second-level decryption or re-encryption oracle as all the re-encryption keys are available to $\mathcal{A}$.

Definition 2. *Given a single-hop unidirectional PRE scheme, the advantage of any PPT adversary $\mathcal{A}$ denoted by $Adv_{\mathcal{A}}$ in the game shown below is defined by the probability:*

$$Pr[\{(pk_i, sk_i) \leftarrow KeyGen(\lambda)\}_{i \in CU \cup HU}, (pk_i^*, sk_i^*) \leftarrow KeyGen(\lambda);$$
$$\{RK_{i \rightarrow j} \leftarrow ReKeyGen(sk_i, pk_j)\}_{i,j \in CU \cup HU \cup \{i^*\}},$$
$$(m_0, m_1, St) \leftarrow \mathcal{A}^{\mathcal{O}_{ReDec}}(pk_i^*, \{pk_j, sk_j\}_{j \in CU},$$
$$\{pk_j\}_{j \in HU}, \{RK_{i \rightarrow j}\}_{i,j \in CU \cup HU \cup \{i^*\}});$$
$$b \in_R \{0, 1\}, C^* \leftarrow Re{-}Encrypt(Encrypt(m_b, pk_i), RK_{i \rightarrow i^*})_{i \in HU \cup CU};$$
$$b' \leftarrow \mathcal{A}^{\mathcal{O}_{ReDec}}(C^*, St) : b' = b]$$

Note that $|m_0| = |m_1|$ and St is the state information maintained by $\mathcal{A}$. A single hop unidirectional PRE scheme is said to be IND-PRE-CCA secure for first level ciphertext if for any IND-PRE-CCA adversary $\mathcal{A}$, $|Adv_\mathcal{A} - \frac{1}{2}|$ is negligibly small.

4   Non-transferability

In order to achieve non-transferability, Alice's ciphertext must possess the property that if a malicious user has the private key of Bob and the re-encryption key, only then it can obtain the plaintext, else it shall obtain nothing useful. Our security definition of non-transferability follows from the definition of non-transferability proposed in [6].

In the following definition, we use the following subscripts $i^*, h \in HU, c_i \in CU, j$ to denote a target honest delegator, an honest user, a corrupted delegatee and a malicious user respectively, where $i \in \{1, \cdots L\}$ and L is polynomially bounded.

Definition 3 [6]. *Non-transferability: A single-hop unidirectional PRE scheme is non-transferable if there exists a polynomial time algorithm $\mathcal{J}'$, such that*

$$Pr[(pk_i^*, sk_i^*) \leftarrow Keygen(1^\lambda); (pk_h, sk_h) \leftarrow Keygen(1^\lambda);$$
$$\{(pk_{c_i}, sk_{c_i} \leftarrow Keygen(1^\lambda)\}; (pk_j, sk_j) \leftarrow Keygen(1^\lambda);$$
$$\{RK_{i^* \rightarrow c_i} \leftarrow ReKeyGen(sk_i^*, pk_{c_i})\}; \{RK_{h \rightarrow c_i} \leftarrow ReKeyGen(sk_h, pk_{c_i})\};$$
$$m \leftarrow \mathcal{M}; C^* \leftarrow Encrypt(m, pk_i^*); \{m_i \leftarrow \mathcal{M}\}; \{C_i \leftarrow Encrypt(m_i, pk_{c_i})\};$$
$$\{m_i' \leftarrow \mathcal{M}\}; \{C_i' \leftarrow Re{-}Encrypt(RK_{h \rightarrow c_i}, Encrypt(m_i', pk_h))\};$$
$$X \leftarrow \mathcal{C}(pk_i^*, \{(pk_{c_i}, sk_{c_i})\}, \{RK_{i^* \rightarrow c_i}\}); m_\mathcal{J} \leftarrow \mathcal{J}(X, (pk_j, sk_j), C^*);$$
$$m_{\mathcal{J}'} \leftarrow \mathcal{J}'(X, (pk_j, sk_j), \{C_i\}, \{C_i'\})$$
$$: m \neq m_\mathcal{J} \vee m_{\mathcal{J}'} \in \{m_i\} \cup \{m_i'\}]$$

is overwhelming for any polynomial time algorithm $\mathcal{C}$, $\mathcal{J}$ and polynomial L.

In the above definition, $\mathcal{C}$ denote the set of colluders and $\mathcal{J}, \mathcal{J}'$ denotes the malicious users. The definition states that, if $\mathcal{C}$ tries to construct an illegal decryption box X for the second level ciphertext of the target honest user i^* to re-delegate the decryption rights to $\mathcal{J}$, then $\mathcal{J}'$ can exploit X to compromise the decryption capabilities of $\mathcal{C}$. Informally, the colluders should not be able to generate a decryption-box to decrypt the delegator's ciphertext, without compromising the private keys of the delegatee. The main challenge for constructing such a scheme lies in extracting the decryption capability of the delegatee from this illegal decryption box.

5   Analysis of a CPA-Secure Non-transferable PRE Scheme by Wang et al. [13]

5.1   Review of the Scheme

- **Setup(λ):** $\mathbb{G}_1$ and $\mathbb{G}_2$ are multiplicative groups of order p. $\hat{e} : \mathbb{G}_1 \times \mathbb{G}_1 \to \mathbb{G}_2$ is a bilinear map. PKG computes $g_1 = g^\alpha \in \mathbb{G}_1$ where g is a generator of $\mathbb{G}_1$ and $\alpha \in \mathbb{Z}_p^*$. Also, $g_2, \eta \in \mathbb{G}_1$ are chosen at random. $H : \{0,1\}^l \to \mathbb{G}_1$ is a cryptographic hash function. the system parameters are $params = \{\mathbb{G}_1, \mathbb{G}_2, p, \hat{e}, g, g_1, g_2, \eta, H\}$, and $msk = g_2^\alpha$.
- **Extract(id):** Choose $u \in \mathbb{Z}_p^*$, set $sk_{id} = (d_0, d_1) = (g_2^\alpha H(id)^u, g^u)$, where $u = h_{msk}(id)$. Validation of key by user id with sk sk_{id} is done by

$$\hat{e}(d_0, g) \stackrel{?}{=} \hat{e}(g_1, g_2)\hat{e}(H(id), d_1)$$

- **ReKeyGen(id, id'):** PKG returns seed of re-key to delegator id:

$$\tilde{rk}_{id \to id'} = \left(\frac{H(id)}{H(id')} \right)^{u'}$$

Here, u' is selected by PKG to generate private key of id'. User id selects $\delta \in \mathbb{Z}_p^*$ at random and computes rekey as:

$$rk_{id \to id'} = (rk_1, rk_2) = \left(\eta^\delta \left(\frac{H(id)}{H(id')} \right)^{u'}, g^\delta \right)$$

- **Encryption($m \in \mathbb{G}_2, id$):** Encryptor chooses $r \in \mathbb{Z}_p^*$ and computes

$$C = (C_1, C_2, C_3, C_4) = (m.\hat{e}(g_1, g_2)^r, g^r, H(id)^r, \eta^r)$$

- **Re-Encryption(m, id'):** The proxy conducts a consistency check for the received 2nd level ciphertext: $\hat{e}(C_2, \eta) \stackrel{?}{=} \hat{e}(C_4, g)$. If it holds, compute:

$$C' = (C_1', C_2, C_3) = \left(C_1 . \frac{\hat{e}(C_4, rk_2)}{\hat{e}(C_2, rk_1)}, C_2, C_3 \right)$$

- **Decryption(C, sk_{id}):** m is obtained from the second level ciphertext by computing:

$$m = C_1 . \frac{\hat{e}(C_3, d_1)}{\hat{e}(C_2, d_0)}$$

- **Re-Decryption($C', sk_{id'}$):** m is obtained from the first level ciphertext by computing:

$$m = C_1' . \frac{\hat{e}(C_3, d_1')}{\hat{e}(C_2, d_0')}$$

5.2   Attack on the Scheme

We show an attack on the non-transferable property of the ID-PRE scheme proposed in [13]. As per the definition of non-transferability in Sect. 4, the adversary is allowed to obtain one pair of keys $(rk_{id_{i*} \to id_j}, sk_{id_j})$ wherein the delegatee id_j is a corrupt user. So, consider the following attack where the adversary queries for a re-encryption key $(rk_{id_i \to id_j}) = (rk_1, rk_2)$ and a private key for id_j to obtain the corresponding private key $sk_{id_j} = (d_0, d_1) = (g_2^{\alpha} H(id_j)^{u_j}, g^{u_j})$. Now, given the second level ciphertext $C = (C_1, C_2, C_3, C_4)$, the adversary does the following computation:

1. Pick $\beta \in \mathbb{Z}_q^*$.
2. Define $d' \overset{\Delta}{=} d_1 \cdot g^{\beta} = g^{u_j + \beta}$.
3. Compute the value of a partial decryption key $psk_{id_i} = (rk_1 \cdot d_0 \cdot H(id_i)^{\beta})$
   $= \eta^{\delta} \left(\frac{H(id_i)}{H(id_j)} \right)^{u_j} \cdot g_2^{\alpha} H(id_j)^{u_j} \cdot H(id_i)^{\beta}$
   $= \eta^{\delta} \cdot H(id_i)^{u_j + \beta} \cdot g_2^{\alpha}$ (Note that this gives the adversary a function of the private key of user id_i which can be used to compute a decryption box for ciphertexts encrypted under id_i)
4. Construct a decryption box for a second level ciphertext of id_i as:

$$m = \frac{C_1}{\hat{e}(C_2, psk_{id_i}) \cdot \hat{e}(C_3, d')^{-1} \cdot \hat{e}(C_4, rk_2)^{-1}}$$

The malicious users can obtain the second level ciphertext $C = (C_1, C_2, C_3, C_4)$ of user id_i and obtain obtain the plaintext m as follows:

$$\frac{C_1}{\hat{e}(C_2, psk_{id_i}) \cdot \hat{e}(C_3, d')^{-1} \cdot \hat{e}(C_4, rk_2)^{-1}}$$
$$= \frac{C_1}{\hat{e}(C_2, \eta^{\delta} \cdot H(id_i)^{u_j + \beta} \cdot g_2^{\alpha}) \cdot \hat{e}(C_3, d')^{-1} \cdot \hat{e}(C_4, rk_2)^{-1}}$$
$$= \frac{m \cdot \hat{e}(g_1, g_2)^r}{\hat{e}(g_1, g_2)^r \cdot \hat{e}(C_4, rk_2) \cdot \hat{e}(d', C_3) \cdot \hat{e}(C_4, rk_2)^{-1} \cdot \hat{e}(d', C_3)^{-1}}$$
$$= m.$$

Note that the private key of the delegatee (d_0, d_1) is not compromised and the second level encrypted message of user id_i is exposed to the malicious users violating the non-transferable property of Proxy Re-encryption.

6   A CCA-secure Non-transferable Scheme

6.1   Our Scheme

- Setup(λ): Let λ be the security parameter, $\mathbb{G}_1, \mathbb{G}_2$ are two groups of prime order q, $e : \mathbb{G}_1 \times \mathbb{G}_1 \to \mathbb{G}_2$ is a bilinear map. Let P be a generator of the group $\mathbb{G}_1$ and randomly choose $Q \in \mathbb{G}_1$. Set $\alpha = \hat{e}(P, P)$. Choose five hash functions

$\tilde{H} : \mathbb{G}_1 \leftarrow \mathbb{Z}_q^*, H_1 : \mathbb{G}_1 \times \mathbb{G}_1 \times \mathbb{G}_1 \times \mathbb{G}_1 \rightarrow \mathbb{Z}_q^*, H_2 : \mathbb{G}_2 \rightarrow \{0,1\}^{l_m+l_\omega}, H_3 :$
$\{0,1\}^{l_m+l_\omega} \rightarrow \mathbb{Z}_q^*, H_4 : \mathbb{G}_1 \times \mathbb{G}_1 \times \{0,1\}^{l_m+l_\omega} \times \mathbb{G}_1 \rightarrow \mathbb{G}_1$, where l_m, l_ω denote the message space $\mathcal{M}$. The hash functions are modelled as random oracles in the security proof. The global parameters are:

$$params := \{\mathbb{G}_1, \mathbb{G}_2, q, P, Q, \tilde{H}, H_1, H_2, H_3, H_4, \alpha\}$$

- $KeyGen(\lambda,\text{params})$: Pick $x_i, y_i, z_i \leftarrow \mathbb{Z}_q^*$, set the private key $sk_i = (x_i, y_i, z_i)$, public key $pk_i = (X_i, Y_i, Z_i, Q_i) = (x_i P, y_i P, z_i P, y_i Q)$ and set $h_i = H_1(pk_i)$.
- $ReKeyGen(sk_i, pk_i, pk_j, \text{params})$: Given as input the public key $pk_j = (X_j, Y_j, Z_j, Q_j)$ and private key $sk_i = (x_i, y_i, z_i)$ of user i and the public key $pk_j = (X_j, Y_j, Z_j, Q_j)$ of user j, pick $s, \delta, \beta \leftarrow \mathbb{Z}_q$ at random, and compute the re-encryption key as follows:

$$T = \frac{z_i + h_i}{\delta + \beta} \in \mathbb{Z}_q^*,$$

$$R = x_i^{-1}(\delta Y_j + sP) + x_i^{-1}\tilde{H}(X_j)Q$$
$$= x_i^{-1}(\delta y_j + s)P + x_i^{-1}\tilde{H}(X_j)Q \in \mathbb{G}_1,$$

$$S = y_i^{-1}(\beta Y_j - sP) + y_i^{-1}Q_j$$
$$= y_i^{-1}(\beta y_j - s)P + y_i^{-1}Q_j \in \mathbb{G}_1.$$

Return the re-encryption key $RK_{i \rightarrow j} = (R, S, T)$.
- $Encrypt(m, pk_i)$: Given a message $m \in \mathcal{M}$ and a public key $pk_i = (X_i, Y_i, Z_i, Q_i)$ as input:
  - Choose $\omega \in_R \mathbb{Z}_q^*$.
  - Set $r = H_3(m, \omega) \in \mathbb{Z}_q^*$.
  - Compute $C_1 = rX_i \in \mathbb{G}_1$.
  - Compute $C_2 = rY_i \in \mathbb{G}_1$.
  - Compute $C_3 = (m||\omega) \oplus H_2(\hat{e}(Z_i + h_i P, P)^r) = (m||\omega) \oplus H_2(\hat{e}(P, P)^{(z_i+h_i)r})$.
  - Compute $C_4 = r \cdot H_4(C_1, C_2, C_3, C_5) \in \mathbb{G}_1$.
  - Compute $C_5 = r \cdot Q \in \mathbb{G}_1$.

The second level ciphertext $C = (C_1, C_2, C_3, C_4, C_5)$ is returned.
- $Re\text{-}Encrypt(C, RK_{i \rightarrow j})$: On input of a second level ciphertext $C = (C_1, C_2, C_3, C_4, C_5)$ and a re-key $RK_{i \rightarrow j} = (R, S, T)$, check the validity of C by testing if condition (1) and (2) holds:

$$\hat{e}(C_4, X_i) \stackrel{?}{=} \hat{e}(H_4(C_1, C_2, C_3, C_5), C_1) \tag{1}$$

$$\hat{e}(X_i + Y_i, C_5) \stackrel{?}{=} \hat{e}(C_1 + C_2, Q) \tag{2}$$

If the above check fails, return $invalid$, else compute

$$D_1 = \left[\frac{\hat{e}(C_1, R) \cdot \hat{e}(C_2, S)}{\hat{e}(\tilde{H}(X_j)P, C_5) \cdot \hat{e}(Y_j, C_5)} \right]^T = \hat{e}(P, P)^{(z_i+h_i)ry_j} \in \mathbb{G}_2, \tag{3}$$

Set $D_2 = C_3, D_3 = C_5$; return $D = (D_1, D_2, D_3)$ as the first level ciphertext.

- *Decrypt*(C, sk_i): Given as input the private key sk_i and second level ciphertext $C = (C_1, C_2, C_3, C_4, C_5)$, first check if conditions (1) and (2) hold. If they do not hold, return "invalid", else compute

$$(m||\omega) = H_2(\hat{e}((C_1 + C_2), \frac{1}{(x_i + y_i)}P)^{(z_i + h_i)}) \oplus C_3 \qquad (4)$$

Remark 1. Conditions (1) and (2) allow for the public verifiability of the ciphertext C. After conditions (1) and (2) are checked, recover $(m||\omega)$ and it suffices to verify any one of the conditions from (6) to (9) in $Verify(pk_i, (m||\omega), C)$.

Remark 2. To avoid checking conditions (1) and (2) as it incurs heavy computation cost as indicated in Table 2 due to bilinear pairing, recover $(m||\omega)$, ensure if C is well-formed by checking if $Verify(pk_i, (m||\omega), C) = valid$ and return $(m||\omega)$, else return *invalid*.

- *Re-Decrypt*$(D, sk_j,)$: Given as input a private key sk_j and first level ciphertext $D = (D_1, D_2, D_3)$, compute

$$(m||\omega) = H_2(D_1^{y_j^{-1}}) \oplus D_2 \qquad (5)$$

Return $(m||\omega)$.
- *Verify*$((pk_i, m||\omega, C))$: Given as input a second level ciphertext $C = (C_1, C_2, C_3, C_4, C_5)$, a public key pk_i and a message $(m||\omega)$, compute $r = H_3(m||\omega)$ and check if the following conditions hold:

$$C_1 \overset{?}{=} r \cdot X_i \qquad (6)$$

$$C_2 \overset{?}{=} r \cdot Y_i \qquad (7)$$

$$C_4 \overset{?}{=} r \cdot H_4(C_1, C_2, C_3, C_5) \qquad (8)$$

$$C_5 \overset{?}{=} r \cdot Q \qquad (9)$$

If all the conditions (6)–(9) are satisfied, return *valid* else return *invalid*.

6.2   Security Proof

We prove the second level security under a variant of the m-DBDH assumption.

Lemma 1. *The variant of the modified decisional bilinear diffie-hellman (m-DBDH) assumption is said to hold if, given the elements $(P, aP, a^{-1}P, a^{-2}P, bP, cP)$ and $T \in \mathbb{G}_2$, there exists no probabilistic polynomial-time adversary which can determine whether $T = \hat{e}(P, P)^{abc}$ or a random element from $\mathbb{G}_2$ with a non-negligible advantage, where P is a generator of $\mathbb{G}_1$ and $a, b, c \in_R \mathbb{Z}_q^*$.*

Table 1. Comparative analysis of the properties of uni-directional single-hop PRE schemes studied in the literature and our scheme.

Property	[13]	[7]	[6]	[5]	Our scheme
Model	Random Oracle	Random Oracle	Standard	Standard	Random Oracle
Security	CCA	CCA	RCCA	CPA	CCA
Non-interactive	No	No	Yes	Yes	Yes
Proxy invisibility	Yes	Yes	Yes	Yes	Yes
Collusion-safe	Yes	Yes	Yes	Yes	Yes
Non-transitive	Yes	Yes	Yes	Yes	Yes
Non-transferable	No	Yes	No	Yes	Yes
Non-key escrow	Yes	No	Yes	Yes	Yes

Theorem 1. *Our proposed scheme is CCA-secure for the second level ciphertext under the variant of the m-DBDH assumption.*

Theorem 2. *Our proposed scheme is CCA-secure for the first level ciphertext under the 1-wDBDHI assumption.*

Remark 3. The proof of Lemma 1, Theorems 1 and 2 is shown in the full version of this paper [11].

Remark 4. The proposed scheme is non-transferable as the proxy and a set of colluding delegatees cannot re-delegate decryption rights to a third party. We can observe this from the following. In order to re-delegate decryption rights to an illegal user, the colluding delegatee will construct the decryption box $(D'_1 \oplus C_3)$ by defining $D'_1 \overset{\Delta}{=} D_1^{y_j^{-1}} = e(P,P)^{(z_i+h_i)r \cdot y_j \cdot y_j^{-1}} = e(P,P)^{(z_i+h_i)r}$. Given $C = (C_1, C_2, C_3, C_4, C_5)$, which is the second level ciphertext encrypted under the public key of the delegator, any malicious user can decrypt C by computing $D'_1 \oplus C_3$. However, this re-delegation will only succeed when the delegatee sends his private key component y_j explicitly to the malicious user as y_j^{-1} must be used to exponentiate D_1 to compute D'_1 and extract $(m||\omega)$. Since the value of D_1 changes in every delegation as a fresh random element $\omega \in \mathbb{Z}_q^*$ is used for every encryption, the value of $D^{y_j^{-1}}$ cannot be computed offline and hence must be explicitly provided by the delegatee to the malicious users. Hence, the delegatee must expose his private key for the illegal transference of decryption rights to a third party. Therefore, as per the definition in Sect. 4, non-transferable property is achieved in our scheme.

7 Comparison

We give a comparison of our scheme with the existing single-hop PRE schemes studied in the literature with respect to the non-transferable property. In Table 1, we show the various properties of a PRE scheme which are satisfied by the existing schemes alongside our scheme. In Table 2, we show the computational

Table 2. The Efficiency comparisons among unidirectional schemes in the literature with our scheme. * $O(n) = O(logN)$, where N is the maximum number of delegatees for each delegator in [9]. ** denotes the computation complexity for decrypt algorithm when conditions (1) and (2) are used for public verification along with any one of conditions (6) to (9) of the $Verify()$ algorithm.

Scheme	Encrypt	Decrypt	Re-Encrypt	Re-Decrypt
[5]	$5t_e + 5t_{et} + 8t_{bp}$	$t_e + 6t_{et} + 4t_{bp}$	$t_e + t_{et} + t_{bp}$	$2t_e + 2t_{et} + 3t_{bp}$
[9]	$((n+2)t_e + t_{et})^*$	$t_e + t_{bp}$	$2t_{bp}$	t_{et}
[6]	$t_s + 4t_e + t_{et} + t_{bp} + t_{me}$	$t_e + t_{et} + 9t_{bp} + t_v$	$t_e + 8t_{bp} + t_v$	$t_e + 2t_{et} + 18t_{bp} + t_v$
[13]	$3t_e + t_{et} + t_{bp}$	$2t_{bp}$	$4t_{bp}$	$2t_{bp}$
Our scheme	$5t_e + t_{et} + t_{bp}$	$5t_e + t_{et} + t_{bp}$ or $(2t_e + t_{et} + 5t_{bp})^{**}$	$t_{et} + 8t_{bp}$	t_{et}

efficiency of a few well-known PRE schemes. Note that we use t to denote the time required for the various computations subscripted with bp, e, et, me, s, v to denote the time taken for a bilinear pairing, exponentiation in $\mathbb{G}_1$, exponentiation in $\mathbb{G}_2$, multi-exponentiation in group $\mathbb{G}_1$, signing algorithm and verification algorithm respectively. The comparisons show that our proposed design is the first scheme that achieves non-transferability with minimal efficiency loss and satisfies all the properties of an unidirectional single-hop PRE scheme.

8 Conclusion

Although there are several protocols achieving PRE in the literature, only two schemes [7] (ID-based settings) and [5] have reported the non-transferable property. To resolve the problem of non-transferability in PRE, [5] uses indistinguishability obfuscation ($i\mathcal{O}$), which involves very complex operations and is highly impractical. In [7], the IB-PRE protocol involves multiple rounds of interaction for partial-key generations and key validations which incurs computational overhead as indicated in the comparison Table 2. Our non-transferable PRE scheme is practical, based on direct manipulation in groups. Our scheme is shown to be CCA secure in the random oracle model for both the first and second level ciphertext and meets the non-transferability definition wherein the colluders (delegatee and proxy) cannot re-delegate the decryption rights of the delegator. An attempt to construct an illegal decryption box to decrypt the second level ciphertexts of the delegator reveals the private key components of the colluding delegatee. We have proposed an efficient non-transferable PRE scheme that affirmatively resolves the problem of illegal transference of decryption rights.

References

1. Ateniese, G., Fu, K., Green, M., Hohenberger, S.: Improved proxy re-encryption schemes with applications to secure distributed storage. In Proceedings of the Network and Distributed System Security Symposium, NDSS 2005, San Diego, California, USA, pp. 29–43 (2005)
2. Blaze, M., Bleumer, G., Strauss, M.: Divertible protocols and atomic proxy cryptography. In: Nyberg, K. (ed.) EUROCRYPT 1998. LNCS, vol. 1403, pp. 127–144. Springer, Heidelberg (1998). doi:10.1007/BFb0054122
3. Canetti, R., Halevi, S., Katz, J.: Chosen-ciphertext security from identity-based encryption. In: Cachin, C., Camenisch, J.L. (eds.) EUROCRYPT 2004. LNCS, vol. 3027, pp. 207–222. Springer, Heidelberg (2004). doi:10.1007/978-3-540-24676-3_13
4. Chow, S.S.M., Weng, J., Yang, Y., Deng, R.H.: Efficient unidirectional proxy re-encryption. In: Bernstein, D.J., Lange, T. (eds.) AFRICACRYPT 2010. LNCS, vol. 6055, pp. 316–332. Springer, Heidelberg (2010). doi:10.1007/978-3-642-12678-9_19
5. Guo, H., Zhang, Z., Jing, X.: Non-transferable proxy re-encryption. IACR Cryptology ePrint Archive 2015:1216 (2015)
6. Hayashi, R., Matsushita, T., Yoshida, T., Fujii, Y., Okada, K.: Unforgeability of re-encryption keys against collusion attack in proxy re-encryption. In: Iwata, T., Nishigaki, M. (eds.) IWSEC 2011. LNCS, vol. 7038, pp. 210–229. Springer, Heidelberg (2011). doi:10.1007/978-3-642-25141-2_14
7. He, Y.J., Chim, T.W., Hui, L.C.K., Yiu, S.M.: Non-transferable proxy re-encryption scheme. In: 5th International Conference on New Technologies, Mobility and Security, Istanbul, Turkey, NTMS 2012, 7–10 May 2012, pp. 1–4 (2012)
8. Isshiki, T., Nguyen, M.H., Tanaka, K.: Attacks to the proxy re-encryption schemes from IWSEC2011. In: Sakiyama, K., Terada, M. (eds.) IWSEC 2013. LNCS, vol. 8231, pp. 290–302. Springer, Heidelberg (2013). doi:10.1007/978-3-642-41383-4_19
9. Libert, B., Vergnaud, D.: Tracing malicious proxies in proxy re-encryption. In: Galbraith, S.D., Paterson, K.G. (eds.) Pairing 2008. LNCS, vol. 5209, pp. 332–353. Springer, Heidelberg (2008). doi:10.1007/978-3-540-85538-5_22
10. Libert, B., Vergnaud, D.: Unidirectional chosen-ciphertext secure proxy re-encryption. IEEE Trans. Inform. Theory **57**(3), 1786–1802 (2011)
11. Sharmila Deva Selvi, S., Paul, A., Pandu Rangan, C.: An efficient non-transferable proxy re-encryption scheme (full version). Cryptology ePrint Archive, May 2017
12. Sree Vivek, S., Sharmila Deva Selvi, S., Radhakishan, V., Pandu Rangan, C.: Efficient conditional proxy re-encryption with chosen ciphertext security. Int. J. Network Secur. Appl. **4**(2), 179–199 (2012)
13. Wang, L., Wang, L., Mambo, M., Okamoto, E.: New identity-based proxy re-encryption schemes to prevent collusion attacks. In: Joye, M., Miyaji, A., Otsuka, A. (eds.) Pairing 2010. LNCS, vol. 6487, pp. 327–346. Springer, Heidelberg (2010). doi:10.1007/978-3-642-17455-1_21
14. Yu, S., Wang, C., Ren, K., Lou, W.: Attribute based data sharing with attribute revocation. In: Proceedings of the 5th ACM Symposium on Information, Computer and Communications Security, ASIACCS 2010, Beijing, China, 13–16 April 2010, pp. 261–270 (2010)

Rounding Technique's Application in Schnorr Signature Algorithm: Known Partially Most Significant Bits of Nonce

Wenjie Qin[✉] and Kewei Lv[✉]

Institute of Information Engineering,
Data Assurance and Communication Security Research Center,
University of Chinese Academy of Sciences,
Beijing 100093, People's Republic of China
qinwenjie_wenky@126.com, lvkewei@iie.ac.cn

Abstract. In 1996, Boneh and Venkatesan proposed the Hidden Number Problem (HNP) and proved the most significant bits (MSB) of computational Diffie-Hellman key exchange scheme and related schemes are unpredictable. They also gave a lattice rounding technique to solve HNP in non-uniform model. In this paper, we analyse the security of the most significant bits of random nonce in Schnorr signature. We put forward the Schnorr-MSB-HNP and use the lattice rounding technique to solve the Schnorr-MSB-HNP in uniform model. We prove that if there is an oracle which inputs the random nonce and outputs $\lceil 2\log\log q \rceil + 4$ most significant bits of nonce, the signature private key will be obtained by choosing $2\lceil \log q \rceil$ signature pairs randomly. Thus the security of the private key can be reduced to the $\lceil 2\log\log q \rceil + 4$ most significant bits of random nonce.

Keywords: Rounding technique · Most significant bits · Schnorr signature algorithm · Nonce · Schnorr-MSB-HNP

1 Introduction

In 1996, Boneh and Venkatesan [1] proposed the Hidden Number Problem(HNP, for simplicity): For a sufficiently large prime q and an integer k, g is the root of cycle group Z_q^*. Let $Oracle_{\alpha,g}(x)$ be an oracle which given x, outputs the k most significant bits of $\alpha g^x \bmod q$. The task is to recover the hidden number $\alpha \bmod q$, using the oracle $Oracle_{\alpha,g}(x)$. That is, given $(g^{x_i}, MSB_k(\alpha g^{x_i}))$ for $1 \leq i \leq d$, we try to compute $\alpha \bmod q$. Here the k most significant bits $MSB_k(\alpha g^x \bmod q)$ is defined as the integer t such that $(t-1)q/2^k \leq \alpha g^x \bmod q < tq/2^k$ and $d = O(logq)$. They proved that computing the $\sqrt{\log q}$ most significant bits of the secret key in Diffie-Hellman and related schemes is as hard as computing the secret key itself. The proof method is based on the Babai's approximation theorem [2,3] and uniqueness theorem.

This work is partially supported by NSF No. 61272039.

L. Batten et al. (Eds.): ATIS 2017, CCIS 719, pp. 48–57, 2017.
DOI: 10.1007/978-981-10-5421-1_5

There are a lot of studies on HNP. Shparlinski et al. extended some results of [1] to arbitrary multiplicative order T using the bounds of exponential sums [4–6]. Boneh and Shparlinski [7] showed that just predicting one bit of the elliptic curve Diffie-Hellman secret in a family of curves is as hard as computing the entire secret. Jetchev and Venkatesan [8] proved that if one can efficiently predict the LSB with non-negligible advantage on a polynomial fraction of all the curves defined over a given finite field F_q, then with polynomial factor overhead, one can compute the entire Diffie-Hellman secret on a polynomial fraction of all the curves over the same finite field. Recently, Shani [9] gave the first bit security result for the elliptic curve Diffie-Hellman key exchange protocol for elliptic curves defined over prime fields and showed that about 5/6 of the most significant bits of the x-coordinate of the Diffie-Hellman key are as hard to compute as the entire key. They used the ideas behind the solution to the modular inversion hidden number problem given in [10] and followed the formal proof given by Ling, Shparlinski, Steinfeld and Wang [11]. Fazio et al. [12] extened the idea of [7] in two novel ways, one is that they generalized it to the case of finite fields F_{q^2}, the other is that they proved that any bit is hard using the list decoding techniques of Akavia et al. [13] as generalized at CRYPTO'12 by Duc and Jetchev [14]. Galbraith and Shani [15] showed that if one can find the significant Fourier coefficients of some function, then one can solve the multivariate hidden number problem for that function, using tools from discrete Fourier analysis introduced by Akavia [13]. In 2007 Garefalakis extended the HNP to non-prime modulus N and proved that computing roughly $\sqrt{\log N}$ bits of RSA or Rabin function is equivalent to computing the entire value [16]. In 2010, Su Dong et al. proved that computing Rabin-Pailier trap function $\lceil 3\sqrt{2n}/2 \rceil + \lceil log2n \rceil$ MSB is as hard as computing the entire cipher [17], where n is the binary length of the RSA modulus N.

HNP as a method to study bit security can also be used to analyse the security of private key in digital signature. We know that ElGamal signature and other variants, such as Schnorr, DSA, are all in one feature that is the random nonce which is generated in each signature. Special care must be taken with the nonce. It is well known that if the random nonce is disclosed, the secret key α can be recovered. In 1997, Bellare et al. [18] showed that if the random nonce in DSS is produced by a weak pseudo-random generator with known parameters, then α can also be recovered using only a few signatures. Howgrave-Graham and Smart [19] showed that Babai's nearest plane algorithm [2] could heuristically recover α, provided that sufficiently many DSA signatures and sufficiently many bits of the corresponding nonces in DSA signatures are known. Although Howgrave-Graham and Smart referenced Boneh-Venkatesan paper [1], they did not notice how close their problem was to the hidden number. In 1999, Nguyen [20] showed a connection between solving HNP and breaking DSA signature. It was then extended together with Shparlinski in [21].

In 1997, Boneh and Venkatesan put forward another idea to solve the HNP, which is the lattice rounding technique [22], and they improved the result to $\log \log q$ bits in the non-uniform model. In this paper, firstly, they gave a lattice and introduced the rounding algorithm. Then they proved that if there exists a basis in the lattice space which satisfied the Lemma 1, and the lattice roudning technique can be used to solve the HNP. Accordind to the condition of the Lemma 1, they could obtain the satisfied basis in the dual lattice. By inverting and transposing the matrix of lattice, they got the dual lattice, and multiplied the matrix of dual lattice on the left by two carefullly constructed unimodular matrices. At last, they got the dual lattice basis which satisfied the Lemma 1. In this way, they could use the rounding technique to solve the HNP. In 2008, Su Dong et al. [23] proved that the security of generalized SRA intellectual poker protocol can be reduced to the hardness of computing the $\lceil (\log\log q)/2 + 1\rceil MSB$ bits of plaintext and the $\lceil 2\log\log q\rceil MSB$ bits of key using the rounding technique. We will use this method to analyse the security of the most significant bits of random nonce in Schnorr signature.

Our Works: We know the Schnorr signature algorithm requires the signer to generate a new random number with every signature, usually called the nonce. Thus, in our paper, we analyse the security of the most significant bits of random nonce in Schnorr signature. Based on the idea that DSA signature was reduced to the HNP, we put forward the Schnorr-MSB-HNP. Using the lattice rounding technique, we solve the Schnorr-MSB-HNP in uniform model, and prove that if there is an oracle which inputs the random nonce and outputs $\lceil 2\log\log q\rceil + 4$ most significant bits of nonce. The signature private key will be obtained by choosing $2\lceil \log q\rceil$ signature pairs randomly. Thus the security of the private key can be reduced to the $\lceil 2\log\log q\rceil + 4$ most significant bits of random nonce.

Notations: We define q is a sufficiently large prime and $[x]_q = x \equiv a \bmod q$, the integer $a \in [0, q-1]$. Let Z be the set of integer number and R be the set of real number. Let $L_1(w_i)$ denote the L_1 norm of w_i. For a matrix W whose columns are the vectors $w_1, \cdots, w_d$, we define $L_{1,\infty}(W) \overset{def}{=} \max_i L_1(w_i)$.

Organization: In Sect. 2, we give some basic concepts, introduce the Schnorr digital signature and propose the Schnorr-MSB-HNP. In Sect. 3, we introduce the lattice rounding technique. In Sect. 4, we present our main result. In Sect. 5, we give our conclusion.

2 Preliminaries

2.1 Basic Concept

Definition 1. *For any rational n, l, $APP_{l,q}(n)$ denotes any rational r such that $|n - r|_q \leq q/2^{l+1}$, where the symbol $|\cdot|_q$ is defined as $|z|_q = min_{b\in Z}|z - bq|$ for any rational number.*

Definition 2. *q is a prime number, for many known random number $t \in Z_q^*$, and approximation $APP_{l,q}(\alpha t)$, the problem of recovering the number $\alpha \in Z_q^*$ is called the HNP.*

Definition 3. *Let $b_1, \cdots, b_s$ be a set of linearly independent vectors in R^s. The set of vectors*

$$L = \{\sum_{i=1}^{s} x_i b_i | x_i \in Z, 1 \leq i \leq s\}$$

is called an s-dimensional full rank lattice. The set $b_1, \cdots, b_s$ is called a basis of L, and L is said to be spanned by $b_1, \cdots, b_s$.

Definition 4. *The dual lattice of L, denoted L^*, is the set of vectors*

$$L^* = \{y \in R^s s.t. \forall x \in L :< x, y >\in Z\}$$

2.2 Schnorr Digital Signature

Schnorr digital signature is a variant of ElGamal digital signature [24]. Let p and q be large prime numbers with $q|p-1$, generally $p \approx 2^{1024}$ and $q \approx 2^{160}$. Let $g, g \in Z_p^*$ be a fixed element of multiplicative order q, that is $[g^q]_p \equiv 1, q \neq 1$. The signer randomly select $\alpha, \alpha \in Z_q^*$, as the secret key and computes $y = g^{-\alpha}$ mod p. Let $h : \{0,1\}^* \to Z_p^*$, be a safe hash function.

To sign a message μ, the signer chooses a random integer $k \in Z_q^*$ called nonce, which must be kept secret, and computes $r = [g^k]_p$ as well as the hash value $e = h(\mu \parallel r)$. In the last, the signer computes $s = [(k + \alpha e)]_q$. The pair (e, s) is the Schnorr signature of the message μ with a nonce k.

The receiver gets the message μ and the signature pair (e, s), then he needs to verify it. He needs to compute

$$r' \equiv g^s y^e \equiv g^s g^{-\alpha e} \equiv g^{s-\alpha e} \equiv g^k$$

If $r' = r$ then $e' = h(\mu \parallel r') = h(\mu \parallel r) = e$, and the signature is valid.

2.3 Schnorr-MSB-HNP

The connection between the Schnorr digital signature and the HNP can be easily explained. In the process of digital signature, we assume that we know the l most significant bits of random nonce k. That is, we are given an integer a such that $0 \leq k - aq/2^l < q/2^l$. The congruence $s = [(k+\alpha e)]_q$ from the process of sigature can be written as $\alpha e \equiv [s - k]_q$. So we can get:

$$0 \leq \alpha e - s - aq/2^l < q/2^l.$$

Let $t = \lfloor e \rfloor_q, u = s + aq/2^l$, we obtain

$$0 \leq \alpha t - u < q/2^l.$$

Therefore,

$$|\alpha t - u - q/2^{l+1}|_q < q/2^{l+1}.$$

We note that both t and u can be easily computed by attacker from the publicly known information. Thus, the approximation $APP_{l,q}(\alpha t)$ is known. Collecting several signature pairs of Schnorr and the corresponding l most significant bits of nonce, the problem of recovering the secret key α is called the Schnorr-MSB-HNP.

The HNP in [1] is that if we are given an oracle to predict partial relevant information about the hidden number, then we try to find out the hidden number. In this method, we choose a series of samples uniformly and randomly to query oracle. The oracle answers partial information about the hidden number. Then we use these samples and answers of oracle to construct a lattice and resolve the problem.

The Schnorr-MSB-HNP is that we also are given an oracle to get the most significant bits of nonce, we try to find out the secret key. We mainly choose a series of signature pairs uniformly and randomly, and we can get the leaked most significant bits of the nonce in every signature satisfying the approximation $APP_{l,q}(\alpha t)$. Then we use these signatures and the leaked most significant bits to consturct a lattice and resolve the problem.

3   Rounding Technique

Let q be a prime, choose $t_1, \cdots, t_d$ integers uniformly and independently at random in the range $[0, q-1]$. The hidden number is α. We assume that there is an oracle, the inputs are $t_1, \cdots, t_d, 1$, and the outputs are numbers $a_1, \cdots, a_d, a_{d+1}$ such that $|[\alpha t_i]_q - a_i| < R$. The value a_{d+1} is obtained by querying the oracle at the point $t = 1$.

We construct the lattice L spanned by the rows of the matrix:

$$
L = \begin{bmatrix}
q & 0 & \cdots & 0 & 0 \\
0 & q & \cdots & 0 & 0 \\
\vdots & \vdots & \ddots & \vdots & \vdots \\
0 & 0 & \cdots & q & 0 \\
t_1 & t_2 & \cdots & t_d & 1
\end{bmatrix}
$$

Set $u = (a_1, \cdots, a_d, a_{d+1})$ and define the lattice vector $v_\alpha \in L$ by $v_\alpha = ([t_1\alpha]_q, [t_2\alpha]_q, \cdots, [t_d\alpha]_q, \alpha)$. We want to recover α from the vector v_α. The rounding technique is to find the lattice point v_α given the vector u.

Let $b_1, \cdots, b_{d+1}$ be some basis of L, the technique performs two steps:

1. Write $u = \sum_{i=1}^{d+1} y_i b_i$ for some $y_i \in R$.
2. Set $v = \sum_{i=1}^{d+1} \lfloor y_i \rceil b_i$ where $\lfloor y_i \rceil$ is the integer closet to y_i.

If the basis $b_1, \cdots, b_{d+1}$ satisfies the next Lemma 1, we can get the right answer, that is $v_\alpha = v$, then we obtain the hidden number α.

Lemma 1. *Let A be the matrix whose rows are the basis vectors b_i. If*

$$L_{1,\infty}(A^{-1}) < 1/(2R)$$

then the vector v constructed by rounding technique satisfies $v = v_\alpha$.

Lemma 2. *Let $q, d, t_1, \cdots, t_d$ as above. Set $m = \lceil \log \log q \rceil + 4$ and $n = m + \lfloor \log q \rfloor$. By assumption $d > n$. Then with probability at least $1/2$ for all $k = m + 1, m + 2, \cdots, n$ there exist subsets $S_k \subseteq 1, \cdots, k - 1$ satisfying:*

$$2^{n-k} \leq [t_k + \sum_{i \in S_k} t_i]_q < 2 \cdot 2^{n-k}$$

The proofs of Lemmas 1 and 2 are from [22].

4   Main Result

We assume that there is an oracle. With this oracle, we can get $l = 2\lceil \log \log q \rceil + 4$ MSB of the random nonce in Schnorr signature. We can express it as $Oracle_l$ which inputs k, returns $MSB_l([k]_q)$.

Theorem 3. *Given an oracle $Oracle_l$ as above. For Schnorr signature, we can get an efficient polynomial-time algorithm using the oracle, calls to the $Oracle_l$ about $d = 2\lceil \log q \rceil$ times, computes the signature private key α.*

Proof.
step1: We choose $d = 2\lceil \log q \rceil$ signature pairs randomly, $(e_1, s_1), (e_2, s_2), \cdots,$ (e_d, s_d). The random nonces denote $k_1, \cdots, k_d$. We can also get the $l = 2\lceil \log \log q \rceil + 4$ most significant bits of the random nonce k_i by calling the $Oracle_l$, which defined as the number a'_i. We use $t'_1, \cdots, t'_d$ and $u'_1, \cdots, u'_d$ to replace $e_1, \cdots, e_d$ and $(s_1 + a'_1 q / 2^l), \cdots, (s_d + a'_d q / 2^l)$ separately. we obtain

$$|\alpha t'_i - u'_i - q/2^{l+1}| < q/2^{l+1}$$

Thus, we get the Schnorr-MSB-HNP. Let R in Lemma 1 is $q/2^{l+1}$. If using the rounding technique to solve Schnorr-MSB-HNP, we need to find the lattice basis to satisfy the Lemma 1. Therefore we have to find the basis to meet the conditions through the next steps.

step2: According to the signature, we construct a lattice L' as follow:

$$L' = \begin{bmatrix} q & 0 & \cdots & 0 & 0 \\ 0 & q & \cdots & 0 & 0 \\ \vdots & \vdots & \ddots & \vdots & \vdots \\ 0 & 0 & \cdots & q & 0 \\ t'_1 & t'_2 & \cdots & t'_d & 1/2^{l+1} \end{bmatrix}$$

Set $u' = (u'_1 + q/2^{l+1}, \cdots, u'_d + q/2^{l+1}, q/2^{l+1})$, and define the lattice vector $v'_\alpha = ([\alpha t'_1]_q, \cdots, [\alpha t'_d]_q, \alpha/2^{l+1})$. Notice that $||u' - v'_\alpha|| < q/2^{l+1}\sqrt{d+1}$. Thus the vector u' is close to the lattice point v'_α.

step3: We have to find the dual lattice of L', denoted L'^*. We know that if the lattice L' is full rank, the dual lattice L'^* can be obtained By inverting and transposing the matrix L', thus

$$L'^* = \frac{1}{q} \begin{bmatrix} 1 & 0 & \cdots & 0 & -t'_1 \\ 0 & 1 & \cdots & 0 & -t'_2 \\ \vdots & \vdots & \ddots & \vdots & \vdots \\ 0 & 0 & \cdots & 1 & -t'_d \\ 0 & 0 & \cdots & 0 & q2^{l+1} \end{bmatrix}$$

step4: In order to construct the basis that satisfies the condition, we need to multiply the matrix L'^* on the left by two constructed unimodular matrices.

1. According to the Lemma 2, we can construct the unimodular matrices W, and define the $d+1 \times d+1$ matrix $W = (w_{i,j})$ by

$$w_{i,j} = \begin{cases} 0 & \text{if } j \in S_i \text{ or } i = j \\ 1 & \text{otherwise} \end{cases}$$

After multiplying the matrix W on the left, we can get the matrix

$$L'^* = \frac{1}{q} \begin{bmatrix} 1 & 0 & \cdots & 0 & & -t'_1 \\ 0 & 1 & \cdots & 0 & & -t'_2 \\ \vdots & \vdots & \ddots & \vdots & & \vdots \\ 0 & 0 & \cdots & 0 & & -t'_m \\ 0 & 0 & \cdots & 0 & -t'_{m+1} + \sum_{i \in S_{m+1}}(-t_i) \\ \vdots & & \vdots & & \vdots \\ 0 & 0 & \cdots & 0 & -t'_h + \sum_{i \in S_h}(-t_i) \\ \vdots & & \vdots & & \vdots \\ 0 & 0 & \cdots & 0 & -t'_n + \sum_{i \in S_n}(-t_i) \\ 0 & 0 & \cdots & 0 & -t'_{n+1} \\ \vdots & & \vdots & & \vdots \\ 0 & 0 & \cdots & 1 & -t'_d \\ 0 & 0 & \cdots & 0 & q2^{l+1} \end{bmatrix}$$

Though the elementary row transformation of WL'^*, we get

$$L'^* = \frac{1}{q} \begin{bmatrix} & & w_1 \\ & & w_2 \\ & D & \\ & & w_d \\ & & q2^{l+1} \end{bmatrix}$$

2. Constructing the unimodular matrices V. Let $x^{(h)}$ be the right most entry in the matrix L'^* e.g. $x^{(1)} = w_1, x^{(2)} = w_2, \cdots, x^{(d+1)} = q2^{l+1}$. Let

$$x^{(h)} = \sum_{i=1}^{h-1} x_i^{(h)} x^{(i)}, x_i^{(h)} = 0, 1, 2, 3$$

We get the unimodular matrix V as follow:

$$V = \begin{bmatrix} 1 & 0 & 0 & \cdots & 0 \\ -x_1^{(2)} & 1 & 0 & \cdots & 0 \\ -x_1^{(3)} & -x_2^{(3)} & 1 & \cdots & 0 \\ & & \vdots & & \vdots \\ -x_1^{(d+1)} & -x_2^{(d+1)} & -x_3^{(d+1)} & \cdots & 1 \end{bmatrix}$$

Then we can get matrix

$$L'^* = \frac{1}{q} \begin{bmatrix} & \begin{matrix} 1 \\ 0 \end{matrix} \\ D' & \vdots \\ & 0 \end{bmatrix}$$

where D' is a $d+1 \times d$ matrix whose entries in absolute are all less $3(n-m) <$ $3 \log q$, and the dual satisfies

$$L_{1,\infty}(L'^*) < 3(n-m)d/q < 3 \cdot 2 \log q \cdot \log q/q < 2^{\lceil \log \log q \rceil + 4}/q < 1/(2R)$$

Thus there is a basis in the Lattice L' satisfying the Lemma 1.

setp5: By inverting we get

$$C = [c_1, \cdots, c_{d+1}] = (L'^*)^{-1} = \left(\frac{1}{q} \begin{bmatrix} & \begin{matrix} 1 \\ 0 \end{matrix} \\ D' & \vdots \\ & 0 \end{bmatrix} \right)^{-1}$$

Using the rounding technique with the basis $C = [c_1, \cdots, c_{d+1}]$, we can find the vector $u = \sum_{i=1}^{d+1} y_i c_i$, and get the value of y_i. Thus the vector v can be resolved, $v_\alpha = v = \sum_{i=1}^{d+1} \lfloor y_i \rceil c_i$, we can get the secret key α.

5   Conclusion

We reduce the security of private key to the most significant bits of random nonce in Schnorr signature. Given an oracle which outputs the most significant bits of nonce, we try to attack the secret key. We choose $2\lceil \log q \rceil$ signature pairs uniformly and randomly, and get the leaked most significant bits of the nonce in every signature satisfying the approximation $APP_{l,q}(\alpha t)$. Then we use these signatures and the leaked most significant bits to consturct a lattice. Finally we have come to the conclusion that if there is an oracle which inputs the random nonce and outputs $\lceil 2 \log \log q \rceil + 4$ most significant bits of nonce, the signature private key will be obtained by choosing $2 \log q$ signature messages randomly, using the rounding technique. We avoid the discrete logarithm problem and do not need the advice bits include discrete-log of t_i to the base g in the [22] and get the result in uniform model. The idea can also be applied to research the security of the least significant bits of random nonce in the Schnorr digital scheme and can get the result that if there is an oracle which inputs the random nonce and outputs $\lceil 2 \log \log q \rceil + 4$ least significant bits of nonce, the signature private key will be obtained by choosing $2 \lceil \log q \rceil$ signature messages randomly.

References

1. Boneh, D., Venkatesan, R.: Hardness of computing the most significant bits of secret keys in diffie-hellman and related schemes. In: Koblitz, N. (ed.) CRYPTO 1996. LNCS, vol. 1109, pp. 129–142. Springer, Heidelberg (1996). doi:10.1007/3-540-68697-5_11
2. Babai, L.: On lovasz' lattice reduction and the nearest lattice point problem. Combinatorica **6**, 1–13 (1986)
3. Lenstra, A., Lenstra, H., Lovasz, L.: Factoring polynomial with rational coefficients. Mathematiche Annalen **261**, 515–534 (1982)
4. Gonzalez Vasco, M.I., Shpailinski, I.E.: On the security of diffie-hellman bits. In: Proceedings of the Workshop on Cryptography and Computational Number Theory, Singapore, Birkhauser, pp. 257–268 (2001)
5. Gonzalez Vasco, M.I., Shpailinski, I.E.: Security of the most signficant bits of the shamir message passing scheme. Math. Comp. **71**, 333–342 (2002)
6. Konyagin, S.V., Shpailinski, I.E.: Charater Sums with Exponential Functions and their Applications. Cambridge University Press, Cambridge (1999)
7. Boneh, D., Shparlinski, I.E.: On the unpredictability of bits of the elliptic curve diffie-hellman scheme. In: Kilian, J. (ed.) CRYPTO 2001. LNCS, vol. 2139, pp. 201–212. Springer, Heidelberg (2001). doi:10.1007/3-540-44647-8_12
8. Jetchev, D., Venkatesan, R.: Bits security of the elliptic curve diffie–hellman secret keys. In: Wagner, D. (ed.) CRYPTO 2008. LNCS, vol. 5157, pp. 75–92. Springer, Heidelberg (2008). doi:10.1007/978-3-540-85174-5_5
9. Shani, B.: On the bit security of elliptic curve diffie–hellman. In: Fehr, S. (ed.) PKC 2017. LNCS, vol. 10174, pp. 361–387. Springer, Heidelberg (2017). doi:10.1007/978-3-662-54365-8_15
10. Boneh, D., Halevi, S., Howgrave-Graham, N.: The modular inversion hidden number problem. In: Boyd, C. (ed.) ASIACRYPT 2001. LNCS, vol. 2248, pp. 36–51. Springer, Heidelberg (2001). doi:10.1007/3-540-45682-1_3
11. Ling, S., Shparlinski, I.E., Steinfeld, R., Wang, H.: On the modular inversion hidden number problem. J. Symbolic Comput. **47**(4), 358–367 (2012)
12. Fazio, N., Gennaro, R., Perera, I.M., Skeith, W.E.: Hard-core predicates for a diffie-hellman problem over finite fields. In: Canetti, R., Garay, J.A. (eds.) CRYPTO 2013. LNCS, vol. 8043, pp. 148–165. Springer, Heidelberg (2013). doi:10.1007/978-3-642-40084-1_9

13. Akavia, A., Goldwasser, S., Safra, S.: Proving hard-core predicates using list decoding. In: IEEE Symposium on Foundations of Computer Science-FOCS, pp. 146–157 (2003)

14. Duc, A., Jetchev, D.: Hardness of computing individual bits for one-way functions on elliptic curves. In: Safavi-Naini, R., Canetti, R. (eds.) CRYPTO 2012. LNCS, vol. 7417, pp. 832–849. Springer, Heidelberg (2012). doi:10.1007/978-3-642-32009-5_48

15. Galbraith, S.D., Shani, B.: The multivariate hidden number problem. In: Lehmann, A., Wolf, S. (eds.) ICITS 2015. LNCS, vol. 9063, pp. 250–268. Springer, Cham (2015). doi:10.1007/978-3-319-17470-9_15

16. Garefalakis, T.: The hidden number problem with non-prime modulus. JP J. Algebra Number Theory Appl. **8**(2), 193–211 (2007)

17. Dong, S., Wang, K., Kewei, L.: The bit security of two variants of paillier trapdoor function. Chin. J. Comput. **33**(6), 1020–1059 (2010)

18. Bellare, M., Goldwasser, S., Micciancio, D.: "Pseudo-random" number generation within cryptographic algorithms: the DDS case. In: Kaliski, B.S. (ed.) CRYPTO 1997. LNCS, vol. 1294, pp. 277–291. Springer, Heidelberg (1997). doi:10.1007/BFb0052242

19. Howgrave-Graham, N.A., Smart, N.P.: Lattice attacks on digital signature schemes. Design Codes Cryptog. **23**, 283–290 (2001)

20. Nguyen, P.Q.: The dark side of the hidden number problem: lattice attacks on DSA. In: Lam, K.-Y., Shparlinski, I.E., Wang, H., Xing, C. (eds.) Proceedings of the Workshop on Cryptography and Computational Number Theory (CCNT 1999), Singapore, pp. 321–330. Birkhauser, Basel (2001)

21. Nguyen, P.Q., Shparlinski, I.E.: The insecurity of the digital signature algorithm with partially known nonces. J. Cryptology **15**(3), 151–176 (2002)

22. Boneh, D., Venkatesan, R.: Rounding in lattices and its cryptographic applications. In: Proceedings of the 8th Annual ACM-SIAM Symposium on Discrete Algorithms, pp. 675–681. ACM (1997)

23. Dong, S., Kewei, L.: Research on the security of generalized SRA intelligence poker protocol based on hidden number problem. In: National Conference on Information Confidentiality (2008)

24. Schnorr, C.P.: Efficient signature generation by smarts cards. J. Cryptology **4**, 161–174 (1991)

On the Practical Implementation
of Impossible Differential Cryptanalysis
on Reduced-Round AES

Sourya Kakarla$^{(\boxtimes)}$, Srinath Mandava, Dhiman Saha,
and Dipanwita Roy Chowdhury

Crypto Research Lab, Department of Computer Science and Engineering,
IIT Kharagpur, Kharagpur, India
{skakarla,smandava,dhimans,drc}@cse.iitkgp.ernet.in

Abstract. In this work, we give a practical implementation of the well known impossible differential attack on 5 round AES-128 given by Biham and Keller. The complexity of the original attack is in the order of the practical realm with time complexity 2^{31} and data complexity $2^{29.5}$. However, the primary memory required to execute the attack was 4 TB making it difficult to implement which is supported by the fact that there are no reported implementations of the attack. We propose a data-memory tradeoff for the attack which lets us reduce memory needed at the expense of increased data complexity. We have been able to implement the attack using 128.5 GB of primary memory and 2^{32} data complexity. Though the data complexity is increased by about 4.65 times, it makes up for the fact that we decreased the memory usage by about 32 times. We also extend the implementation to 5 round AES-192/256. To the best of our knowledge, the implementations of attacks in this work are the first ones available publicly.

Keywords: AES · Impossible differential · Cryptanalysis · Data structure · Implementation · Data-memory tradeoff · Key recovery

1 Introduction

AES [6] has become the standard symmetric key cipher used across the internet since the Rijndael family of ciphers were selected for Advanced Encryption Standard by the U.S National Institute of Standards and Technology. Its security is of utmost importance to the security of the internet thereby making it one of the most widely studied ciphers. Though there are no practical attacks possible on full round AES, round-reduced versions were attacked with complexities significantly less than the brute force complexity. These attacks help in developing greater insight into the security of AES. One such family of attacks is impossible differential attacks [2]. Impossible differential cryptanalysis is a form of differential cryptanalysis [4]. While traditionally differential cryptanalysis tracks the probabilities of differences through the rounds of a cipher that are

© Springer Nature Singapore Pte Ltd. 2017
L. Batten et al. (Eds.): ATIS 2017, CCIS 719, pp. 58–72, 2017.
DOI: 10.1007/978-981-10-5421-1_6

highly probable, impossible differential cryptanalysis tracks difference patterns that are impossible to occur at an intermediate state i.e. their probability is zero. Generally, two plaintexts are taken and their difference is tracked down in the encryption direction to an intermediate state. Their corresponding ciphertexts are taken and their differences are tracked in the direction of the decryption to the same intermediate state. If at this intermediate state, the probability of both the paths holding is 0, then these patterns are called *impossible differential paths*. Using impossible differential paths, we can mount an attack by eliminating all keys which give the impossible differential path thereby leaving behind the right key.

The first impossible differential attack on AES is an attack on 5 round AES-128 by Biham and Keller [3]. This was extended to a 6 round attack by Cheon *et al.* [5]. Later in 2004, Phan [10] extended the attack to 7 round AES-192 and AES-256. There have been several other impossible differential attacks [1,8,9] on the different variants of AES since then. Among these attacks, the ones [3,5] on AES-128 which do not exploit the key schedule of AES are extendable to AES-192 and AES-256.

Almost all of the impossible differential attacks on AES with the exception of [3] are not practical attacks since their time and/or data complexities are highly infeasible to be implemented in real life. As the 5 round attack on AES-128 is practical with time complexity only 2^{31}, we were surprised to observe that there are no readily available public implementations of the attack. We deduced that the memory needed for the attack which was 4 TB might have been the reason for it not having been implemented. So we set out to achieve probably the first implementation of a full key recovery impossible differential attack on 5 round AES.

Our contribution is as follows:

- First, we propose a data-memory tradeoff to the attack given by Biham and Keller [3] on 5 round AES-128. This tradeoff enables us to implement the attack with flexible resources.
- We implement full key recovery attack on 5 round AES-128 using the data-memory tradeoff. This implementation uses 128.5 GB of primary memory and 2^{34} chosen plaintexts.
- We used customized data structures which lead to a time and space efficient implementation.
- Using the techniques above, we implement the attack on 5 round variants of AES-192 and AES-256.

The rest of the paper is organized as follows. Section 2.1 provides a brief description of AES with its operations. In Sect. 2.2, notations for some of the aspects of AES are furnished. Section 2.4 gives an explanation of the attack given in [3]. The data-memory tradeoff for the attack is given in Sect. 3. The implementation details of the attacks on AES-128, AES-192, and AES-256 are given in Sect. 4. Finally, we finish with concluding remarks in Sect. 5.

2 Background and Preliminaries

2.1 AES

AES is a block cipher which operates on blocks of 128 bits using key sizes of 128, 192 or 256 bits. The intermediate state of AES can be arranged as 4×4 matrix as shown in Fig. 1 The number of rounds varies with the key size, 10 for AES-128, 12 for AES-192 and 14 for AES-256. Each round of AES encryption consists of the following operations in the given order:

1	2	3	4
5	6	7	8
9	10	11	12
13	14	15	16

Fig. 1. Byte positions in AES state

- SubBytes(SB): Each byte is substituted by the value from S-box. This is the only non-linear operation in AES.
- ShiftRows(SR): Each row in the state is shifted cyclically to the left. The ith row is shifted by i bytes to the left ($0 \leq i \leq 3$).
- MixColumns(MC): Each column is multiplied by a constant 4×4 matrix over the $GF(2^8)$.
- AddRoundKey(ARK): The state is XORed with the 128-bit round key.

The decryption of AES consists of the inverse of the above operations in the reverse order. Last round of AES does not contain a MixColumns operation. It is assumed that this is true for round reduced AES too. An additional AddRoundKey is applied at the start of the first round. Thus for n rounds, there are $n+1$ round keys. The round keys are supplied by the key schedule algorithm.

2.2 Notation

We define notations to represent intermediate states and other aspects of the AES algorithm. There are n rounds and $1 \leq i \leq n$. The key is represented by K.

- s_i is the state at the beginning of ith round.
- s_0 is the initial state which is generally the plaintext.
- s_{n+1} is the final state which is generally the ciphertext.
- s_1 is the state after the initial AddRoundKey.
- s_i^B is the state after SubBytes of ith round.
- s_i^R is the state after ShiftRows of ith round.
- s_i^M is the state after MixColumns of ith round ($i \neq n$).
- s_i^A is the state after AddRoundKey of ith round.

- $s_{i,j}^{\mathcal{X}}$ is the jth byte of $s_i^{\mathcal{X}}$ ($1 \leq j \leq 16$, $\mathcal{X} \in \{\varnothing, \mathcal{B}, \mathcal{R}, \mathcal{M}, \mathcal{A}\}$).
- K_i denotes the round key used in round i. K_0 corresponds to the key used in the initial AddRoundKey.
- $\mathcal{D}_p$: The set of byte positions in $s_1^{\mathcal{B}}$ which move to the same column after ShiftRows in $s_1^{\mathcal{R}}$.

$$\mathcal{D}_p = ((1, 6, 11, 16), (2, 7, 12, 13), (3, 8, 9, 14), (4, 5, 10, 15))$$

- $\mathcal{D}_c$: The set of byte positions in $s_n^{\mathcal{A}}$ which move to the same column after ShiftRows^{-1} in $s_n^{\mathcal{R}}$.

$$\mathcal{D}_c = ((1, 8, 11, 14), (2, 5, 12, 15), (3, 6, 9, 16), (4, 7, 10, 13))$$

We can see that $s_i^{\mathcal{A}} = s_{i+1}$, $1 \leq i \leq n$.

2.3   4 Round Impossible Differential

In this subsection, the 5 round attack on AES-128 given by Biham and Keller [3] is explained. A 4 round impossible differential path which is used in the attack is shown in Fig. 2. The difference between the two states are traced through the rounds of AES. The last round does not contain the MixColumns operation. The grey squares represent bytes where the difference is non-zero. These bytes are called *active bytes*. The white squares represent bytes where the difference is zero i.e. the bytes where the states are equal. These bytes are called *passive bytes*.

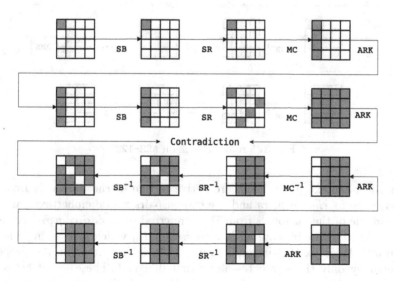

Fig. 2. 4 round impossible differential path

If the two states are p and q, the difference between the states is represented as another state, d, where $d_i^{\mathcal{X}} = p_i^{\mathcal{X}} \oplus q_i^{\mathcal{X}}$, $\forall \mathcal{X} \in \{\varnothing, \mathcal{B}, \mathcal{R}, \mathcal{M}, \mathcal{A}\}$. The path shows that if there is a single active byte in d_0, all the bytes are active in $d_2^{\mathcal{A}}$. If all the bytes along one of the diagonals in $\mathcal{D}_c$ are passive in $d_4^{\mathcal{A}}$ (ciphertext pair), then at least 4 bytes are passive in d_3. This is a contradiction since $d_2^{\mathcal{A}} = d_3$. This proves that if the starting states differ only in one byte, then it is impossible to obtain ciphertext states that are passive along one of the diagonals in $\mathcal{D}_c$.

2.4   5 Round Attack on AES-128 by Biham and Keller

A round is added at the top to the 4-round impossible differential path to mount an attack on 5 round AES-128 as shown in Fig. 3. All keys which give the impossible condition in the last 4 rounds can be deemed as wrong keys and be eliminated.

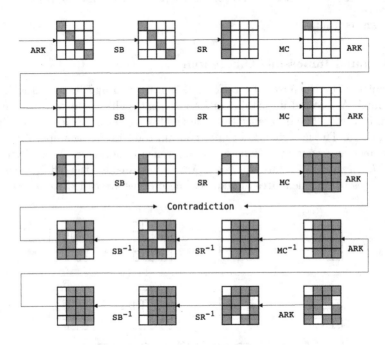

Fig. 3. 5 round attack on AES-128

Let the plaintext pairs which are active in one of the diagonals from $\mathcal{D}_p$ be referred to as *chosen pairs* and the chosen pairs whose ciphertext pairs are passive in one of the diagonals from $\mathcal{D}_c$ be referred to as *desired pairs*. For each desired pair we can eliminate all key guesses of K_0 which give a single active byte in $d_1^{\mathcal{M}}$. If we fix the diagonal (from $\mathcal{D}_p$) in plaintext pairs, the property is affected by only the key bytes along that diagonal. These set of bytes are called as a *partial key* corresponding to that diagonal. Thus a partial key can be independently eliminated irrespective of the other partial keys of K_0.

Instead of taking a desired pair and checking whether the property satisfies for all the 2^{32} partial key guesses, pre-computation is used to speedup the elimination of wrong partial keys. A hash table is created using Algorithm 1 which

---

Algorithm 1. Compute Hash Table

1: HashTable← INITIALIZATION()
2: **for all** $a, a', b, c, d \in \{0, 1, \cdots, 2^8 - 1\}, a \neq a'$ **do**　　　　▷ These are bytes.
3:　　$col \leftarrow$ INITIALIZECOLUMN(a, b, c, d)
4:　　$col' \leftarrow$ INITIALIZECOLUMN(a', b, c, d)
5:　　$col \leftarrow$ MixColumn^{-1}(SubBytes$^{-1}(col)$)　　▷ The column version of the operations
　　are used
6:　　$col' \leftarrow$ MixColumn^{-1}(SubBytes$^{-1}(col')$)
7:　　$hkey \leftarrow col \oplus col'$
8:　　HashTable$[hkey].Append(col)$
9: **end for**

---

gives the partial keys eliminated by a desired pair. The hash table contains 2^{40} values stored in 2^{32} indexes averaging 2^8 values per index.

Given a desired pair with plaintexts P_1, P_2, we can compute all the partial keys eliminated by calculating $x \oplus P_1$ over all the values x in hash table at the index $P_1 \oplus P_2$. On an average, 2^8 partial keys are eliminated per desired pair. The probability that a chosen pair is a desired pair is $2^{-32} \cdot 4 = 2^{-30}$. We take chosen plaintexts which are varied over the 2^{32} possibilities along a diagonal from $\mathcal{D}_p$ with all the other bytes fixed. From these chosen plaintexts, we get 2^{63} chosen pairs. The corresponding ciphertexts are obtained and desired pairs are taken from the chosen pairs. We get $2^{63} \cdot 2^{-30} = 2^{33}$ desired pairs. We iterate over these desired pairs and eliminate the wrong partial keys using the hash table. The expected number of wrong partial keys remaining is

$$2^{32} \cdot (1 - 2^{-32})^{2^{33} \cdot 2^8} \approx 0 \tag{1}$$

It is given in the original attack that using 2^{28} desired pairs would suffice for the attack which would mean using about $2^{29.5}$ chosen plaintexts. Iterating through the 2^{28} pairs, we make 2^8 XOR and hash table lookups per pair making it a total of 2^{36} XOR calculations and hash table computation. If the computation cost of XOR calculation and hash table lookup is equated to 2^{-5} part of computation of 1 encryption, the total time complexity is about 2^{31} encryptions. Similarly, the precomputation of hash table is calculated as 2^{36} encryptions. The data complexity is $2^{29.5}$ chosen plaintexts. The memory used is at least 4 TB as 2^{42} bytes are used for the hash table. Although this memory can be deemed as practical, a server with 4 TB of primary memory is not yet commonly available. Thus the memory usage is a bottleneck for implementing the attack. We introduce measures in the following section to tackle this.

3 Memory Reduction Techniques

In this section, we introduce methods to reduce the primary memory needed for the attack. First, we give a simple 50% reduction in the memory needed with no extra cost and then introduce a data-memory tradeoff.

Reducing the hash table size to 2 TB
We first look to reduce the size of the hash table without any other increased costs. In the original attack both the ordered pairs $((a, b, c, d), (a', b, c, d))$ and $((a', b, c, d), (a, b, c, d))$ are used in the computation of the hash table. We can remove this redundancy by replacing the condition $a \neq a'$ with $a > a'$ in line 2 of Algorithm 1. The hash table size is reduced by half to 2 TB. Given a desired pair, (P_1, P_2) we eliminate the partial keys $x \oplus P_2$ and $x \oplus P_1$ (as opposed to only $x \oplus P_1$ in the original attack) over the values x at the index $P_1 \oplus P_2$. This makes up for the fewer values in the hash table. Even though now we have only an average of 2^7 values per index in the hash table, still on an average 2^8 partial keys are eliminated per desired pair. Note that the time and data complexities are not changed with this alteration.

Data-Memory Tradeoff
To further reduce the hash table, we need to look at the equation which calculates number of remaining partial keys. If we have an average of 2^x ($0 \leq x \leq 7$) values per index in the hash table, 2^{x+1} partial keys are expected to be eliminated per desired pair. If 2^y desired pairs are used, the expected number of remaining partial keys is given by

$$2^{32} \cdot (1 - 2^{-32})^{2^y \cdot 2^{x+1}} = 2^{32} \cdot (1 - 2^{-32})^{2^{x+y+1}} \tag{2}$$

In the original attack with 2^8 values per index, 2^{33} desired pairs sufficed. Thus we have,

$$x + y + 1 = 8 + 28 \Rightarrow y = 35 - x. \tag{3}$$

$$2^{32} \cdot (1 - 2^{-32})^{2^{35-x} \cdot 2^{x+1}} \approx 483 \tag{4}$$

If we have 2^x values per index in the hash table, then the number of desired pairs required for the attack would be 2^{35-x}. For 2^y desired pairs used, $2^{(y+31)/2}$ chosen plaintexts are needed. We have to be careful when computing a hash table (smaller than the original) such that the values are not extremely skewed across the indices. If we have a skewed hash table, it might be possible that all the desired pairs used might get values from the sparse part of the table, thus resulting in fewer keys eliminated than expected. In practice it is found that randomly sampling a subset of all values of (a, a', b, c, d) when calculating the hash table leads to a distribution which is not too skewed.

Thus we can reduce the memory usage by reducing x to a suitable value and increasing y to the corresponding value. It is preferable not to reduce x to a value as low as 0. Even though there is 1 entry per index on an average for $x = 0$, a skewed hash table might lead to 0 entries at some indexes. If we take $x = 2$, $y = 35 - 2 = 33$. Number of chosen plaintexts required is 2^{32}. The memory needed for the hash table is 64 GB (for storing 2^{34} 4-byte values). Though the data complexity is increased by $2^{2.5}$ times, it makes up for the fact that primary memory usage is greatly reduced from 4 TB to 64 GB provided optimal implementation of the hash table.

Reducing data complexity. There might be scenarios where the attacker is equipped with abundant memory but has less data to attack with. From the data-memory tradeoff (Eq. 3), we can see that decreasing the data complexity is possible if the average number of entries per index in the hash table increases. This is actually possible if we alter the computation of the hash table. Instead of only considering pairs such as $((a, b, c, d), (a', b, c, d))$, we can also consider the pairs $((a, b, c, d), (a, b', c, d)), b \neq b'$ and similar pairs with the different byte at c or d. Now the maximum of average number of entries per index in the hash table is increased from 2^7 to 2^9.

Thus either the memory usage or the data complexity can be decreased based on the requirements. The memory used and the data complexity for different x is given in Table 1.

Table 1. Attack on 5 round AES-128 data-memory tradeoff (partial key)

Average number of hash table entries per index x	Hash table entries 2^{32+x}	Hash table size 2^{x+4} GB	Desired pairs 2^{35-x}	Chosen plaintexts $2^{33-0.5x}$
9	2^{41}	8 TB	2^{26}	$2^{28.5}$
7	2^{39}	2 TB	2^{28}	$2^{29.5}$
4	2^{36}	256 GB	2^{31}	2^{31}
3	2^{35}	128 GB	2^{32}	$2^{31.5}$
2	2^{34}	64 GB	2^{33}	2^{32}
1	2^{33}	32 GB	2^{34}	$2^{32.5}$

Time Complexity. One might expect that with increase in data complexity, time complexity might increase. This is in fact not true. The data-memory tradeoff has no effect on the time-complexity of the attack. The main operation in the attack is calculating the partial keys eliminated for each desired pair from the hash table. Thus time complexity is proportional to $2^x \cdot 2^y = 2^{x+y}$, which is constant as per Eq. 3. So we expect that time complexity to not be affected by changes in x.

4   Implementation Details and Experimental Results

The implementation of the attacks was coded in C. The code was run on a server with Intel(R) Xeon(R) CPU E5-2697 v2 @ 2.70GHz processors. The total primary memory of the server was 256 GB under a NUMA setting. An AES implementation using AES-NI [7] instructions was used. Other subroutines of the attack which involved AES operations also used these instructions. Now we give some high level implementation details of the attack.

4.1   Implementation for AES-128

From the data-memory tradeoff, we take $x = 2$, meaning the hash table has an average of 2^2 entries per index. The number of chosen plaintexts used is 2^{32} per partial key.

Hash Table. For any hash table implementation, we expect the size to be at least 64 GB. But as the number of entries per index vary, it is difficult to implement the table without using any extra memory. We implemented a data structure for the hash table as shown in Fig. 4.

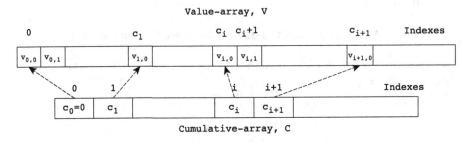

Fig. 4. The hash table data structure with the arrays V and C. $v_{i,j}$ is the jth value in the index i.

If n_i is the number of values at index i, the cumulative count c_i is given by

$$c_i = \begin{cases} 0, & \text{for } i = 0 \\ \sum_{k=0}^{i-1} n_k, & \text{for } i > 0 \end{cases}$$

V is the *value-array* where all the values of the hash table are stored in the order of their hash table indexes. C is the *cumulative-array* where $C[i] = c_i$. The hash table values at index i are given by

$$\texttt{HashTable}[i] = \Big\{ V[j] \mid C[i] \leq j < C[i+1] \Big\}$$

Each element of V is 4 bytes in size since hash table values are 4 byte values. As there are 2^{34} hash table values, size of V is 64 GB. For elements in C, 4 bytes is not sufficient as $\exists i, C[i] \geq 2^{32}$. Therefore, we use 8 byte sized elements. There are 2^{32} elements in C making its size 32 GB. Thus, the total size of hash table is 96 GB.

Desired Pairs. We would be needing 2^{33} desired pairs from 2^{32} chosen plaintexts for a partial key. However, it is not feasible to enumerate the 2^{63} pairs of chosen plaintexts to obtain the desired pairs. This is avoided by fixing the ciphertext diagonal (from $\mathcal{D}_c$) and storing the chosen plaintexts in a hash table called *desired-table*. This table is indexed by the value of the diagonal bytes of the corresponding ciphertexts. We only need to store the bytes of the plaintext along the plaintext diagonal as all the chosen plaintexts are equal across the other bytes. The procedure for constructing the desired-table is given in Algorithm 2. Once the desired-table is constructed, all the pairs of plaintexts at the same index are desired pairs. This process is repeated for different ciphertext diagonals to get all the desired pairs.

Algorithm 2. Desired Pair Generation 5 round AES-128

Require: $pdiag, cdiag \in \{0, 1, 2, 3\}$ ▷ indexes of the plaintext and ciphertext diagonals resp.

1: **procedure** BUILDDESIREDTABLE($pdiag, cdiag$)
2:      DesiredTable← INITIALIZATION()
3:      **for all** $a, b, c, d \in \{0, 1, \cdots, 2^8 - 1\}$ **do**   ▷ These are bytes
4:          $p \leftarrow$ INITIALIZESTATEPDIAGONAL($(a, b, c, d), pdiag$)   ▷ Bytes not in diagonal are fixed
5:          $c \leftarrow$ ENCRYPTIONORACLE(p)
6:          $dc \leftarrow$ GETCDIAGONALBYTES($c, cdiag$)   ▷ Obtain bytes in ciphertext diagonal
7:          DesiredTable[dc].$Insert((a, b, c, d))$
8:      **end for**
9:      **return** DesiredTable
10: **end procedure**

As the number of entries per index in the desired-table is not known, we use a linked-list like data structure shown in Fig. 5 which is highly space efficient. H is the *head-array*. $H[i]$ gives the first node at index i. N is the *node-array*. $N[i]$ is the next node in the list. Ending of a list is represented by a self-reference at the last node of the list. There are 2^{32} 4-byte sized elements in both the arrays. Thus, the size of each array is 16 GB making the total size of desired-table 32 GB. The procedures of desired-table are given in Algorithm 3. Some details of null references in H are skipped for brevity. Elements of H are initialized to 0 while elements of N are initialized as $N[i] = i$.

Key Elimination. Once the desired-table for a ciphertext diagonal is obtained, we eliminate the partial keys over the corresponding desired pairs using the hash table. This is repeated for all the diagonals. The overall implementation is given as a procedure in Algorithm 4. 2^{32} bits are needed to keep track of the eliminated partial keys. Therefore, 0.5 GB is used for the *key-array*. The over all memory usage is displayed in Table 2.

From Eq. 4, it is expected that around 483 partial keys to be not eliminated. In practice we have found that around 450 to 520 partial keys remain after the elimination process. It took 12 h to get these keys for one partial key. We get the

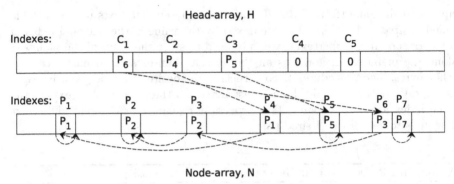

(a) $\{P_2, P_3, P_6\}$ have the same ciphertext diagonal value C_1. Similarly, $\{P_1, P_4\}$ have C_2 as their ciphertext diagonal. Only P_5 has C_3 as its ciphertext diagonal. P_7 has not been processed yet. C_4 and C_5 have no entries yet.

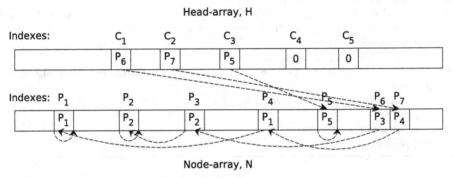

(b) P_7 is processed and it is found that its ciphertext diagonal is C_2. Hence, now $\{P_1, P_4, P_7\}$ are the plaintexts which have C_2 as their ciphertext diagonal.

Fig. 5. Two intermediate states of the desired-table during its construction.

correct key, $K = K_0$, by brute forcing over all the possible keys computed from the partial key sets (Table 3).

As the attack on AES-128 does not involve key schedule, we can apply it to the 5 round AES-192 and AES-256 variants by making a few alterations which are explained in the following sub-section.

4.2   Implementation for AES-192/256

Here we explain the implementation for AES-256 which can be applied for AES-192 without any changes. The first round key K_0 is obtained in the same way as for AES-128. For the second round key K_1, we give a new differential path that shifts the previous path by one round forward as shown in Fig. 6. Note that the definition of desired pair needs to be modified as in the ciphertext pair, only one passive byte is required for it to be a desired pair for K_1. Thus data complexity for K_1 is significantly less than that for K_0. Similarly we

Algorithm 3. Desired Table Procedures

```
 1: procedure INSERT(p, c)                                    ▷ Insert p in index c
 2:     if H[c] = 0 then                                ▷ List at index c is empty
 3:         H[c] ← p
 4:     else
 5:         N[p] ← H[c]
 6:         H[c] ← p                       ▷ Inserting p at the start of the list at H[c]
 7:     end if
 8: end procedure
 9: procedure GETENTRIES(c)                          ▷ Returns all entries at index c
10:     set ← ∅
11:     next ← H[c]
12:     if next = 0 then                          ▷ If list at index c is empty
13:         return set
14:     else
15:         set = set ∪ {next}
16:         while N[next] ≠ next do                       ▷ Iterate till end of list
17:             next = N[next]
18:             set = set ∪ {next}
19:         end while
20:     end if
21:     return set
22: end procedure
```

Algorithm 4. 5 round AES-128 Attack (Partial Key)

Require: $pdiag \in \{0, 1, 2, 3\}$

```
 1: procedure ATTACKPARTIAL(pdiag)          ▷ pdiag is the index of diagonal of the
        partial key
 2:     HashTable ← LOADHASHTABLE()
 3:     IK ← INITIALIZEIK()  ▷ IK is the key-array used to keep track of elimination
        of keys
 4:     for cdiag = 0 to 3 do              ▷ cdiag is the index of the ciphertext diagonal
 5:         DesiredTable ← BUILDDESIREDTABLE(pdiag, cdiag)
 6:         for dkey = 0 to 2^32 − 1 do
 7:             for all {P_1, P_2} ∈ DesiredTable[dkey] do
 8:                 hindex ← P_1 ⊕ P_2
 9:                 for all x ∈ HashTable[hindex] do
10:                     ELIMINATEKEY(IK, x ⊕ P_1)          ▷ The partial key x ⊕ P_1 is
        eliminated
11:                     ELIMINATEKEY(IK, x ⊕ P_2)
12:                 end for
13:             end for
14:         end for
15:     end for
16:     KeySet ← GETVALIDKEYS(IK)          ▷ Get the partial keys which were not
        eliminated
17:     return KeySet
18: end procedure
```

Table 2. Memory usage of implementation

Data structure	Memory used
Hash table	96 GB
Desired table	32 GB
Key array	0.5 GB
Total	128.5 GB

Table 3. Full key recovery attack on 5 round AES-128

Key retrieved	Chosen plaintexts	Memory used	Time taken
$K = K_0$	$2^{32} \cdot 4$	128.5 GB	$4 \times 12 = 48\,\text{h}$

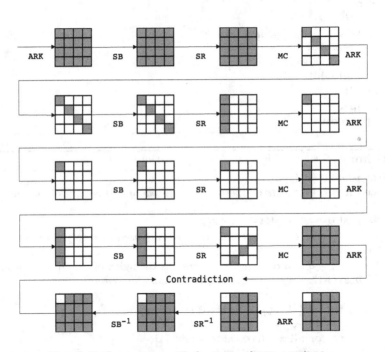

Fig. 6. Path to retrieve K_1 for 5 round AES-192/256

need to redefine chosen plaintexts. Chosen plaintexts are plaintexts s_0, whose bytes in the state s_1^M vary along a diagonal from $\mathcal{D}_p$ with other bytes fixed. We choose plaintexts by choosing s_1^M and decrypt back using K_0 to obtain the actual plaintext s_0. The rest of the implementation follows along the same lines of the implementation on AES-128. The results are given in Table 4.

Table 4. Full key recovery attack on 5 round AES-256

Key retrieved	Chosen plaintexts	Memory used	Time taken
K_0	$2^{32} \cdot 4$	128.5 GB	$4 \times 12 = 48\,\text{h}$
K_1	$2^{25} \cdot 4$	98 GB	2 h
K	$2^{32} \cdot 4$	128.5 GB	50 h

5 Conclusion

In this work, we have given a data-memory tradeoff for the impossible differential attack on 5 round AES-128 by Biham and Keller. This data-memory tradeoff enables implementation of the attack with flexible resources to tackle the high memory requirement of 4 TB of the original attack. We have implemented the attack on AES-128 with a decrease in primary memory from 4 TB to 128.5 GB and increase in data complexity from $2^{29.5}$ to 2^{32} with the time complexity, 2^{31}, not affected. Custom data structures were devised to make the implementation efficient. This attack was extended to AES-192 and AES-256 and implemented using the same techniques. This is the first reported implementation of all the attacks mentioned to the best of our knowledge.

This implementation might be useful to future impossible differential attacks on higher number of rounds with practical complexities as the basic primitives of computation in impossible differential attacks are implemented in an efficient way. It might also be useful for gaining insight into the distribution of hashes in the hash table and the key elimination patterns per pair and can be a future extension of this work.

References

1. Bahrak, B., Aref, M.R.: Impossible differential attack on seven-round AES-128. IET Inform. Secur. **2**(2), 28–32 (2008). http://dx.doi.org/10.1049/iet-ifs:20070078
2. Biham, E., Biryukov, A., Shamir, A.: Cryptanalysis of skipjack reduced to 31 rounds using impossible differentials. In: Stern, J. (ed.) EUROCRYPT 1999. LNCS, vol. 1592, pp. 12–23. Springer, Heidelberg (1999). doi:10.1007/3-540-48910-X_2
3. Biham, E., Keller, N.: Cryptanalysis of Reduced Variants of Rijndael. In: 3rd AES Conference, vol. 230 (2002)
4. Biham, E., Shamir, A.: Differential cryptanalysis of DES-like cryptosystems. J. Cryptology **4**(1), 3–72 (1991). http://dx.doi.org/10.1007/BF00630563
5. Mala, H., Dakhilalian, M., Rijmen, V., Modarres-Hashemi, M.: Improved impossible differential cryptanalysis of 7-round AES-128. In: Gong, G., Gupta, K.C. (eds.) INDOCRYPT 2010. LNCS, vol. 6498, pp. 282–291. Springer, Heidelberg (2010). doi:10.1007/978-3-642-17401-8_20
6. Daemen, J., Rijmen, V.: The Design of Rijndael: AES - The Advanced Encryption Standard. Information Security and Cryptography. Springer (2002). http://dx.doi.org/10.1007/978-3-662-04722-4

7. Gueron, S.: Intel® Advanced Encryption Standard (AES) New Instructions Set. Intel Corporation (2010). https://software.intel.com/sites/default/files/article/165683/aes-wp-2012-09-22-v01.pdf

8. Lu, J., Dunkelman, O., Keller, N., Kim, J.: New impossible differential attacks on AES. In: Chowdhury, D.R., Rijmen, V., Das, A. (eds.) INDOCRYPT 2008. LNCS, vol. 5365, pp. 279–293. Springer, Heidelberg (2008). doi:10.1007/978-3-540-89754-5_22

9. Mala, H., Dakhilalian, M., Rijmen, V., Modarres-Hashemi, M.: Improved impossible differential cryptanalysis of 7-round AES-128. In: Gong, G., Gupta, K.C. (eds.) INDOCRYPT 2010. LNCS, vol. 6498, pp. 282–291. Springer, Heidelberg (2010). doi:10.1007/978-3-642-17401-8_20

10. Phan, R.C.: Impossible differential cryptanalysis of 7-round Advanced Encryption Standard (AES). Inf. Process. Lett. **91**(1), 33–38 (2004). http://dx.doi.org/10.1016/j.ipl.2004.02.018

Privacy Preserving Techniques

Private Distributed Three-Party Learning of Gaussian Mixture Models

Kaleb L. Leemaqz[✉], Sharon X. Lee, and Geoffrey J. McLachlan

School of Mathematics and Physics, University of Queensland,
Brisbane, Australia
k.leemaqz@uq.edu.au

Abstract. This paper presents a scheme for privacy-preserving clustering in a three-party scenario, focusing on cooperative training of multivariate mixture models. With modern-day big data often collected and stored across multiple independent parties, preservation of private data is an important issue during cross-party communications when carrying out statistical analyzes of the joint data. We consider the situation where the data are horizontally distributed among three parties and that each data owner wants to learn the global parameters while data from other parties are kept private. The inter-party communications must not expose any information that may potentially disclose details of the private data, including how the data are partitioned across the parties. In addition, unlike most existing methods, the proposed scheme does not require a special trusted party to be involved. Clustering plays an important role in statistical learning and is one of the most widely used data mining methods. We shall illustrate our scheme using a Gaussian mixture model (GMM) based cluster analysis.

1 Introduction

Distributed knowledge discovery has emerged as an active field of research due to the need of analyzing extremely big data. In these settings, cross-party data mining raises important privacy and security concerns. The data might, for example, contain sensitive information such as personal details, credit records, sales data, and medical history, which can lead to serious consequences, whether legally, commercially, or ethically, if disclosed to other parties. However, it is inevitable that some privacy will be lost if cooperative data mining is to be carried out. The challenges then rest on finding the optimal balance between privacy and utility, that is, to maximize the utility of data in each party while minimizing information leakage. This has led to significant growth in the development of privacy preserving data mining techniques. Two streams of approaches seem to have emerged from the literature, namely, auxiliary-based and encryption-based methods. The former focuses on preventing the miner from learning about the original data by instead working on auxiliary data derived from the original one. To this end, techniques such as randomization, transformation, and noise-contamination have been proposed; see, for example, [2,5,6]. The encryption-based approach,

© Springer Nature Singapore Pte Ltd. 2017
L. Batten et al. (Eds.): ATIS 2017, CCIS 719, pp. 75–87, 2017.
DOI: 10.1007/978-981-10-5421-1_7

on the other hand, utilizes cryptographic methods to enable cooperative computation without disclosure of any private data [9, 10, 17, 19]. For surveys of recent developments in this area, the reader is to referred to papers by, for example, [1, 16, 18].

Most of the existing methods consider only the case where one intends to utilize untrusted computational resources. A typical example of such situation is cloud computing, where the data are to be shared with an untrusted party (in this case, it is the service provider). This leads to the existence of an hierarchical arrangement of participating parties, commonly in the form of master and slave nodes, with the results of the algorithm only known by the master nodes. This implicitly leads to the situation of multiple levels of trust between parties, where, to a slave node, a master node has a higher level of trust.

A less discussed scenario in multi-party computation is where parties of equal levels of trust (or distrust) intend to analyze their data as a joint set without revealing their private data. One solution might be to entrust their data to a third party, and for them to perform the analysis. In practice, however, it can be difficult to find such a trusted third party. Here we focus on the rarely considered situation where there is no trusted third party and no master/slave-type arrangements.

This paper proposes a method for performing private joint analysis on data stored between three parties, set in the latter scenario of equal trust levels between the parties. However, in contrast to existing works, we do not require a special trusted party (that is, a party with a higher level of trust than others). Based on a cyclic communication strategy, our scheme does not adopt the more commonly-used broadcast communication topology and hence avoid leakage of party-specific information. In the event that one of the parties is corrupted, private data from the other two parties will not be leaked to the adversary. Other side-channel information such as the partitioning or distribution of data across the parties is also protected from disclosure to any parties.

Mixture models (MM) are powerful tools for clustering and density estimation. They provide a formal but very flexible framework to model data comprising of heterogeneous populations, facilitating probabilistic classification/clustering of the data [13, 15]. As such, they are widely used in machine learning, data mining, artificial intelligence, and in numerous applications in related fields ranging from signal processing, image analysis, social science, finance, ecological and environmental modelling, to biological and medical data analysis. Among many parametric finite mixture models proposed in the literature, the Gaussian mixture model (GMM) is the one of the most commonly used models due to its mathematical tractability and formal properties. Hence, we shall adopt the GMM as an illustration of our protocol. It should be noted that the proposed approach can be implemented for more complex clustering tools based on non-normal mixture models (for example, those described in [3, 11, 12])

The rest of this paper is organised as follows. In Sect. 2, we briefly define the GMM model. Section 3 briefly outline a learning algorithm for the GMM model. In Sect. 4, we discuss the encryption schemes used as well as the privacy model used for later analysis in Section 6. In Sect. 5, we present a novel scheme for learning a global GMM model across multiple parties while preserving individual private data. In Sect. 6, a privacy analysis of the proposed algorithm is performed. Finally, concluding remarks are given in Sect. 8.

2   The GMM Model

We begin by giving an overview of model-based clustering via the Gaussian mixture model (GMM). A finite mixture model is a convex combination of component densities, the latter typically taken to belong to the same parametric family. In the case of the GMM, its component densities are taken to be a (multivariate) Gaussian distribution given by

$$\phi_p(\boldsymbol{y}; \boldsymbol{\mu}, \boldsymbol{\Sigma}) = (2\pi)^{-\frac{p}{2}} |\boldsymbol{\Sigma}|^{-\frac{1}{2}} e^{-\frac{1}{2}(\boldsymbol{y}-\boldsymbol{\mu})^T \boldsymbol{\Sigma}^T (\boldsymbol{y}-\boldsymbol{\mu})}, \tag{1}$$

where $\boldsymbol{y}$ denotes a p-dimensional random vector, $\boldsymbol{\mu}$ is a p-dimensional mean vector, and $\boldsymbol{\Sigma}$ is a $p \times p$ positive definite covariance matrix. In the above, $|\boldsymbol{\Sigma}|$ denotes the determinant of $\boldsymbol{\Sigma}$.

The density of a g-component mixture of Gaussian distributions can be expressed as

$$f(\boldsymbol{y}; \boldsymbol{\Psi}) = \sum_{i=1}^{g} \pi_i \phi_p(\boldsymbol{y}; \boldsymbol{\mu}_i, \boldsymbol{\Sigma}_i), \tag{2}$$

where π_i $(i = 1, \ldots, g)$ are the mixing proportions satisfying $\pi_i \geq 0$ and $\sum_{i=1}^{g} \pi_i = 1$. The vector $\boldsymbol{\Psi}$ is the vector containing all the unknown parameters of the mixture model and is given by $\boldsymbol{\Psi} = (\pi_1, \ldots, \pi_{g-1}, \boldsymbol{\theta}_1, \ldots, \boldsymbol{\theta}_g)$. Here, $\boldsymbol{\theta}_i$ denotes the vector of unknown parameters of the ith component density, which contains the elements of $\boldsymbol{\mu}_i$ and the distinct elements of $\boldsymbol{\Sigma}_i$.

Under the mixture model framework, a probabilistic clustering of a data set can be easily obtained by applying the *maximum a posteriori* (MAP) rule to each observation; that is, an observation is assigned to the component to which it has the highest estimated posterior probability [15].

In many application, constraints are applied to the covariance matrices $\boldsymbol{\Sigma}_i$ or other parameters of the GMM to achieve parsimony or sometimes simply for computational convenience. For example, the widely popular k-means algorithms is a special case of the GMM assuming common spherical covariance matrices and equal mixing proportions. In this paper, we will work with the general GMM without imposing any constraints on the parameters of the model.

3   The EM Algorithm

The training or fitting of a GMM can be carried out by maximum likelihood (ML) via the Expectation–Maximization (EM) algorithm [14]. Given a set of initial parameters, the EM algorithm iterates between the E- and M-steps until some convergence criterion is satisfied. The E-step calculates the conditional expectation of the complete-data log likelihood $\log L_c(\boldsymbol{\Psi})$ given the observed data $\boldsymbol{y}$ (that is, the so-called Q-function), using the current estimates of $\boldsymbol{\Psi}$. In the case of a GMM, the missing data are the latent component indicators Z_{ij} (which takes the value of one if $\boldsymbol{y}_j$ belongs to the ith component of the mixture model, and zero otherwise) and hence the E-step involves only the calculation of the conditional expectation of Z_{ij} given the observed data. This is because $\log L_c(\boldsymbol{\Psi})$ is linear with Z_{ij}. The M-step updates the estimate of the parameters of the model (that is, the elements of $\boldsymbol{\Psi}$) by maximizing the Q-function with respect to $\boldsymbol{\Psi}$.

3.1   E-Step

Let $\boldsymbol{y}_j$ $(j = 1, \ldots, n)$ be a random sample of n observations. It follows that the conditional expectation of Z_{ij} given $\boldsymbol{y}$ is given by

$$\tau_{ij}^{(k)} = E_{\boldsymbol{\Psi}^{(k)}}\{Z_{ij} = 1 \mid \boldsymbol{y}\} = \frac{\pi_i^{(k)} f_i(\boldsymbol{y}_j : \boldsymbol{\theta}_i^{(k)})}{\sum_{h=1}^{g} \pi_h^{(k)} f_h(\boldsymbol{y}_j : \boldsymbol{\theta}_h^{(k)})}, \tag{3}$$

where the superscript (k) is used to denote the value of the parameter after the kth iteration of the EM algorithm. The above quantity $\tau_{ij}^{(k)}$ is the value after the kth iteration of the posterior probability of the jth observation $\boldsymbol{y}_j$ belonging to the ith component of the mixture model given $\boldsymbol{y}_j$.

3.2   M-Step

The M-step of the $(k+1)$th iteration of the EM algorithm for a GMM is implemented by updating the parameters π, $\boldsymbol{\mu}_i$, $\boldsymbol{\Sigma}_i$ $(i = 1, \ldots, g)$, respectively, as follows:

$$\pi_i^{(k+1)} = \frac{n_i^{(k)}}{n}, \tag{4}$$

$$\boldsymbol{\mu}_i^{(k+1)} = \frac{\sum_{j=1}^{n} \tau_{ij}^{(k)} \boldsymbol{y}_j}{n_i^{(k)}}, \tag{5}$$

$$\boldsymbol{\Sigma}_i^{(k+1)} = \frac{\sum_{j=1}^{n} \tau_{ij}^{(k)} (\boldsymbol{y}_j - \boldsymbol{\mu}_i^{(k)+1})(\boldsymbol{y}_j - \boldsymbol{\mu}_i^{(k+1)})^T}{n_i^{(k)}},$$

where $n_i^{(k)} = \sum_{j=1}^{n} \tau_{ij}^{(k)}$.

3.3   Implementation

Concerning the starting values for the parameters, these are typically obtained from a given initial clustering of the data (for example, via k-means clustering or random partitions) and subsequently applying the M-step described above by taking τ_{ij} to be defined according to the initial clustering.

Concerning the stopping criterion, we adopt the approach of monitoring the progress of the likelihood function. The algorithm terminates when the relative difference log likelihood values between the current and previous iteration is smaller than a specified threshold ϵ, that is, when

$$\frac{|L^{(k+1)} - L^{(k)}|}{L^{(k)}} < \epsilon, \tag{6}$$

where $L^{(k)}$ denotes the value of the log likelihood function evaluated at the completion of the kth iteration of the EM algorithm. The log likelihood function is defined as $L^{(k)} = \sum_{j=1}^{n} \log(f(\boldsymbol{y}_j, \boldsymbol{\Psi}^{(k)}))$.

4 Privacy

There is a large amount of data involved in the process of learning a GMM model that may be of interest to an adversary. This includes not only information on the observations themselves, but also side channel information that may be leaked the process such as the distribution of the partitions. In brief, attributes that are to remain private include: the total number of observations n, the dimensions of the observations p, the distribution of the data between parties π_i ($i = 1, \ldots, g$), and the parameters of each component of the mixture model $\boldsymbol{\theta}_i$. Likewise, with regards to the results of the clustering process, the parameters of the mixture density $\boldsymbol{\Psi}$, as well as their respective cluster labels (which are derived from the estimate of τ_{ij}) are to remain private.

4.1 Cryptographic Schemes

The scheme proposed in this paper requires the use of only two cryptographic protocols, a message exchange scheme and an additive homomorphic encryption scheme.

Any message exchange protocol that satisfies the required security properties can be used for the sending and receiving of messages between parties. Therefore the proposed scheme can be used with any well-studied key-exchange/ establishment and message exchange protocols. Thus we assume that the chosen protocol will provide any required authentication, integrity, confidentiality, and forward/backward secrecy properties. For the purpose of our proposed scheme, we only require that the homomorphic encryption scheme used is additive.

Additive Homomorphic Encryption. A homomorphic encryption scheme is additive, if given two plaintext, p_1, p_2, an encryption scheme $\boldsymbol{Enc}_k()$ provides the property: $\boldsymbol{Enc}_k(p_1 \oplus p_2) = \boldsymbol{Enc}_k(p_1) \oplus \boldsymbol{Enc}_k(p_2)$
That is, the product of two cipher texts will decrypt to the sum of their corresponding plaintexts.

4.2 Adversary Model

Since the main concern of the proposed scheme is to minimize the leakage of information rather than the analysis of the chosen message exchange and encryption scheme, the security and privacy properties are to be guaranteed by their semantic security assumption. Thus it can be assumed that the external communicational attacks are mitigated by the use of secure communication channels.

To analysis the privacy properties of the algorithm, we utilize the notion of a Semi-Honest adversary and the Malicious adversary.

Semi-Honest Adversary Model. In the Semi-Honest adversary model, sometimes also referred to as the Honest-but-Curious model, an adversary can control some subset of the participating parties with the aim of gathering as much private information as possible. Under this model, the adversary will follow the protocol as specified, but will also attempt to gain as much information as possible through normal protocol message exchange.

Thus at the completion of the protocol, an adversary will have all the information stored at the parties it controls as well as the transcripts of all message interactions between parties. For the proposed scheme, information stored at a party at the completion of the algorithm includes the parameters of the resulting model, its partition of the data, the number of clusters, the number of iterations, and the size of the complete data set.

Malicious Adversary Model. In MPC (multi-party computation) there also exists a stronger Malicious adversary which, in addition to possessing the powers of the semi-honest adversary, does not necessarily follow the protocol specification and may also attempt to gain private information by sending malicious messages or altering protocol messages to its advantage. It has been shown that a protocol that is secure under the Semi-Honest Adversary Model is also secure under the Malicious Adversary Model by the use of zero-knowledge proofs to ensure the soundness of executed protocol.

5 Privacy-Preserving Distributed GMM Algorithm

This section presents an algorithm for three-party learning of a GMM for horizontally partitioned data. At the completion of the algorithm all parties would have common (but undisclosed) knowledge of the global model parameters without revealing their private data sets. Each party will also be able to derive the predicted cluster labels for their private data, but not the labels for the data held by other parties. Under our communication scheme, there is no master or slave nodes and each party is treated as equal in term of trust level. Furthermore, communications between parties are one-way, that is, node A can only either receive or send messages to/from node B, but not both send and receive from the node B. One of the benefits of adopting this cyclic-like topology is that it can help minimize the extraction of node-specific information from the received messages. Before presenting our algorithm, we shall establish some notation (Table 1) to be used in this section.

Table 1. Notations used in Algorithms 1 and 2

Symbol	Definition
P	Number of parties
m	Index for a party
n	Number of observations in the complete dataset
sk_p	Secret key of party p
pk_p	Public key of party p
$\boldsymbol{Enc}_k$	Encryption function with key k
$\boldsymbol{Dec}_k$	Decryption function with key k

5.1   Initialization

Before the commencement of the main algorithm, a secure communication channel is to be established between all parties. Key generation and exchange are also to be completed for all chosen encryption schemes. Let $m = 1, \ldots, P$ denote the index of the P parties. Note that for notational convenience, the indices are consecutively numbered but in practice they are assigned randomly and that this assignment is known by all parties. For the required homomorphic encryption scheme, each party p should at minimum possess its secret key sk_p and the P public keys pk_1, ..., pk_m.

Through the established secure communication channel, there is common information that must be shared. Most of the required information such as the number of desired clusters and number of participating parties are not considered to be private knowledge as they are directly related to the data but only ensure the functioning of the algorithm.

One essential piece of information required, however, is the overall size of the dataset n. To minimize information leakage, this must be distributed in a way such that the proportion of the (joint) data held by each party remains private. To achieve this, we propose a scheme for computing n without revealing n_m, the number of observation held by Party m. Throughout this paper, we shall use the subscript m to denote the data stored or quantities to be calculated by Party m; for example, $\boldsymbol{y}_{jm}$ $(j = 1, \ldots, n_m)$ denotes the n_m observations stored by Party m. An overview of the scheme is shown in Algorithm 1.

Lastly, concerning the starting values required for the EM algorithm, these can be computed using an existing distributed privacy preserving k-means algorithm (for example [8] or [4]), or by sharing some disclosable quantities over the existing secure channel.

5.2   E-Step

The E-step is computed as per Sect. 3.1 for all parties on their respective data sets. Thus for Party m $(m = 1, ..., P)$, this step involves calculating the posterior

Algorithm 1. Algorithm for Privately Determining n for Party m

---

Input: index of parties $m = 1, \ldots, P$, secret key of m sk_m, public key of all parties
$pk = pk_1, \ldots, pk_P$, size of data n_m
Compute message $\mathcal{T}_m = (M_m, m)$ where $M_m = \boldsymbol{Enc}_{pk_m}(n_m)$
Send $\mathcal{T}_m$ to m_{+1}
On receiving $\mathcal{T}_{m*} = (M_{m*}, m*)$
If: $m* \neq m$
$\mathcal{T}_{m*+1} = M_{m*} \oplus \boldsymbol{Enc}_{pk_{m*}}(n_m), m*$
Send $\mathcal{T}_{m*+1}$ to $m_{+1 \bmod P}$
Else if: $m^* = m$
$n = \boldsymbol{Dec}_{sk_m}(\mathcal{T}_{m*})$
Output: n

---

probabilities of component membership τ_{ijm} $(i = 1, \ldots, g)$ for observation $\boldsymbol{y}_{jm}$
$(j = 1, \ldots, n_m)$, as given by

$$\tau_{ijm}^{(k)} = \frac{p_{ijm}^{(k)}}{\sum_{h=1}^{g} p_{hjm}^{(k)}}, \tag{7}$$

where $p_{ijm}^{(k)} = \pi_i^{(k)} f_i(\boldsymbol{y}_{jm}; \boldsymbol{\theta}_i^{(k)})$. As noted previously, the superscript (k) is used
to denote the kth iteration of the EM algorithm. The computed quantities $\tau_{ijm}^{(k)}$
are to remain private and not to be disclosed to other parties as these may reveal
information about individual observations.

5.3   M-Step

Since the M-Step requires the corporation of all parties, we need to disclose at
least some sufficient statistics in order for other parties to evaluate the values of
the global parameters. Thus, each party will calculate the following summarizing
quantities and communicate them to the designed 'send to' party:

$$T_{1im} = \sum_{j=1}^{n_m} \tau_{ijm}^{(k)}, \tag{8}$$

$$T_{2im} = \sum_{j=1}^{n_m} \tau_{ijm}^{(k)} \boldsymbol{y}_{jm}, \tag{9}$$

$$T_{3im} = \sum_{j=1}^{n_m} \tau_{ijm}^{(k)} (\boldsymbol{y}_{jm} - \boldsymbol{\mu}_i^{(k)})(\boldsymbol{y}_{jm} - \boldsymbol{\mu}_i^{(k)})^T. \tag{10}$$

In addition, unless the algorithm is at its initial iteration (that is, $k = 1$),
Party m will also need to communicate an encrypted message containing (14)
from the previous iteration together with the quantities (8) to (10) above.

As all parties will disclose the above mentioned encrypted quantities, Party
m will need to perform the chosen additive function on messages received from

---

Algorithm 2. M-Step EM Algorithm for Party m

Input: data $\boldsymbol{y}_{jm}$ $(j = 1, \ldots, n)$, number of components g

Compute T_{1im}, T_{2im}, and T_{3im} using (8), (9), and (10), respectively.

Compute $T_m = (M_{1m}, M_{2m}, M_{3m}, m)$ where

$M_{1m} = \boldsymbol{Enc}_{pk_m}(T_{1im})$,

$M_{2m} = \boldsymbol{Enc}_{pk_m}(T_{2im})$,

$M_{3m} = \boldsymbol{Enc}_{pk_m}(T_{3im})$

Send T_m to m_{+1}

On receiving $T_{m*} = (M_{1m*}, M_{2m*}, M_{3m*}, m)$

If: $m* \neq m$

$T_{m*+1} = (M_{1m*} \oplus \boldsymbol{Enc}_{pk_m*}(T_{1im})$,

$M_{2m*} \oplus \boldsymbol{Enc}_{pk_m*}(T_{2im})$,

$M_{3m*} \oplus \boldsymbol{Enc}_{pk_m*}(T_{3im}), m*)$

Send T_{m*+1} to $m_{+1 \bmod P}$

Else if: $m^* = m$

$T_{1im} = \boldsymbol{Dec}_{sk_m}(T_{1im*})$

$T_{2im} = \boldsymbol{Dec}_{sk_m}(T_{2im*})$

$T_{3im} = \boldsymbol{Dec}_{sk_m}(T_{3im*})$

Compute $\pi_i, \boldsymbol{\mu}_i$, and $\boldsymbol{\Sigma}_i$ using (13).

Output: labels, parameters $\pi_i, \boldsymbol{\mu}_i$, and $\boldsymbol{\Sigma}_i$

---

its 'receive from' party and pass them to its 'send to' party; see Algorithm 2 for details. If the received message is at the end of its cycle (that is, it had passed through all the parties once), we can proceed to complete the M-step as follows:

$$\pi_i = \frac{1}{n} \sum_{m=1}^{P} T_{1im}, \tag{11}$$

$$\boldsymbol{\mu}_i = \frac{\sum_{m=1}^{P} T_{2im}}{n_i}, \tag{12}$$

$$\boldsymbol{\Sigma}_i = \frac{\sum_{m=1}^{P} T_{3im}}{n_i}, \tag{13}$$

where $n = \sum_{m=1}^{P} \sum_{i=1}^{g} T_{1im}$ and $n_i = \sum_{m=1}^{P} T_{1im}$.

5.4 Stopping Criteria

After the completion of the E- and M-steps as described above, each party will also need to calculate the value of the log likelihood function corresponding to its part of data given by (14) and communicate it on the next iteration.

$$L_m^{(k)} = \sum_{j \in 1}^{n_m} \log \left(\sum_{i=1}^{g} p_{ijm}^{(k)} \right). \tag{14}$$

Each party will also receive the sum corresponding to (14) from other parties, from which the global log likelihood value can be derived. The algorithm terminates once the stopping criterion is met (see Sect. 3.3).

6   Privacy and Information Leakage

Definition. Under the semi-honest privacy model, we say that for parties x, y, protocol ϕ is secure if for the function f there exists a probabilistic polynomial time simulators S_1 and S_2, where the ith party's view is $view_i^\pi(x, y)$ and x, y the party's respective private inputs. Such that

$$\{S_1(x, f(x,y))\}_{x,y \in \{0,1\}*} \overset{c}{\equiv} \{ view_1^\phi(x,y)\}_{x,y \in \{0,1\}*}$$
$$\{S_2(x, f(x,y))\}_{x,y \in \{0,1\}*} \overset{c}{\equiv} \{ view_2^\phi(x,y)\}_{x,y \in \{0,1\}*}$$

where $|x| = |y|$.

Informally, a protocol is said to be secure, if from each party's viewpoint, the outputs of the protocol is indistinguishable from that of a simulated one, where only its private input and output of the algorithm is being computed.

For the proposed algorithm, the security of the messages are guaranteed by the semantic security property of the chosen homomorphic encryption scheme, where it is not possible for a probabilistic polynomial time-bounded adversary to distinguish between an outputted ciphertext and random output of the same length with non-negligible greater than $1/2$.

Malicious Adversary. When considering a Malicious adversary, the possibility of incorrect values or unexpected terminations must be considered. In the prior case, it can be argued that the adversary actually learns less information. Since the purpose of the algorithm is to learn the model parameters of the combined data between all parties, if the adversary returns false or incorrect values to other parties, all subsequent intermediate and final outputs will no longer be representative of the combined data.

In the latter case, the adversary will only learn of the intermediate values from the last iteration before the algorithm is terminated. The amount of information gained is discussed in the subsequent section.

Information Leakage. Since the proposed algorithm does not modify or alter the chosen encryption schemes, for any party m, message $\mathcal{T} = \boldsymbol{Enc}_{pk_m*}(M)$ is indistinguishable from a randomly generated message of the same length. Thus the focus on the analysis is to be on the amount of information a party can learn through normal execution of the algorithm.

A list of information that might be of possible interest to an adversary is given in Table 2 with their respective level of privacy. As shown in the table, model parameters and inputs of the algorithm are shared knowledge as they need to be synchronized at every party for the algorithm to function. Thus the main pieces of information that is required to remain private are the observations and the meta-data of the observations. We shall now examine the information available to the adversary with corruption capabilities.

Table 2. Information of interest

Information	Type
Number of observations	Private
Distribution of observations	Private
Distribution of observations for each component	Private
Likelihood values	Shared
Mean vectors	Shared
Covariance Matrices	Shared
Class labels	Private
Number of clusters	Shared
Number of dimensions	Shared
Number of iteration	Shared

A corrupted party is considered to be controlled by the adversary and thus have knowledge of all its shared and private data. In the event that a secure k-means scheme was not used for the initialization of the algorithm, summarization quantities may have been shared between the parties depending on the initialization scheme used, but no other sensitive information should have been transmitted. Although there is a possibility for an adversary of exploiting this initialization step, it would nevertheless require a significant effort to learn the total number of observations. Evidently, a large number of protocol initializations would be considered by other parties to be malicious behavior.

The remaining issue is the consideration of what an adversary can learn from a controlled party. An adversary will learn of all the observations, and any shared or private information held, when it has been controlled. As one may recognize, in a three party protocol, little information would be unknown to the adversary if it controls more than a single party. Thus the focus should be of learning the partition sizes of the observations held by each party when the adversary is in control of a single party. In this scenario, through normal execution of the algorithm, the adversary will have knowledge of the total number of observations n and the total number of participating parties P. Thus from the perspective of the adversary, the number of possible different distributions of the observations between the remaining two honest parties. An adversary can attempt to discover this information from the intermediate parameters that are cooperatively calculated at every iteration during the secure summation process shown in (9). However, knowing only the values n, an $\mathcal{A}_n$, the number of possible observation distributions can be expressed by the following *Stirling partition number* [7]

$$S_r(n+1, 2) = 2S_r(n, 2) + \binom{n}{0} S_r(n-2, 1), \tag{15}$$

where r denotes the minimal number of observations held by a party. In the above, the operator $\begin{pmatrix} a \\ b \end{pmatrix}$ denotes the binomial coefficient defined as $\begin{pmatrix} a \\ b \end{pmatrix} = \frac{a!}{(a-b)!b!}$, where $a!$ denotes the factorial of a.

Alternatively, the adversary may attempt to learn the number of observations at each party for each component (n_i), where $n_i = \sum_{q=1}^{m} n_{mi}$. This reduced number of possible distributions of the observations between parties based on the component i can be expressed as

$$S_r(n_i + 1, 2) = 2S_r2 + \begin{pmatrix} n \\ -1 \end{pmatrix} S_r(n_i - 2, 1). \tag{16}$$

As one may observe, the number of possible distributions are directly affected by the total number of observations and the number of components. Thus it can be considered that the algorithm is most suitable for applications with a large amount of data.

7   Performance

The performance overhead of the scheme is heavy dependent on the chosen communication and encryption scheme as well as the increase in the number of messages required compared to a non-privacy preserving counterpart. In a typical distributed GMM implementation, all parties would be computing their part of observations and then combining their results at the end of each iteration. Thus assuming a cyclic communication topology, the proposed algorithm is required to send three times the number of messages as each party is required to compute intermediate parameters independently with the help of the other two parties. Due to this, there is also a slight computational penalty, as each part is also required to perform one additive encryption operation per message.

8   Conclusion

In this paper, we have presented an algorithm for training a GMM between three parties without revealing their private data. Unlike existing methods that typically uses a ring or mesh topology, we adopt a ring-like topology that can effectively minimise the risk of leaking party-specific information (such as the number of observations held by each party) in the event of a corrupted party. Upon completion of the algorithm, all parties will learn the parameters of the global model as if the analysis were performed on the joint data set. In addition, each party will also be able to derive the predicted cluster labels for each of its own private observations. We also investigated the amount of side-channel information that may be gain by an adversary with corruption capabilities.

References

1. Aggarwal, C.C., Yu, P.S.: A general survey of privacy-preserving data mining models and algorithms. In: Privacy-Preserving Data Mining and Algorithms, pp. 11–52 (2008)
2. Agrawal, S., Haritsa, J.R.: A framework for high-accuracy privacy-preserving mining. In: Proceedings of the 21st ICDE, Japan (2005)
3. Azzalini, A., Capitanio, A.: The Skew-Normal and Related Families. Institute of Mathematical Statistics Monographs. Cambridge University Press, UK (2014)
4. Beye, M., Erkin, Z., Lagendijk, R.L.: Efficient privacy preserving k-means clustering in a three-party setting. In: 2011 IEEE WIFS, pp. 1–6 (2011)
5. Evfimevski, A., Gehrke, J., Srikant, R.: Limiting privacy breaches in privacy preserving data mining. In: Proceedings of ACM SIGMOD/PODS Conference (2003)
6. Evfimievski, A.: Randomization in privacy preserving data mining. ACM SIGKDD Explor. Newsl. **4**, 43–48 (2002)
7. Graham, R.L., Knuth, D.E., Patashnik, O.: Concrete Mathematics. Addison Wesley, Reading (1988)
8. Jagannathan, G., Wright, R.N.: Privacy-preserving distributed k-means clustering over arbitrarily partitioned data. In: Proceedings of the Eleventh ACM SIGKD-DICKDDM, New York, NY, USA, pp. 593–599 (2005)
9. Jha, S., Kruger, L., McDaniel, P.: Privacy preserving clustering. In: Vimercati, S.C., Syverson, P., Gollmann, D. (eds.) ESORICS 2005. LNCS, vol. 3679, pp. 397–417. Springer, Heidelberg (2005). doi:10.1007/11555827_23
10. Kantarcoglu, M., Vaidya, J.: Privacy preserving naive bayes classifier for horizontally partitioned data. In: Proceedings of the IEEE ICDM PPDM, pp. 3–9 (2003)
11. Lee, S., McLachlan, G.J.: Finite mixtures of multivariate skew t-distributions: some recent and new results. Stat. Comput. **24**, 181–202 (2014)
12. Lee, S.X., Leemaqz, K.L., McLachlan, G.J.: A simple parallel EM algorithm for statistical learning via mixture models. In: Liew, A.W.-C., et al. (eds.) Proceedings of DICTA 2016, pp. 295–302. IEEE eXpress, Los Alamitos, California (2016)
13. McLachlan, G.J., Basford, K.E.: Mixture Models: Inference and Applications. Marcel Dekker, New York (1988)
14. McLachlan, G.J., Krishnan, T.: The EM Algorithm and Extensions. Wiley, Hoboken (1997)
15. McLachlan, G.J., Peel, D.: Finite Mixture Models. Wiley, New York (2000)
16. Vaidya, J.: A survey of privacy-preserving methods across vertically partitioned data. In: Privacy-Preserving Data Mining and Algorithms, pp. 337–358 (2008)
17. Vaidya, J., Clifton, C.: Privacy preserving association rule mining in vertically partitioned data. In: Proceedings of the Eighth ACM SIGKDD ICKDDM, pp. 639–644. ACM Press (2002)
18. Verykios, V.S., Bertino, E., Fovino, I.N., Provenza, L.P., Saygin, Y., Theodoridis, Y.: State-of-the-art in privacy preserving data mining. In: Proceedings of ACM SIGMOD Record, New York, USA, pp. 50–57 (2004)
19. Wu, D., Atallah, M.: Privacy-preserving cooperative statistical analysis. In: Proceedings of the 17th ACSAC. pp. 103–110 (2001)

A Privacy Preserving Platform for MapReduce

Sibghat Ullah Bazai[1(✉)], Julian Jang-Jaccard[1], and Xuyun Zhang[2]

[1] CS/IT, INMS, Massey University, Palmerston North, New Zealand
{s.bazai,j.jang-jaccard}@massey.ac.nz
[2] Department of ECE, University of Auckland,
Auckland, New Zealand
xuyun.zhang@auckland.ac.nz

Abstract. Big data applications typically require a large number of clusters, running in parallel, to process data fast and more efficiently. This is typically controlled and managed by MapReduce. In MapReduce operations, Mappers transform input original key/value pairs to a set of intermediate key/value pairs while Reducers aggregate a set of intermediate values, compute and write to the output. The output however can bring serious privacy concerns. Firstly, the output can directly leak sensitive information because it contains the global view of the final computation. Secondly, the output can also indirectly leak information via composite attacks where the adversary can link it with public information published via different sources such as Facebook or Twitter. To address such privacy concerns, we propose a privacy preserving platform which can prevent privacy leakage in MapReduce. Our platform can be plugged into the Reduce phase to sanitize the final output in such a way that the privacy is preserved while it yet provides a high data utility. We demonstrate the feasibility of our platform by providing empirical studies and highlights that our proposal can be used for real life applications.

Keywords: MapReduce · Differential privacy · K-anonymity · New york taxi data

1 Introduction

Tremendous work in data analytics has made an impressive progress to assist in critical data-driven decision-making processes. What makes scalable data analytics possible is the emergence of MapReduce which provides a parallel computing paradigm for big data applications. The name MapReduce comes from its two main functions: Map and Reduce. In the Map function, input data is usually spilt into smaller chunks and computed in a completely parallel manner by independent cluster nodes. The Reduce function consolidates the smaller chunks into a group. The several groups from different cluster nodes are computed and are written as an output. The MapReduce platform provides libraries which can provide everything meant for computing on larger clusters from parallelization, data distribution, load balancing, and fault tolerance.

L. Batten et al. (Eds.): ATIS 2017, CCIS 719, pp. 88–99, 2017.
DOI: 10.1007/978-981-10-5421-1_8

One considerable privacy concern raised in the way the Reducer handles the output and writes it to the file system. The concern is raised because the Reducer often runs on third-party infrastructure (i.e., public clouds). The administrators of the third party (or adversaries) can easily infer the sensitive knowledge simply by directly examining the output files. Or indirectly, they can also infer the original input by linking the output with other types of data, for example with non-sensitive data published in social media such as Facebook, Twitter or background auxiliary information gained via a friend or family - this is known as composite attacks [1]. To solve such a privacy concern, a variety of data anonymization techniques have been used such as data masking and grouping, K-anonymity [2], t-closeness [3], l-diversity [4] and differential privacy (DP) [5]. However, these techniques exist in isolation from each other in which often are tailored to address a specific problem for a specific domain.

We proposed a privacy preserving platform to prevent MapReduce privacy leakage. Our platform is designed in such a way that it can accommodate many different privacy preserving mechanisms and corresponding algorithms that can implement different strategies for different data anonymization results. Our platform can be plugged in the Reducer phase to sanitize the final output so that it can prevent adversaries to inference the original data or other privacy related data within dataset. We demonstrate the feasibility of our platform by providing empirical studies which aim to highlight that our proposal can be used for real life application. The studies illustrate the concrete examples of applying two state-of-art privacy preserving mechanisms, Differential Privacy and K-anonymity respectively along with New York Taxi dataset in our platform.

The rest of paper is organized as follows. In Sect. 2, we describe the major technologies and their important features involved in our platform. In Sect. 3, we describe the related work that provides different types of solutions to addressing MapReduce privacy problems. In Sect. 4, we describe our proposed platform in detail. In Sect. 5, the results of our experiment analysis based on our empirical study are demonstrated. Finally, we conclude our work and discuss some future directions in Sect. 6.

2 Background

2.1 MapReduce

The MapReduce have been a critical technology in processing big data analytics. MapReduce was originally proposed by Google in 2002 [6]. As a typical data batch processing technology, its applications have been developed for the fields in data mining, machine learning, data analytics and other fields. Due to its powerful parallel processing support, MapReduce has become the key technology for data processing.

Big Data processing is typically performed by feeding a large dataset to mappers that split the data into smaller more manageable chunks for different nodes of clusters. Mapper is responsible for reading each data, line by line, and saving that each assigned information into key/value pairs where the key is the data from the input file and the value is the number of times that the key appears in the data. After completing this process, mapper stores the key/value pairs in a temporary location. The temporarily located data is then processed using shuffle and sort then forwards this intermediate value to a reducer. The reducer performs the collective combining job, that is, to collect all intermediate data with the same key/value pairs and store them into HDFS.

2.2 K-Anonymity

K-anonymity is the first data anonymization technique with formal mathematical support as a proof. Sweeney [7] introduced K-anonymity in 2002 by stating that without ensuring k individuals in aggregation a single aggregate statistic should not be published. In his definition, Quasi- Identifiers (QID) are attributes in dataset which may be linked from publicly available dataset. The main goal to achieve K-anonymity is to replace QID values with more general values, for example generalizing 3 different values "15", "17", and "19" into a more general single value "15–20".

K-anonymity is considered as one of the most popular techniques thus has been studied well in the data anonymization community. In typical processing of K-anonymity, it utilizes two distinct techniques known as *generalization* and *suppression* with the aim to decrease the granularity of quasi identifier. Using *generalization*, more granular values are combined together to create a broader category. This can be achieved both for numerical variables (e.g., number of passenger in single taxi 3, 4, and 5 into a broader category of 3–5) and for categorical variables (e.g., generalizing pickup time data from "2013-08-07 17:38:43" to "2013-08-07"). *Generalization* replaces the original record attributes with less exact but constant values. QIDs may become generalized to a certain point where a few conclusions can be drawn about their relationships with other records. However, caution should be taken as repeated generalization could decrease the quality of the entire data set. *Suppression* works differently from generalisation by removing any records that violate anonymity standards from the data set entirely. Also caution should be taken that *suppression* can skew the integrity of data set when values are eliminated disproportionately to the original distribution of the data. More often than not, *suppression* is used in conjunction with the *generalization* to improve the anonymization efficiency, for example, the records that were not within the boundary of K-anonymity after generalization can be automatically suppressed.

2.3 Differential Privacy (DP)

Formally DP [8] can be defined as; if datasets D_1 and D_2 are only differ from a single record the function f over the range of output R is ε- Differentially private [14] for all subset S_b of R by satisfying the following condition

$$\Pr[f(D_1) \in S_b] \le e^{\varepsilon} . \Pr[f(D_1) \in S_b] \tag{1}$$

DP ensures that output will not raise the probability of any adversary learning any individual data by more than the factor. To measure the perturbation in any mechanisms sensitivity plays a vital role. Mainly two types of sensitivities are measured; *global sensitivity* and *local sensitivity*. The *global sensitivity* G_s [10] is considered as an essential notation of DP noise calculation, and defined as maximal differences between query results on neighbouring datasets, and indicates how much the difference should be hidden in mechanisms. *Local sensitivity* calibrates the record-based differences between query results on neighbouring datasets and also satisfies the DP.

Privacy budget- ε controls privacy guarantee level of any noisy-based anonymisation mechanisms. For types of applications which require higher degree of privacy, the lower privacy budget is more efficient which can range from 0.001 to max 1. The ultimate privacy guarantee depends on the step with the maximal ε. *Laplace* and *Exponential* mechanisms are the two most common mechanisms to provide noise for DP. *Laplace* mechanism adds controlled noise to the query result before returning it to the adversary [16]. The noise is generated using Laplace distribution, typically applied in the continuous data and it controls the random noise by Laplace distribution. Let a function f: $D' \rightarrow R$ over a dataset D', the Laplace mechanism is used to achieve ε-differential privacy.

$$M(D) = f\left(D'\right) + Lap(\frac{\Delta f}{\varepsilon}) \tag{2}$$

Where Δf represents the sensitivity of query f. For non-numeric queries exponential mechanism perform much better then Laplace mechanism [11]. The *exponential* mechanism takes a set of possible outputs, a quality score that assigns to each element in the range a number, and the dataset itself. The quality score is at most s-sensitive in the dataset, and here we allow this sensitivity to be passed in as a parameter. The algorithm privately outputs an element of the range that approximately maximizes the quality score [12]. The formal definition of *Exponential* mechanism is: Let $E : (D, \psi)$ be a quality function of dataset D that measures the score of output r $\in$ R. Then an Exponential mechanism is Mc is ε-differential privacy if

$$M(D) = Return r \text{ with the Probability } \alpha \exp \varepsilon\frac{E(D,r)}{2\Delta f} \tag{3}$$

Where Δf represents the sensitivity of query f.

3 Related Work

In this section, we describe existing works that discuss security and privacy issues in MapReduce in different stage of its operations.

A number of works in this area focuses protecting the intermediate values that are produced after Mapper function. The intermediate values which are stored in a temporary file by MapReduce platform are not supported with any protection mechanism [9] therefore these values can be easily accessed by adversaries. The deletion of the intermediate (i.e., temporary) files happens at the end of mapper and reduce job [13]. Pig allow user to run high level scripting language on MapReduce platform in the Hadoop ecosystem. Pig does not handle temporary files deletion if the script execution failed or killed. Once this happens, the deletion task is left to the developers to handle it on their own without any support from the MapReduce platform. The authors in [14] discuss three main challenges of MapReduce when used in cloud platform: Scalability and Dynamic, Cost effectiveness and Data utility and Compatibility. Zhang et al. [15] addresses these issues by proposing a privacy preserving layer over MapReduce, which satisfies privacy demands itemized by data publishers built on diverse MapReduce privacy models.

More closed work to us which provides the protection on the reducer is described by Airavat [16] which proposed a secure framework for MapReduce by defining mandatory access control (MAC) with DP on secure Operating system SELinux. Airavat MAC is activated when privacy leakage exceeds from define limit, ensuring high utility and privacy. However, Airavat add pre-configured noise for query which limits its application. Tran and Sato [17] addresses Airavat limitation by allowing users to write reducer code by modifying System's access control, however, if adversary manage to sneak reducer code by changing user right as a trusted user, the proposed solution fail to provide privacy guarantee.

4   Proposed Solution

In this section, we describe the details of our proposed platform including the major components and their responsibilities.

4.1   The Proposed Platform

We propose a privacy-preserving platform that works collaboratively with Mapper and Reducer in such a way that it hides the details of the final output by providing mechanisms for various data sanitization while it still provide a high data utility. The approach taken by our platform essentially provides a better flexibility of executing different privacy preserving mechanisms and corresponding algorithms while ensuring any part of data is not leak during any MapReduce operations. The proposed platform is illustrated in Fig. 1.

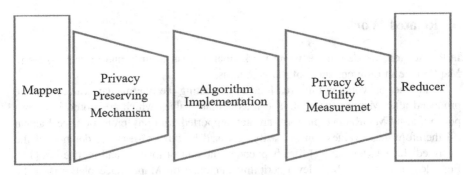

Fig. 1. Proposed platform

Our platform consists of three components: Privacy Preserving Mechanism layer, Algorithm Implementation layer, and Privacy and Utility Measurement layer. The privacy preserving mechanism layer can accommodate many state-of-art data anonymization mechanisms. Once this mechanism is determined, an algorithm which can produce a specific sanitized dataset can be implemented by the algorithm layer. Finally, Privacy and Utility Measurement layer can measure the different privacy and utility values using different formulas in order to verify the sanitized data is still ensuring the privacy and yet provide enough useful information.

4.2   Components

In this section, we provide the details of the components in our proposed model.

Privacy Preserving Mechanism layer: This layer receives data from trusted Mapper(s) and defines a privacy protection mechanism to preserve the privacy from unprotected reducer and dishonest system administrator. The list of privacy protection mechanisms which can be applied in this layer include for example but not limited to, K-anonymity, l-diversity, t-closeness and differential privacy. Each of these mechanisms has their own strengths and weaknesses and is most often applicable to use in a specific use case. Providing a single privacy preserving technique is often too limiting to accommodate many different applications scenarios. In our proposal, we address this limitation by allowing the data scientist to decide and pick a mechanism that best suitable for their business demands.

Algorithm Implementation layer: Algorithms deal with the process of transforming the original data into a sanitized data under the umbrella of the privacy preserving mechanism that was defined in the privacy preserving mechanism layer. This layer allows the data scientist to choose a suitable algorithm for data transformation, for example, it can be a simple aggregation algorithm implementation using a sum and mean value of the data set under the group of K, or it can be the implementation of Naïve Bayers or Decision Trees for classification task, or K-means for clustering task.

Privacy and Utility Measurement layer: This layer is responsible for providing a functionality where data scientist can measure the privacy and utility trade-off after the original data has been transformed into a sanitized one.

Data utility can ensure that the data still contain enough information where data analytics can still find the relationships and correlations between data. This can be done by a utility measurement (e.g., RMSE, MAE). The utility measure can be done in many different ways depending on the type of algorithms it dealt with. For example, to measure data utility in the aggregation, the data utility can be measured by comparing the accuracy of answering aggregate queries between the original dataset and the sanitized data. For a classification algorithm, the utility measure can be done by comparing the percentage of samples that are correctly classified between the original dataset and the sanitized version. A noise added statistical utility measure can be achieved by calculating the total variance of perturbed data or calculating the length confidence interval of the estimator. Additionally, utility measure can be achieved by using the techniques such as generalization height, privacy information loss ratio, workload aware anonymization. Each approach has its own unique way for calculating a data utility.

Privacy measure can ensure that the data is protected from any privacy attack after the data has been sanitized. The privacy measure is typically done by measuring the uniqueness of data (e.g., the number of unique data). For example, record-based privacy measure, it can measure the ratio of counts that are related to unique record before and after transformation.

5 Empirical Studies

This section provides empirical studies to illustrate a number of different ways to utilise our proposed platform for a real life application. To this end, we choose two state-of-the-art privacy-preserving mechanisms, differential privacy (DP) and K-anonymity, respectively, to demonstrate the effectiveness and usefulness of our proposed platform along with the widely-used New York taxi data [18]. The experiments are performed on Intel(R) Xeon(R) CPU E5-1650 v3 @ 3.50 GHz, 3501 MHz, 6 Core(s), and 12 Logical Processor(s) with 4 Tara bytes hard drive and 32 GB of RAM. As to the New York Taxi trip data, we specifically use the 2013–2016 version of this dataset. The original New York Taxi trip data includes 19 features in total. However, we specifically use a subset of the original dataset and only consider four commonly-used features: pickup date time, pickup longitude, pickup latitude, and total fare amount, in order to focus on the discussion of our main idea in this paper.

5.1 Applying Differential Privacy (DP) on Aggregation Algorithm

Let's suppose a data scientist wants to execute a query to find the average of total amount of taxi fare charged to passengers from JFK airport New York to see how much the driver earns from this location collectively in the year between 2013 and 2016. Typically, New York Taxi Workers Alliance (NYTWA) Repair Services have the details of every taxi visited for JFK airport. The NYTWA could use this knowledge to link with non-sensitive published results to deduce the exact salary of a particular driver. To prevent such privacy violation from occurring, rather than using a real value (i.e., the total exact amount of taxi income), it would protect privacy better if a statistically approximate of the total taxi fare is used instead.

With that goal in mind, we implemented DP as a privacy preservation mechanism to see the effect of using a noisy mechanism-based technique to provide privacy. For an algorithm implementation, we utilise an aggregation scenario with the following details in the pseudocode.

For the implementation of adding the controlled noise for our algorithm, we use the Laplacian mechanism which generates the random noise in terms of the Laplace

---

Algorithm DPAA (Differential Privacy on Aggregation Algorithm)

INPUT: Privacy Budget as PB, Location Density as LD, Sensitivity Sen,
                Total Amounts as TA

OUTPUT: Root Mean Square Error as $RMSE$

ALGORITHM:

1:   **for each** $i \in PB$ **do** /* **outer loop** */
2:       initialize Actual Sum AS = 0
3:       initialize Sanitized Sum SS = 0;
4:       Calculate $Noise$ using $Lap(Sen/PB[i])$
5:       **for each** $j \in TA$ **do** /* **inner loop** */
6:           Add $TA[j]$ to AS
7:           Add $TA[j]$ and $Noise$ to SS
     end inner for each
     end outer for each
8:   Calculate RMSE[i] to be sqrt (square((SS-AS)/LD))
9:   Output $RMSE$;

---

distribution from Eq. (2). This Laplace noise is added to each raw data (i.e., individual total amount). The value with noise then is summed. To understand the effect of noise in different data size and distribution, our experiments were carried out on different location density scale which is denoted as LD. We used 5 different scales: LD-10, LD-100, LD-1000, LD-2500, and LD-5000, respectively where the number after LD- indicates the size of the data; for example, LD-10 represents the 10 pickup locations in the sample. Our experiment study used a fixed sensitive = 1. For each location density, we apply four different privacy budgets (i.e., ε-0.001, ε-0.01, ε- 0.1 and ε-1) to understand the effect of noise between the privacy budget and the data size. The overall privacy verses utility trade-off, based on different privacy budget and the data size, is calculated using the Root Mean Square Error (RMSE) which measures the difference between the raw data and the sanitized data (i.e., the noised injected raw data). Assuming n test samples with raw data values $\psi_1,\dots, \psi_n$, and sanitized values $\hat{\psi}_1,\dots,\hat{\psi}_n$, the RMSE is then given by:

$$RMSE = \sqrt{\frac{\sum_{i=1}^{n}(\hat{\psi}_i - \psi_i)^2}{n}} \qquad (4)$$

The RMSE calculation on the privacy budget on different LD is shown in Fig. 2.

The results in Fig. 2 show differences on the privacy budget value ε for different location densities. We make the following observations;

- For the privacy budget ε-0.001, it provides the lowest error rate denoted by the smallest $RMSE$ values. Most likely, the noise is relatively small compared to other privacy budget. This privacy budget may be applicable for the types of applications where it requires relatively high accuracy but privacy is not a main concern.
- The privacy budgets ε-0.01 and ε-1 illustrates similar $RMSE$ values no matter the data size. We see a big difference in $RMSE$ result on the LD size 10. This is most likely that the LD size 10 is too skewed to get any meaningful value.

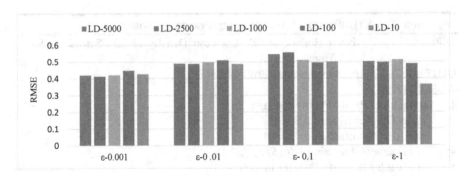

Fig. 2. Privacy utility trade-off using RMSE on DP

- Using the privacy budget ε-0.01, it provides the most uniform distribution of the error rate regardless the different size of location density. It also demonstrates the highest *RMSE* values which mean that the most noise was introduced. This privacy budget may be applicable for the types of applications where it requires relatively high privacy but accuracy is not a main concern.

5.2 Applying K-Anonymity on Aggregation Algorithm

For our second empirical study, we used K-anonymity as a privacy preservation mechanism to anonymise the total taxi fare. For an algorithm implementation, we use the following pseudocode which calculates the approximate total taxi fare within different group sizes of *k*.

Algorithm KAA (<u>K</u>-anonymity on <u>A</u>ggregation <u>A</u>lgorithm)

INPUT: K group size as KG, Location Density as LD, Total Amounts as TA,
OUTPUT: Root Mean Square Error as $RMSE$
ALGORITHM:
Initialize all variables KG, LD, AVG
1: **for each** $i \in K$ **do**
2:      Calculate the averages of all $K[i]$.
3:      **for each** average **do**
4:          $Noise[i] = Avg - KG[i]$;
          end for each
5:      Repeat Step 2 for every LD
6:      **for each** element in n of $Noise$ **do**
7:          **for each** element j of TA **do**
8:              $RMSE [n] = RMSE [j] + (Noise[i] - [j])$;
              end for each
9:              RMSE[n]=RMSE[n]/LD;
          end for each
      end for each
10: Output $RMSE$;

The aggregation algorithm is applied in the following ways. We first calculate the average value against the total taxi fare (i.e. Total amount) within all records in the same group. The average becomes a new sanitized value for all records. To see the effects of the accuracy against different levels of group size k threshold, we use K to be the one of the sizes of $k \in \{5, 10, 100 \text{ and } 1000\}$. To understand the effect of anonymized value in the different group size, our experiments carried out again on different location density scales: LD-10, LD-100, LD-1000, LD-2500, LD-5000. Here again, we use Root Mean Square Error (RMSE) (4) to understand the overall privacy verses utility trade-off based on different group threshold k and the data size (i.e., location density).

The RMSE calculation on different group threshold k on different LD is shown in Fig. 3.

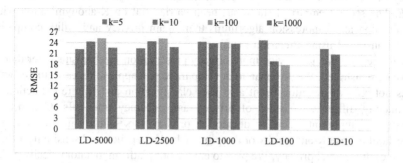

Fig. 3. Privacy utility trade-off using RMSE on K-anonymity

The results in Fig. 3 show differences on the group size k for different location densities. We make the following observations:

- The k group size 5 and 10 do not make much difference in the location density LD-10 which illustrates that the distribution of data within 10 records looks to be fairly uniform (i.e., not so much variations on total taxi fare within the record sets).
- For the location density LD-100, there is a quite large difference in *RMSE* values among different k group sizes. It indicates that the distribution of data in this group is much more skewed. For example, total amount may vary from the minimum value of 0.16 to the maximum value of 375. This indicates that the sample size of 100 is less preferable to use for any meaningful analysis.
- For the location density LD-1000, we experience a good consistency with *RMSE* values across different k group sizes. It is evident that the distribution of data in this group is unvarying or the size of the data is big enough to hide the difference between the data range which contributes to the stable *RMSE* values across different value of k sizes.
- From the location density above 2500, the graphs started looking similar in their *RMSE* value proportion across different k group sizes. The smaller group size k (i.e., $k = 5$) gives the lowest *RMSE* value due to its frequent average sum applied across the data set. Similarly, the largest group size k (i.e., $k = 1000$) also gives relatively low *RMSE* value because there is more chance for the data to be normalised.

6 Conclusions and Future Work

In this paper, we have proposed a privacy preserving platform for the prevention of privacy leakage in MapReduce by adding three middle layers between Mappers and Reducers. The novelty of our Platform is that it allows the users to choose anonymization technique in Layer 1, algorithm to process that technique in Layer 2 and utility-privacy trade-off measurement to verify the impact of algorithm and anonymity technique combination in Layer 3.

We have presented an empirical study on NYC taxi data using our Platform to illustrate the feasibility and practicability of our proposal. The first empirical study been carried out using Differential Privacy with an aggregation algorithm then the privacy verses utility measurements were demonstrated using the accuracy measure and *RMSE*. The second empirical study has been carried out on K-anonymization with a generalization and suppression algorithms then again privacy and utility comparison was demonstrated using Precision measure.

In future, we plan to provide more privacy preservation mechanisms other than the two we demonstrated. We also plan to develop more real application case studies where it uses not only aggregation but it also uses classification and feature extraction and consequently different measures of privacy and accuracy trade-offs. Currently we manually set important values to decide the privacy verses utility measures such as K-threshold in case K-anonymity or the privacy budget epsilon and sensitivity value in the case of differential privacy. We plan to enable our platform to automatically pick up these values in the future, depending on the application scenarios.

References

1. To, Q.C., Nguyen, B., Pucheral, P.: TrustedMR: a trusted MapReduce system based on tamper resistance hardware. In: Debruyne, C., et al. (eds.) On the Move to Meaningful Internet Systems: OTM 2015. LNCS, vol. 9415, pp. 38–56. Springer, Cham (2015). doi:10.1007/978-3-319-26148-5_3
2. Sweeny, L.: K-Anonymity: a model for protecting privacy. Int. J. Uncertainty Puzziness Knowledge-Based Syst. **10**, 557–570 (2002)
3. Ninghui, L., Tiancheng, L., Venkatasubramanian, S.: t-closeness: privacy beyond k-anonymity and L-diversity. In: Proceedings of the International Conference on Data Engineering, pp. 106–115 (2007)
4. Machanavajjhala, A., Kifer, D., Gehrke, J., Venkitasubramaniam, M.: ?-diversity: privacy beyond k-anonymity. ACM Trans. Knowl. Discov. Data. **1**, 3–es (2007)
5. Chen, C.-L., Pal, R., Golubchik, L.: Oblivious mechanisms in differential privacy: experiments, conjectures, and open questions. In: 2016 IEEE Security and Privacy Workshops, pp. 41–48 (2016)
6. Dean, J., Ghemawat, S.: MapReduce: simplified data processing on large clusters. Commun. ACM **51**, 107 (2008)
7. Sweeney, L.: Achieving K -anonymity privacy protection using generalization and suppression. Int. J. Uncertainty Fuzziness Knowl. Based Syst. **10**, 1–18 (2002)
8. Dwork, C.: A firm foundation for private data analysis. Commun. ACM **54**, 86 (2011)

9. Dwork, C., Smith, A.: Differential privacy for statistic: what we know and what we want to learn. J. Priv. Confidentiality **1**, 135–154 (2009)
10. Liu, F., Mathematics, C., Dame, N.: Generalized gaussian mechanism for differential privacy, pp. 1–29. arXiv. 46556 (2016)
11. Barthe, G., Gaboardi, M., Gregoire, B., Hsu, J., Strub, P.-Y.: Proving differential privacy via probabilistic couplings, pp. 1–10. arXiv. 1 (2016)
12. Gaboardi, M., Haeberlen, A., Hsu, J., Narayan, A., Pierce, B.C.: Linear dependent types for differential privacy. In: Popl 2013, vol. 48, pp. 357–370 (2013)
13. Ohrimenko, O., Costa, M., Fournet, C., Gkantsidis, C., Kohlweiss, M., Sharma, D.: Observing and preventing leakage in MapReduce. In: Proceedings of the 22nd ACM SIGSAC Conference on Computer and Communication Security - CCS 2015, pp. 1570–1581 (2015)
14. Chen, G., Cai, Q., Zhan, Y.: Approaches on personal data privacy preserving in cloud: a survey. In: Proceedings of The Third International Conference on Data Mining, Internet Computing, and Big Data, Konya, pp. 36–43. Turkey (2016)
15. Zhang, X., Liu, C., Nepal, S., Dou, W., Chen, J.: Privacy-preserving layer over MapReduce on cloud. In: Proceedings of the 2nd International Conference on Cloud Green Computing, 2nd International Conference on Society Computer Its Applications CGC/SCA 2012, pp. 304–310 (2012)
16. Roy, I., Setty, S.T.V.S.T.V., Kilzer, A., Shmatikov, V., Witchel, E.: Airavat: security and privacy for MapReduce. In: Proceedings of the 7th USENIX Conference on Networked System Design Implementation, vol. 19, pp. 20–20 (2010)
17. Tran, Q., Sato, H.: A solution for privacy protection in mapreduce. In: Proceeding of the International Computer Software Application Conference, pp. 515–520 (2012)
18. Douriez, M., Doraiswamy, H., Freire, J., Silva, C.T.: Anonymizing NYC taxi data: does it matter? In: 2016 IEEE International Conference on Data Science and Advanced Analytics (DSAA), pp. 140–148. IEEE (2016)

Privacy-Preserving Deep Learning: Revisited and Enhanced

Le Trieu Phong[1]([✉]), Yoshinori Aono[1], Takuya Hayashi[1,2], Lihua Wang[1], and Shiho Moriai[1]

[1] National Institute of Information and Communications Technology (NICT), Tokyo, Japan
{phong,aono,wlh,shiho.moriai}@nict.go.jp
[2] Kobe University, Kobe, Japan
t-hayashi@eedept.kobe-u.ac.jp

Abstract. We build a privacy-preserving deep learning system in which many learning participants perform neural network-based deep learning over a combined dataset of all, without actually revealing the participants' local data to a curious server. To that end, we revisit the previous work by Shokri and Shmatikov (ACM CCS 2015) and point out that local data information may be actually leaked to an honest-but-curious server. We then move on to fix that problem via building an enhanced system with following properties: (1) no information is leaked to the server; and (2) accuracy is kept intact, compared to that of the ordinary deep learning system also over the combined dataset. Our system makes use of additively homomorphic encryption, and we show that our usage of encryption adds little overhead to the ordinary deep learning system.

Keywords: Privacy · Deep learning · Neural network · Additively homomorphic encryption

1 Introduction

1.1 Background

In recent years, *deep learning* (aka, *deep machine learning*) has produced exciting results in both acamedia and industry, in which deep learning systems are approaching or even surpassing human-level accuracy. This is thanks to algorithmic breakthroughs and physical parallel hardware applied to *neural networks* when processing massive amount of data.

Massive collection of data, while vital for deep learning, raises the issue of privacy. Individually, a collected photo can be permanently kept on a server of a company, out of the control of the photo's owner. At law, privacy and confidentiality worries may prevent hospitals and research centers from sharing their medical datasets, baring them from enjoying the advantage of large-scale deep learning over the joint datasets.

© Springer Nature Singapore Pte Ltd. 2017
L. Batten et al. (Eds.): ATIS 2017, CCIS 719, pp. 100–110, 2017.
DOI: 10.1007/978-981-10-5421-1_9

As a directly related work, Shokri and Shmatikov [12] presented a system for privacy-preserving deep learning, allowing local datasets of several participants staying home while the learned model for the neural network[1] over the joint dataset can be obtained by the participants. To achieve the result, the system in [12] needs the following: each learning participant, using local data, first computes gradients of a neural network; then a part (e.g. 1%–10%) of those gradients must be sent to a parameter cloud server. The server is *honest-but-curious*: it is assumed to be *curious* in extracting the data of individuals; and yet, it is assumed to be *honest* in operations.

To protect privacy, the system of Shokri and Shmatikov admits an accuracy/privacy tradeoff (see Table 1): sharing no local gradients leads to perfect privacy but not desirable accuracy; on the other hand, sharing all local gradients violates privacy but leads to good accuracy. To compromise, sharing a part of local gradients is the main solution in [12] to keep as less accuracy decline as possible.

1.2 Our Contributions

We demonstrate that, in the system of Shokri and Shmatikov [12], even a small portion of the gradients stored over the cloud server can be exploited: namely, local data can be unwillingly extracted from those gradients. Illustratively, we show in Sect. 3 a few examples on how a small fraction of gradients leaks useful information on data.

We then propose a novel system for deep learning to protect the gradients over the *honest-but-curious* cloud server, using additively homomorphic encryption. All gradients are encrypted and stored on the cloud server. The additive homomorphic property enables the computation over the gradients. Our system is described in Sect. 4, and depicted in Fig. 3, enjoying following properties on security and accuracy:

Security. *Our system leaks no information of participants to the honest-but-curious parameter (cloud) server.*

Accuracy. *Our system achieves identical accuracy to a corresponding deep learning system (Downpour SGD, see below) trained over the joint dataset of all participants.*

Our tradeoff. Protecting the gradients against the cloud server comes with the cost of increased communication between the learning participants and the cloud server. We show in Table 2 that the increased factors are not big: less than 3 for concrete datasets MNIST [2] and SVHN [11]. For example, in the case of MNIST, if each learning participant needs to communicate 0.56 MB[1] of plain gradients to the server at each upload or download; then in our system with LWE-based encryption, the corresponding communication cost at each upload or download becomes

$$\textbf{2.46} \text{ (Table 2's factor)} \times \textbf{0.56} \text{ (original MB)} \approx \textbf{1.38} \text{ MB}$$

---

[1] Size of 140106 gradients each of 32 bits; the size is computed via the formula $\frac{140106 \times 32}{8 \times 10^6} \approx 0.56$.

Table 1. Comparison of techniques.

System	Method to protect gradients (against the curious server)	Tradeoff	Accuracy is declined?
Shokri-Shmatikov [12]	Partial sharing	Accuracy/Privacy	Yes (less than Downpour SGD)
Ours (Sect. 4)	Additively homomorphic encryption	Efficiency/Privacy	No (equal to Downpour SGD)

Table 2. Increased communication factor.

Our system	Increased factor (compared to ordinary Downpour SGD)
LWE-based	**2.46** (MNIST dataset [2]), **2.43** (SVHN dataset [11]), **2.41** (speech dataset [6])

(Using parameters for 128-bit security in encryption)

which needs less than 2 s to be transmitted over a 10 Mbps channel. Technical details are in Sect. 5.

On the computational side, the most frequent operation is ciphertext additions over the server. As each ciphertext is a vector of integers, the addition cost is also small. For example, it takes only 0.013 s to add two LWE-based ciphertexts with parameters for the SVHN dataset over a server (2.60 GHz) with one thread of computation.

A remark on adversary model. We consider the cloud server as the adversary in this paper while learning participants are seen as honest entities. This is because in our scenario learning participants are considered as organisations such as financial institutions or hospitals acting with responsibilities by laws. Our scenario and adversary model is different from Hitaj et al. [8] which examines dishonest learning participants.

1.3   Technical Overviews

A succinct comparison is in Table 1. Below we present the underlying technicalities.

Downpour stochastic gradient decent (Downpour SGD) [6], no privacy protection. Both our system and that of [12] rely on the fact that neural networks can be trained via a variant of asynchronous stochastic gradient decent called Downpour SGD [6]. Specifically, first a global weight vector W_{global} for the neural network is initialised randomly. Then, at each iteration, replicas of the neural network are run over local datasets, and the corresponding local gradient vector G_{local} is sent to a cloud server. For each G_{local}, the cloud server then updates the global parameters as follows:

$$W_{\text{global}} := W_{\text{global}} - \alpha \cdot G_{\text{local}} \tag{1}$$

where α is a constant called learning rate. The updated global parameters W_{global} are broadcasted to all the replicas, who then use them to replace their old weight parameters. The process of updating and broadcasting W_{global} is repeated until a desired minimum for a pre-defined cost function (based on cross-entropy or squared-error) is reached.

The design of Downpour SGD is for large-scale efficiency, and learning accuracy. Data privacy is not considered in Downpour SGD.

Shokri-Shmatikov systems. The system in [12, Sect. 5] can be called as *gradients-selective* Downpour SGD, by following reasons. In [12, Sect. 5], the update rule at (1) is modified as follows:

$$W_{\text{global}} := W_{\text{global}} - \alpha \cdot G_{\text{local}}^{\text{selective}} \tag{2}$$

in which vector $G_{\text{local}}^{\text{selective}}$ contains selective (say 1%–10%) gradients of G_{local}. The update using (2) allows each participant to choose which gradients to share globally, with the hope of reducing the risk of leaking sensitive information on the participant's local dataset to the cloud server.

Putting aside the issue that gradients leak information to the server (showed in Sect. 3), as only a part of local gradients are used to update the weight vector W_{global}, Shokri-Shmatikov's system accuracy is not as good as Downpour SGD (where all local gradients are used), in general.

In [12, Sect. 7], Shokri-Shmatikov showed an additional technique on using differential privacy to counter-measure indirect leakage from gradients. Their strategy is to add Laplace noises into $G_{\text{local}}^{\text{selective}}$ at (2). Due to noises, this method much more declines the learning accuracy.

Our system. The system we designed can be called as *gradients-encrypted* Downpour SGD, by following reasons. In our system in Sect. 4, we make use of the following update formula

$$\mathbf{E}(W_{\text{global}}) := \mathbf{E}(W_{\text{global}}) + \mathbf{E}(-\alpha \cdot G_{\text{local}}) \tag{3}$$

in which $\mathbf{E}$ is homomorphic encryption supporting addition over ciphertexts. The decryption key is only known to the participants and not to the cloud server. Therefore, the honest-but-curious cloud server knows nothing about each

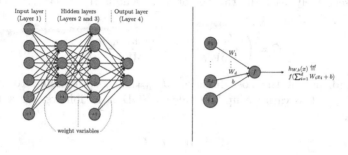

Fig. 1. (left) a neural network with 5 inputs, 2 hidden layers, 2 outputs; **(right)** a network with one neuron.

G_{local}, and hence obtains no information on each local dataset of participants. Nonetheless, as

$$\mathbf{E}(W_{\text{global}}) + \mathbf{E}(-\alpha \cdot G_{\text{local}}) = \mathbf{E}(W_{\text{global}} - \alpha \cdot G_{\text{local}})$$

by the additively homomorphic property of $\mathbf{E}$, each participant will get the correctly updated W_{global} by decryption.

In addition, to ensure the integrity of the homomorphic ciphertexts, each client will use a secure channel such as TLS/SSL (distinct from each other) to communicate the homomorphic ciphertexts with the server.

2 Preliminaries

Deep machine learning can be seen as a set of techniques applied to neural networks. In Fig. 1 is a neural network with 5 inputs, 2 hidden layers, and 2 outputs. The node with $+1$ represents the bias term. The neuron nodes are connected via weight variables. In a deep learning structure of neural network, there can be multiple layers each with thousands of neurons.

Each neuron node (except the bias node) is associated with an *activation function* f. Examples of f in deep learning are $f(z) = \max\{0, z\}$ (rectified linear), $f(z) = \frac{e^z - e^{-z}}{e^z + e^{-z}}$ (hyperbolic tangent), and $f(z) = (1 + e^{-z})^{-1}$ (sigmoid). The output at layer $l+1$, denoted as $a^{(l+1)}$, is computed as $a^{(l+1)} = f(W^{(l)}a^{(l)} + b^{(l)})$ in which $(W^{(l)}, b^{(l)})$ is the weights connecting layers l and $l+1$, and $a^{(l)}$ is the output at layer l.

The learning task is, given a training dataset, to determine these weight variables to minimise a pre-defined cost function such as the cross-entropy or the squared-error cost function [1]. The cost function can be computed over all data items in the training dataset; or over a subset (called mini-batch) of t elements from the training dataset. Denote the cost function for the latter case as $J_{|\text{batch}|=t}$. In the extreme case of $t = 1$, corresponding to maximum stochasticity, $J_{|\text{batch}|=1}$ is the cost function defined over 1 single data item.

Stochastic gradient descent (SGD). Let W be the flattened vector consisting all weight variables, namely we take all weights in the neural network and arrange them consecutively to form the vector W. Denote $W = (W_1, \ldots, W_{n_{gd}}) \in \mathbb{R}^{n_{gd}}$. Let

$$G = \left(\frac{\delta J_{|\text{batch}|=t}}{\delta W_1}, \ldots, \frac{\delta J_{|\text{batch}|=t}}{\delta W_{n_{gd}}} \right) \qquad (4)$$

be the gradients of the cost function $J_{|\text{batch}|=t}$ corresponding to variables $W_1, \ldots, W_{n_{gd}}$. The variable update rule in SGD is as follows, for a learning rate $\alpha \in \mathbb{R}$:

$$W := W - \alpha \cdot G \qquad (5)$$

in which $\alpha \cdot G$ is component-wise multiplication. The learning rate α can also be changed adaptively as described in [1].

Downpour SGD [6]. By (4) and (5), as long as the gradients G can be computed, the weights W can be updated. The data used in computing G can be distributed (does not have to be centrally stored) and the update of W can be done at any time (no waiting after having G). These properties enable the following variant of SGD called Downpour SGD.

Specifically, Downpour SGD uses multiple replicas of a neural network. Before each execution, each replica will download the newest weights from the parameter server; and each replica is run over a data shard, which is a subset of the training dataset. Weight updates are done over the parameter server according to SGD's rule (5). Downpour SGD significantly increases the scale and speed of deep network training, as experimentally shown in [6].

Thanks to the asynchronous property of the SGD's rule (5), in Downpour SGD the replicas can run independently of each other. To reduce the communication overhead, it is possible that each replica send gradients G and retrieve weights W at n_{push} and n_{fetch} steps. In the extreme case, $n_{push} = n_{fetch} = 1$, which corresponds to maximum stochasticity.

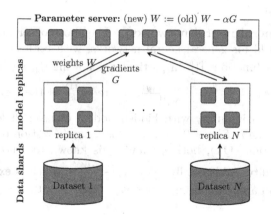

Fig. 2. Downpour SGD [6].

3 Gradients Leak Information

Example 1 (one neuron). For illustration of how gradients leak information on data, we first use the neural network in Fig. 1, with only one neuron. In the figure, real numbers x_i $(1 \le i \le d)$ are the input data, with a corresponding truth label y; real numbers W_i $(1 \le i \le d)$ are the weight parameters to be learned; and b is the bias. The function f is an activation function (either sigmoid, rectified linear, or hyperbolic tangent as described in Sect. 2). The cost function is defined as the distance between the predicted value $h_{W,b}(x) \stackrel{\text{def}}{=} f(\sum_{i=1}^{d} W_i x_i + b)$ and the truth value y: $J(W, b, x, y) \overset{\text{def}}{=} (h_{W,b}(x) - y)^2$ and hence the gradients are

$$\eta_k \overset{\text{def}}{=} \frac{\delta J(W, b, x, y)}{\delta W_k} = 2(h_{W,b}(x) - y)f'(\sum_{i=1}^{d} W_i x_i + b) \cdot x_k \tag{6}$$

$$\eta \overset{\text{def}}{=} \frac{\delta J(W, b, x, y)}{\delta b} = 2(h_{W,b}(x) - y)f'(\sum_{i=1}^{d} W_i x_i + b) \cdot 1. \tag{7}$$

The k-th component x_k of $x = (x_1, \ldots, x_d) \in \mathbb{R}^d$ or the truth label y can be inferred from the gradients by one of the following means:

(**O1**) Observe that $\eta_k/\eta = x_k$. Therefore, x_k is completely leaked if η_k and η are shared to the cloud server. For example, if 1% of local gradients, chosen randomly as suggested in [12], are shared to the server, then the probability that both η_k and η are shared is $(1/100) \times (1/100) = 1/10^4$, which is not negligible.

(**O2**) Observe that the gradient η_k is proportional to the input x_k for all $1 \le i \le d$. Therefore, when $x = (x_1, \ldots, x_d)$ is an image, one can use the gradients to produce a related "proportional" image, and then obtain the truth value y by guessing.

Example 2 (general neural networks). The above observations (**O1**) and (**O2**) similarly hold for general neural networks, with both cross-entropy and squared-error cost functions [1]. In particular, following [1], $\eta_{ik} \overset{\text{def}}{=} \frac{\delta J(W,b,x,y)}{\delta W_{ik}^{(1)}} = \xi_i \cdot x_k + \lambda W_{ik}^{(1)}$, $\eta_i = \xi_i \overset{\text{def}}{=} \frac{\delta J(W,b,x,y)}{\delta b_i^{(1)}}$, where $W_{ik}^{(1)}$ is the weight parameter connecting layer 1's input x_k with hidden node i of layer 2; $b_i^{(1)}$ is the bias associated with node i of layer 2; and $\lambda \ge 0$ is a regularization term.

As in observation (**O1**), both η_{ik} and η_i is known to server with a non-negligible probability. Additionally $\frac{\eta_{ik}}{\eta_i} = x_k + \frac{\lambda W_{ik}^{(1)}}{\xi_i}$ which is exactly the data x_k (if $\lambda = 0$) or an approximation of the data x_k (if $\lambda > 0$).

4   Our System: Privacy-Preserving Deep Learning Without Accuracy Decline

Our system is depicted in Fig. 3, consisting of a common cloud server and N (e.g. $= 10x$) learning participants.

Learning Participants. First, the participants jointly set up the public key pk and secret key sk for an additively homomorphic encryption scheme. The secret key sk is kept confidential against the cloud server, but is known to all learning participants. Each participant will establish a TLS/SSL secure channel, different from each other, to communicate and protect the integrity of the homomorphic ciphertexts.

Then, the participants locally hold their datasets and run replicas of a deep learning based neural network. The initial (random) weight W_{global} to run the local deep learning is downloaded from the cloud server. The gradient vector $G^{(k)}$

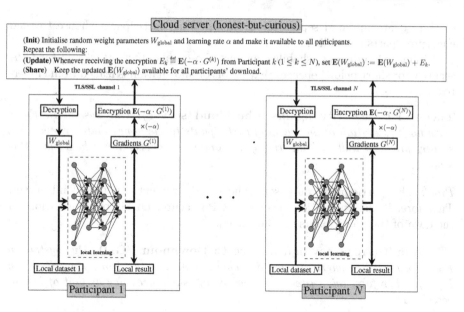

Fig. 3. Our system (*gradients-encrypted* Downpour SGD) for privacy-preserving deep learning, with a cloud server and N participants.

obtained after each execution of the neural network, multiplied by the learning rate α, is then encrypted using the public key pk. At each iteration of running the neural network, the resulting encryption $\mathbf{E}(-\alpha \cdot G^{(k)})$ $(1 \leq k \leq N)$ from each learning participant is sent to the server. Mimicking Downpour SGD, it is possible to split $G^{(k)}$ into many parts, encrypt those part separately, and then send to the server for additively homomorphic encryption.

All learning participants download the encrypted W_{global} at each execution of the local neural network. The secret key sk is used to decrypt, so that the participants will obtain the updated weight W_{global}.

The downloads and uploads of the encrypted W_{global} can be *asynchronous*: a participant does not have to wait for the others in uploading and downloading. Nonetheless, the more local data each participant uses in each local training, the better W_{global} everyone can reach, thanks to the characteristic of stochastic gradient descent.

Cloud Server. The cloud server is a common place to recursively update the encrypted weight parameters. First, initial weight W_{global} and learning rate α are chosen and sent to all participants. After receiving any encryption $\mathbf{E}(\alpha \cdot G^{(k)})$, the server computes $\mathbf{E}(W_{\text{global}}) + \mathbf{E}(-\alpha \cdot G^{(k)}) = \mathbf{E}(W_{\text{global}} - \alpha \cdot G^{(k)})$ where the equality is thanks to the additively homomorphic property of encryption. Therefore, W_{global} is updated to $W_{\text{global}} - \alpha \cdot G^{(k)}$, or notationally $W_{\text{global}} := W_{\text{global}} - \alpha \cdot G^{(k)}$. The encrypted and updated W_{global} is made available for all participants to download. Like in Downpour SGD, it is also possible that parts of W_{global} are updated separately if the learning participants choose to send encrypted parts of gradients.

Ciphertext indistinguishability against chosen plaintext attacks [7] (or CPA security for short below) ensures that no bit of information is leaked from ciphertexts.

Theorem 1 (Security against the cloud server). *Our system in Fig. 3 leaks no information of the learning participants to the honest-but-curious cloud server, provided that the underlying homomorphic encryption scheme is CPA-secure.*

Proof. The participants only send encrypted gradients to the cloud server. Therefore, if the encryption scheme is CPA-secure, no bit of information on the data of the participants can be leaked. □

Theorem 2 (Accuracy equivalence to Downpour SGD). *Our system in Fig. 3, when all ciphertexts are decrypted, functions as Downpour SGD (in Fig. 2). Therefore, our system can achieve the same accuracy as that of Downpour SGD.*

Proof. After decryption, the update rule of weight parameter becomes $W_{\text{global}} := W_{\text{global}} - \alpha \cdot G^{(k)}$ in which $G^{(k)}$ is the gradient vector computed from data samples held by participant k (and the downloaded W_{global}). Since the update rule is identical to (5) and each learning participant in our system functions as a replica (as in Downpour SGD) when encryption is removed, the theorem follows. □

5   An Instantiation of Our System

In this section we show an instantiation of our system using an LWE-based encryption based on [4]. The mark $\xleftarrow{\text{g}}$ is for "sampling randomly from a discrete Gaussian" set, so that $x \xleftarrow{\text{g}} \mathbb{Z}_{(0,s)}$ means x appears with probability proportional to $\exp(-\pi x^2/s^2)$.

- ParamGen(1^λ): Fix $q = q(\lambda) \in \mathbb{Z}^+$ and $l \in \mathbb{Z}^+$. Fix $p \in \mathbb{Z}^+$ so that $\gcd(p, q) = 1$. Return $pp = (q, l, p)$.
- KeyGen($1^\lambda, pp$): Take $s = s(\lambda, pp) \in \mathbb{R}^+$ and $n_{\text{lwe}} \in \mathbb{Z}^+$. Take matrices $R, S \xleftarrow{\text{g}} \mathbb{Z}_{(0,s)}^{n_{\text{lwe}} \times l}$, $A \xleftarrow{\$} \mathbb{Z}_q^{n_{\text{lwe}} \times n_{\text{lwe}}}$. Compute $P = pR - AS \in \mathbb{Z}_q^{n_{\text{lwe}} \times l}$. Return the public key $pk = (A, P, n_{\text{lwe}}, s)$ and the secret key $sk = S$.
- Enc($pk, m \in \mathbb{Z}_p^{1 \times l}$): Take $e_1, e_2 \xleftarrow{\text{g}} \mathbb{Z}_{(0,s)}^{1 \times n_{\text{lwe}}}$, $e_3 \xleftarrow{\text{g}} \mathbb{Z}_{(0,s)}^{1 \times l}$. Compute $c_1 = e_1 A + pe_2 \in \mathbb{Z}_q^{1 \times n_{\text{lwe}}}$, $c_2 = e_1 P + pe_3 + m \in \mathbb{Z}_q^{1 \times l}$. Return $c = (c_1, c_2)$.
- Dec($S, c = (c_1, c_2)$): Compute $\overline{m} = c_1 S + c_2 \in \mathbb{Z}_q^{1 \times l}$. Return $m = \overline{m} \bmod p$.
- Add(c, c'): For addition, compute and return $c_{\text{add}} = c + c' \in \mathbb{Z}_q^{1 \times (n_{\text{lwe}} + l)}$.

Data encoding and encryption. A real number $a \in \mathbb{R}$ can be represented, with prec bits of precision, by an integer $\lfloor a \cdot 2^{\mathsf{prec}} \rfloor \in \mathbb{Z}$. To realise the encryption $\mathbf{E}(\cdot)$ in Fig. 3, because both W_{global} and $\alpha \cdot G^{(k)}$ are in the space $\mathbb{R}^{n_{gd}}$, it suffices to describe an encryption of a real vector $r = (r^{(1)}, \ldots, r^{(n_{gd})}) \in \mathbb{R}^{n_{gd}}$. The encryption is, for $l = n_{gd}$,

$$
\mathbf{E}(r) = \mathsf{lweEnc}_{pk}\Big(\overbrace{\underbrace{\lfloor r^{(1)} \cdot 2^{\mathsf{prec}} \rfloor}_{\in \mathbb{Z}_p} \cdots \underbrace{\lfloor r^{(n_{gd})} \cdot 2^{\mathsf{prec}} \rfloor}_{\in \mathbb{Z}_p}}^{\mathbb{Z}_p^{1 \times n_{gd}}} \Big). \tag{8}
$$

For $r, t \in \mathbb{R}^{n_{gd}}$, the decryption of $\mathbf{E}(r) + \mathbf{E}(-t) \in \mathbb{Z}_q^{1 \times (n_{\mathrm{lwe}} + n_{gd})}$ will yield, for all $1 \leq i \leq n_{gd}$, $\lfloor r^{(i)} \cdot 2^{\mathsf{prec}} \rfloor - \lfloor t^{(i)} \cdot 2^{\mathsf{prec}} \rfloor \in \mathbb{Z}_p \subset (-p/2, p/2]$ and hence $u^{(i)} = \lfloor r^{(i)} \cdot 2^{\mathsf{prec}} \rfloor - \lfloor t^{(i)} \cdot 2^{\mathsf{prec}} \rfloor \in \mathbb{Z}$ if $p/2$ is large enough (see below). The substraction $r^{(i)} - t^{(i)} \in \mathbb{R}$ is computed via $u^{(i)}/2^{\mathsf{prec}} \in \mathbb{R}$, so that finally $r - t \in \mathbb{R}^{n_{gd}}$ is obtained after decryption as desired. In general, to handle n_{gradupd} additive terms without overflow, it is necessary that $p/2 > n_{\mathrm{gradupd}} \cdot 2^{\mathsf{prec}}$, or equivalently, $p > n_{\mathrm{gradupd}} \cdot 2^{\mathsf{prec}+1}$.

Lemma 1 (Choosing parameters). *When $n_{\mathrm{lwe}} \geq 3000$, $s = 8$, it is possible to set $\log_2 q \approx \log_2 p + \log_2 n_{\mathrm{gradupd}} + \log_2(167.9\sqrt{n_{\mathrm{lwe}}} + 33.9) + 1$ in which n_{gradupd} is the number of gradient updates at cloud server in Fig. 3. For example, when $n_{\mathrm{lwe}} = 3000$, $p = 2^{48} + 1$, $n_{\mathrm{gradupd}} = 2^{15}$, it is possible to set $q = 2^{77}$.*

Theorem 3 (Increased communication factor, LWE-based). *The communication cost between the server and participants of our system is $\frac{n_{\mathrm{lwe}} \log_2 q}{n_{gd} \cdot \mathsf{prec}} + \frac{\log_2 q}{\mathsf{prec}}$ times of the communication cost of the corresponding Downpour SGD, in which (n_{lwe}, p, q) is parameters of the encryption scheme, n_{gd} is the number of gradient variables represented by prec bits.*

Proof. In Downpour SGD, each replica sends n_{gd} gradients (each of prec bits) to the parameter server at each iteration, so that the communication cost for one iteration in bits is $\mathsf{PlainBits} = n_{gd} \cdot \mathsf{prec}$. In our system, let us compute the ciphertext length that each participant sends to the cloud parameter server at each iteration. By (8), the ciphertext is in $\mathbb{Z}_q^{1 \times (n_{\mathrm{lwe}} + n_{gd})}$ so that its length is $\mathsf{EncryptedBits} = (n_{\mathrm{lwe}} + n_{gd}) \log_2 q$ (bits). The increased factor is therefore $\frac{\mathsf{EncryptedBits}}{\mathsf{PlainBits}} = \frac{n_{\mathrm{lwe}} \log_2 q}{n_{gd} \cdot \mathsf{prec}} + \frac{\log_2 q}{\mathsf{prec}}$ ending the proof. □

We take $n_{\mathrm{lwe}} = 3000$, $s = 8$, $p = 2^{48} + 1$, $n_{\mathrm{gradupd}} = 2^{15}$, and $q = 2^{77}$ following Lemma 1. These parameters for (n_{lwe}, s, q) conservatively ensure that the LWE assumption has at least 128-bit security according to recent attacks [3,5,9,10].

Let us consider multiple n_{gd}:

- $n_{gd} = 140106$: this number of gradient parameters is used in [12] with the dataset MNIST [2]. Real numbers are represented by 32 bits, so that $\mathsf{prec} = 32$. Theorem 3 tells us that the increased communication factor between our system and the related Downpour SGD is $\frac{n_{\mathrm{lwe}} \log_2 q}{n_{gd} \cdot \mathsf{prec}} + \frac{\log_2 q}{\mathsf{prec}} = \frac{3000 \cdot 77}{140106 \cdot 32} + \frac{77}{32} \approx 2.46$.

- $n_{gd} = 402250$: this is used in [12] with the dataset SVHN [11]. The increased communication factor becomes $\frac{n_{1we} \log_2 q}{n_{gd} \cdot \text{prec}} + \frac{\log_2 q}{\text{prec}} = \frac{3000 \cdot 77}{402250 \cdot 32} + \frac{77}{32} \approx 2.43$.

- $n_{gd} = 42 \cdot 10^6$: this number of gradient parameters is used in [6] for speech data. The increased communication factor becomes $\frac{n_{1we} \log_2 q}{n_{gd} \cdot \text{prec}} + \frac{\log_2 q}{\text{prec}} = \frac{3000 \cdot 77}{42 \cdot 10^6 \cdot 32} + \frac{77}{32} \approx 2.41$.

Acknowledgement. This work is partially supported by JST CREST #JPMJCR168A.

References

1. Stanford Deep Learning Tutorial. http://deeplearning.stanford.edu
2. The MNIST dataset. http://yann.lecun.com/exdb/mnist/
3. Aono, Y., Boyen, X., Phong, L.T., Wang, L.: Key-Private Proxy Re-encryption under LWE. In: Paul, G., Vaudenay, S. (eds.) INDOCRYPT 2013. LNCS, vol. 8250, pp. 1–18. Springer, Cham (2013). doi:10.1007/978-3-319-03515-4_1
4. Aono, Y., Hayashi, T., Phong, L.T., Wang, L.: Efficient key-rotatable and security-updatable homomorphic encryption. In: Fifth ACM International Workshop on Security in Cloud Computing (SCC), 2017, pp. 35–42. ACM (2017)
5. Chillotti, I., Gama, N., Georgieva, M., Izabachène, M.: Faster fully homomorphic encryption: bootstrapping in less than 0.1 seconds. In: Cheon, J.H., Takagi, T. (eds.) ASIACRYPT 2016. LNCS, vol. 10031, pp. 3–33. Springer, Heidelberg (2016). doi:10.1007/978-3-662-53887-6_1
6. Dean, J., Corrado, G., Monga, R., Chen, K., Devin, M., Le, Q.V., Mao, M.Z., Ranzato, M., Senior, A.W., Tucker, P.A., Yang, K., Ng, A.Y.: Large scale distributed deep networks. In: NIPS 2012, pp. 1232–1240 (2012)
7. Goldreich, O.: The Foundations of Cryptography - Volume 2, Basic Applications. Cambridge University Press, Cambridge (2004)
8. Hitaj, B., Ateniese, G., Pérez-Cruz, F.: Deep models under the GAN: information leakage from collaborative deep learning. CoRR abs/1702.07464 (2017)
9. Lindner, R., Peikert, C.: Better key sizes (and Attacks) for LWE-based encryption. In: Kiayias, A. (ed.) CT-RSA 2011. LNCS, vol. 6558, pp. 319–339. Springer, Heidelberg (2011). doi:10.1007/978-3-642-19074-2_21
10. Liu, M., Nguyen, P.Q.: Solving BDD by enumeration: an update. In: Dawson, E. (ed.) CT-RSA 2013. LNCS, vol. 7779, pp. 293–309. Springer, Heidelberg (2013). doi:10.1007/978-3-642-36095-4_19
11. Netzer, Y., Wang, T., Coates, A., Bissacco, A., Wu, B., Ng, A.Y.: Reading digits in natural images with unsupervised feature learning. In: NIPS Workshop on Deep Learning and Unsupervised Feature Learning 2011 (2011)
12. Shokri, R., Shmatikov, V.: Privacy-preserving deep learning. In: ACM CCS 2015, pp. 1310–1321. ACM (2015)

Attacks

Characterizing Promotional Attacks
in Mobile App Store

Bo Sun[1]([✉]), Xiapu Luo[2], Mitsuaki Akiyama[3], Takuya Watanabe[3],
and Tatsuya Mori[1]

[1] Department of Computer Science and Communications Engineering,
Waseda University, Shinjuku, Japan
{sunshine,mori}@nsl.cs.waseda.ac.jp
[2] Department of Computing, The Hong Kong Polytechnic University,
Kowloon, Hong Kong
csxluo@comp.polyu.edu.hk
[3] NTT Secure Platform Laboratories, NTT Corporation, Tokyo, Japan
akiyama.mitsuaki@lab.ntt.co.jp, watanabe@nsl.cs.waseda.ac.jp

Abstract. Mobile app stores, such as Google Play, play a vital role in
the ecosystem of mobile apps. When users look for an app of interest,
they can acquire useful data from the app store to facilitate their decision on installing the app or not. This data includes ratings, reviews,
number of installs, and the category of the app. The ratings and reviews
are the *user-generated content* (UGC) that affect the reputation of an
app. Unfortunately, *miscreants* also exploit such channels to conduct
promotional attacks (PAs) that lure victims to install malicious apps. In
this paper, we propose and develop a new system called *PADetective* to
detect miscreants who are likely to be conducting promotional attacks.
Using a dataset with 1,723 of labeled samples, we demonstrate that the
true positive rate of detection model is 90%, with a false positive rate of
5.8%. We then applied *PADetective* to a large dataset for characterizing
the prevalence of PAs in the wild and find 289 K potential PA attackers
who posted reviews to 21 K malicious apps.

Keywords: Mobile app store · Promotional attacks · Machine learning

1 Introduction

With more than four million apps [20], mobile app markets, such as Google Play
and Apple App Store, play a vital role in distributing apps to customers. To help
users look for apps and for developers to promote their apps, mobile app markets
provide various information about the apps, such as descriptions, screenshots,
and number of installations. In addition, most markets involve *reputation systems*, through which users can rate the apps and write down reviews, to facilitate
other users to select apps. Since apps with higher ratings usually get more downloads [12], recent studies report that some developers adopt unfair approaches
to manipulate their apps' ratings and reviews [22,23], even if such behaviors are

© Springer Nature Singapore Pte Ltd. 2017
L. Batten et al. (Eds.): ATIS 2017, CCIS 719, pp. 113–127, 2017.
DOI: 10.1007/978-981-10-5421-1_10

prohibited by FTC [9] and app markets. Note that attackers also employ such approach to promote malicious apps and lure victims to install them. We call such malicious apps campaign as *promotional attacks* (PAs).

Although a few recent studies have revealed the paid reviews [22] and colluded reviewers [23], there have been no systematic examinations on the promotional attacks in mobile app stores. To fill in the gaps, we conducted the first large-scale investigation on PAs with the aim of answering the following two questions: (1) How can we detect PAs systematically? and (2) How prevalent are PAs in the wild?

It is non-trivial to address these two questions because the solution should be accurate to capture PA attackers with low false positive rate, scalable to handle millions of apps and reviews in app stores, and robust to raise the bar for sophisticated attackers to evade the detection. Existing studies cannot achieve these goals. For example, high computational complexity limits the scalability of [22], and requiring the similar reviews in keyword level affects the accuracy of [17,18]. Moreover, to our best knowledge, none of the existing studies have examined market-scale apps.

To tackle these challenges, we propose and develop a novel system, named *PADetective*, to identify PA attackers accurately and efficiently. PADetective adopts supervised learning to characterize PA attackers according to 15 features (e.g., day intervals, semantic similarity), and then applies the trained model to detect other PA attackers. It is worth noting that these new and effective features are carefully selected from not only UGC but also metadata in order to enhance the robustness of PADetective. In particular, features from metadata have not been used by existing works, and they could contribute to the robustness of PADetective because it is easier for attackers to manipulate UGC than metadata. We employ the information entropy and the coefficient of variation for quantifying the features from metadata, and leverage the state-of-the-art NLP technique (i.e., *Paragraph vector* [14]) to extract features from UGC because it can extract similar reviews at semantic level and therefore increase the accuracy. Moreover, we employ the TRUE-REPUTATION [19] algorithm to calculate the true reputation scores for detecting abnormal ratings. These algorithms are light-weight, and we only need to recompute the true reputation scores and similarity word weight vectors for new UGC and metadata. This feature extraction approach empowers PADetective to handle large-scale dataset. In our evaluation, PADetective processed 57 million reviews in one day. We evaluate PADetective using real PA data, and the result shows that PADetective's true positive rate is up to 90% with a low false positive rate of 5.8%.

Moreover, we conduct the first large-scale investigation on PA by applying PADetective to 1 million apps in Google Play, which has 57 million reviews posted by 14 million users. PADetective flagged 289 K reviewers as suspicious promotional attackers. These reviewers posted reviews to 136 K apps, which included 21 K malicious apps. Among the top 1 K reviewers who were flagged as promotional attackers with high probability score, 136 reviewers posted reviews only for malicious apps, and another 113 reviewers posted reviews for apps where more than half of the apps were detected as malicious. It is worth noting that PAs detected by PADetective can contribute to the detection of potentially malicious apps.

Major contributions of this work are summarized as follows:

- We developed a novel system, named *PADetective*, which aims to detect PA attackers from a large volume of reviewers with high accuracy and low false positive rates. The extensive experiments demonstrated that PADetective can achieve 90% true positive rate with low false positive rate of 5.8% (Sect. 4).
- Using the PADetective, we conducted the first large-scale measurement study on PAs by examining 57 million reviews, posted by 14 million users for 1 million apps in Google Play, and obtained interesting observations and insights (Sect. 5).
- Our extensive analyses revealed that the detected PAs can be used to discover potentially malicious apps, which have not been detected by popular anti-virus scanners (Sect. 5).

2   Problem Statement

This section specifies the problem we address in this paper by first presenting the high-level overview of the problem and then describing its mathematical formulation. Figure 1 presents the high-level overview of the problem. Although this work targets Google Play, the model is applicable to other mobile app stores as well. In the model, a reviewer posts review comments and rating scores for several apps published in the app store. For the apps commented/rated by the reviewer, we can extract the UGC and the metadata associated with the apps. The UGC includes comment posting time, review comment, and rating score; these are generated by the reviewer. The app metadata includes the number of installs, a set of developers of the app, and a set of the categories of the app; these are the data of the apps commented/rated by the reviewer.

Our goal is to determine whether a given reviewer is a PA attacker or not by analyzing the UGC and the metadata associated with apps commented on or rated by the reviewer. To achieve it, we first extract a feature vector from the UGC and app metadata, and then train a classifier using labeled data. After that, we apply the trained classifier to differentiate legitimate reviewers and a PA attackers.

To formulate the problem in a mathematical way, we introduce the variables summarized in Table 1. It is worth noting that we only examine the reviewers with $m_i \geq 3$ because it takes time and efforts for promotional attackers to create zombie accounts for commenting apps and therefore they often reuse these accounts for posting reviews. We discuss how to relax this restriction in Sect. 6. Of the variables shown in Table 1, c_{ij}, s_{ij}, and t_{ij} are UGC data and n_{ij}, d_{ij}, and k_{ij} are the metadata. Using these six values for all the apps in $\mathbf{A}(r_i)$, we compute a feature vector $\mathbf{F}(r_i) = \{f_1^i, f_2^i, \ldots f_{15}^i\}$ for a given reviewer r_i. Our goal is to build an accurate classifier $g(\mathbf{F}(r_i))$ that determines whether r_i is promotional attacker or not. The details of computing a feature vector from the observed variables will be described in the next section.

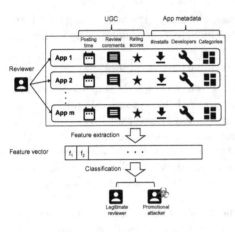

Fig. 1. High-level overview of the problem.

Table 1. Notations used for our problem.

Symbol	Definition
r_i	the i-th reviewer ($i = 1, 2, \ldots$)
$\mathbf{A}(r_i)$	a set of apps reviewed by the reviewer r_i
m_i	number of apps reviewed by the reviewer r_i. $m_i = |\mathbf{A}(r_i)|$
c_{ij}	review comment posted by the reviewer r_i for the j-th app. $j = 1, 2, \ldots, m_i$
s_{ij}	rating score posted by the reviewer r_i for the j-th app. $j = 1, 2, \ldots, m_i$
t_{ij}	time at which the reviewer r_i posted a comment for the j-th app. $j = 1, 2, \ldots, m_i$
n_{ij}	number of installs for the j-th app reviewed by the reviewer r_i. $j = 1, 2, \ldots, m_i$
d_{ij}	developer of the j-th app reviewed by the reviewer r_i. $j = 1, 2, \ldots, m_i$
k_{ij}	category of the j-th app reviewed by the reviewer r_i. $j = 1, 2, \ldots, m_i$

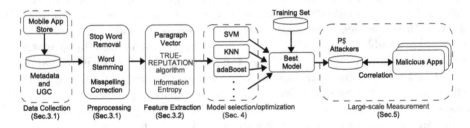

Fig. 2. Overview of PADetective.

3   PADetective System

This section details PADetective (Fig. 2), especially its four major components including: data collection, data preprocessing, feature extraction, and detection.

3.1   Data Collection and Preprocessing

Collection. We first create a list of apps to be downloaded by using the list of package names in [21]. Then, we collect metadata for each app by accessing its description page according to its package name and employing our HTML parser to extract the metadata in the page. Moreover, we develop a UGC crawler by leveraging the review collection API [4] provided by Google Play Store. Figure 3 shows the statistics of the number of reviews in each app. Note that the Google

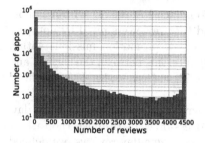

Fig. 3. Histogram for the number of reviews in each app.

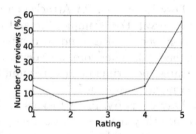

Fig. 4. Percentage of review numbers with different rating.

Play review collection service only allows 4,500 most recent reviews to be crawled for each app. To circumvent this limitation, we could fetch the reviews continuously thanks to our automated process of data collection. To follow the acceptable use policy of the API, we deployed our crawler on 100 servers around the world to collect UGC for a large number of apps. We used the crawler to collect UGC and metadata for 1,058,259 apps from the Google Play app store in November 2015. The data set involved 57,868,301 reviews from 20,211,517 unique users. Figure 4 shows the statistics for the collected rating data. The rating scale in the Google Play Store ranges from 1 to 5. We can see that over 55% of ratings are 5 stars.

Preprocessing. Before creating the feature vector for the classifier, we develop a 8-step process to remove the noisy and meaningless data. **Step 1:** Remove all reviews under the default reviewer name "A Google User", because we cannot extract the string features from the default reviewer name. **Step 2:** Extract the reviewers who have commented on at least three apps. The limitation introduced by this step is discussed in Sect. 6. **Step 3:** Remove reviews written in languages other than English as *PADetective* currently only handles English. **Step 4:** Split all sentences into words. **Step 5:** Transform all letters into lowercase. **Step 6:** Remove all stop words such as "is", "am", "the". **Step 7:** Consolidate variant forms of a word into a common form (i.e., word stemming), for example, convert "running" to "run.". **Step 8:** Correct the misspelled English words for all the reviews. For Steps 3–8, we implement the natural language processing based on NLTK [5] and TextBlob [7]. TextBlob enables us to realize language detection and spelling correction. After data preprocessing, our dataset for feature extraction includes 2,606,791 reviewers.

3.2 Feature Extraction

We profile each reviewer r_i using 15 features extracted from UGC and metadata. These features form a feature vector $\mathbf{F}(r_i) = \{f_1^i, f_2^i, \ldots f_{15}^i\}$, and are described as follows.

f_1^i: **Day intervals.** PA Attackers are likely to launch PA attacks within a short day interval. For example, Xie and Zhu found that reviewers hired by app promotion web services tend to complete their review promotion missions within 120 days [23]. Therefore, we calculated the day intervals between the earliest and the latest post time $\max(\mathbf{T}_i) - \min(\mathbf{T}_i)$, where $\mathbf{T}_i = \{t_{i1}, \ldots, t_{im_i}\}$, and defined $f_1^i = \max(\mathbf{T}_i) - \min(\mathbf{T}_i)$.

f_2^i: **Day entropy.** PA Attackers are likely to write reviews within the same day, because they may use automated posting process or want to finish the task as quickly as possible. To measure the proportion of same-day reviews, we defined f_2^i using the information entropy: $f_2^i = H(X) = -\sum_{j=1}^{m_i} P(t_{ij}) \log P(t_{ij})$, where $P(t_{ij})$ is the frequency of same-day reviews: t_{ij}/sum and $sum = \sum_{j=1}^{m_i} t_{ij}$ is the sum of days reviewed by reviewer r_i. If all the reviews are posted on the same day, the entropy of the post time will be 0.

f_3^i: **Bi-gram matching.** PA attackers often post similar reviews. Detecting similar reviews is important due to the presence of made-up words that are used to express strong feelings, such as "goooooood" and "cooooool". Made-up words cannot be reformed by existing spelling correction algorithms because they are designed to correct misspelled words instead of intentionally created words. To address this problem, we converted each word into a bi-gram and then used bag of bi-gram to build a feature vector for each c_{ij}. Finally we calculated the average of the cosine similarity score of each pair of reviews by the reviewer r_i. In other words, $f_3^i = \sum_{j=1}^{m_i} \sum_{k=1}^{m_i} cosim(c_{ij}, c_{ik})/m_i^2$. Where cosim is cosine similarity score. We set the threshold of cosine similarity as 0.9.

f_4^i: **Semantic similarity.** Since reviewers may use different words and expressions to express the same feeling, we identify similar words and expressions using the the Paragraph Vector (PV) algorithm [14], because it performs a semantic analysis in discovering similar words and expressions. By applying the PV algorithm realized in the Python library gensim [3] to $57, 868, 301$ reviews in our dataset, we get the predicted model after around 1 h. We defined f_4^i as the average of the similarity scores predicted from the trained model for each pair of reviews. $f_4^i = \sum_{j=1}^{m_i} \sum_{k=1}^{m_i} D(c_{ij}, c_{ik})/m_i^2$, Where D is the distance of two different documents computed by PV algorithm. Table 2 presents some examples of the similarity scores computed by the trained PV model. It is clear that the model can infer the correlations between not only different words with the same purpose but also security-related similarity words without using the labeled data. Note that although we used words to demonstrate the effectiveness of the approach, we actually apply the algorithm to the entire review texts.

f_5^i: **Sentiment analysis.** PA attackers usually post positive reviews to promote apps for monetary benefit and/or luring victims to install malicious apps. Sentiment analysis classifies the attitude of a text into three categories: negative, neutral, positive. Using sentiment analysis, we could reveal potential PA attackers if all the reviews are positive. We use TextBlob [7] to conduct the sentiment analysis of all the reviews. The sentiment analysis in TextBlob was implemented by a supervised learning naive Bayes classifier that is trained on the labeled movie reviews provided by NLTK. We define f_5^i as the average score for each

Table 2. Examples of similarity score computed with the trained Paragraph vector model.

word1	word2	similarity score
adware	malware	0.88
ads	spam	0.64
camera	permission	0.74
hack	access	0.71
internet	location	0.62
good	nice	0.60

Table 3. Example of score predicted by sentiment analysis classifier

Sentence	The score of sentiment analysis
That is my opinion	0.0
Awesome game	0.3
Nice graphics and I love it	0.55
Very bad game	−0.65
I hate all the covers I'm here to look for the songs made by the artist not covers	−0.8

pair of reviews predicted by the sentiment analysis classifier. Table 3 shows an example of the scores predicted by the sentiment analysis classifier. If the score is zero, it means the sentiment of the review is neutral. It shows that our classifier can correctly identify the sentiment of the reviews.

f_6^i: **The average length of the reviews.** Fake reviews injected by promotional attackers are likely to be short, because they may use an automated posting process or want to get income as quickly as possible. Therefore, we defined f_6^i as the average length of the reviews written by the reviewer r_i.

f_7^i: **True Reputation Score.** Users often rely on the average ratings of the apps, computed by the app stores, in selecting the apps. Unfortunately, PA attackers can easily manipulate the average ratings by giving high ratings to their target apps. We defined f_7^i as the average of the margin between the app's rating and the reviewer's rating based on the true reputation score of each app instead of the average rating. This score is calculated according to the TRUE-REPUTATION algorithm [19], which takes into account the user confidence in terms of user activity, user objectivity, and user consistency. f_7^i is computed as: $f_7^i = \sum_{i=1}^{m_i}(s_{ij} - u_{aj})/m_i$, where m_i is the number of apps reviewed by reviewer r_i. a is an app and u_a is true reputation score for app a.

f_8^i: **Average ratings.** Since PA attackers give high ratings to malicious apps for attracting more downloads, we defined f_8^i as the average ratings posted by reviewer r_i. f_9^i: **Coefficient of variation of ratings.** We defined f_9^i as the coefficient of variation of all the ratings posted by each reviewer to measure their distribution. It is the ratio of the standard deviation to the mean: $f_9^i = \sigma(\mathbf{S}_i)/\sum_{j=1}^{m_i} s_{ij}$, where σ is standard deviation and $\mathbf{S}_i = \{s_{i1}, \ldots, s_{im_i}\}$. If a reviewer posts identical ratings, f_9^i will be 0.

f_{10}^i: **Average number of installs.** Since the number of installs is an important metric affecting users' selection of apps, we defined f_{10}^i as the average number of installs for reviewer r_i. $f_{10}^i = \sum_{j=1}^{m_i} n_{ij}/m_i$.

f_{11}^i: **Coefficient of variation of the number of installs.** To measure the distribution of the number of installs, we define f_{11}^i as the coefficient of variation of the number of installs for reviewer r_i. The computation of f_{11}^i can be referred to the equation defined by f_{10}^i. If a reviewer posts reviews to apps with the same number of installs, the coefficient of variation will be 0.

f_{12}^i: **Developer Entropy.** PA attackers are more likely to promote apps from the same developer because the targeted malicious apps should be associated with each other. Therefore, we defined f_{12}^i as the entropy of developer for reviewer r_i. The computation of f_{12}^i can be referred to the equation defined by f_2^i. If a reviewer only posts reviews for apps from the same developer, his/her f_{12} will be 0.

f_{13}^i: **Category Entropy.** PA attackers tend to promote apps having a small number of distinct categories, possibly due to the automated posting process. Similar to f_{12}^i, we defined f_{13}^i as the entropy of category for reviewer r_i. The computation of f_{13}^i can also be referred to the equation defined by f_2^i. If a reviewer only posts reviews for apps having a small number of distinct categories, his/her f_{13} will be 0.

f_{14}^i: **Length of reviewer name.** Legitimate reviewers usually use their own name as the reviewer name, whereas the reviewer names selected by PA attackers are likely to be unusually short or long. Hence, we defined f_{14}^i as the length of the reviewer name.

f_{15}^i: **Number of digits and symbols in reviewer name.** The reviewer names of promotional attackers are often randomly generated, and therefore they are likely to contain digits and symbols such as "!", "*", "@." According to this observation, we defined f_{15}^i as the number of digits and symbols in the reviewer names.

3.3   Effectiveness of Feature and Description of Detection Model

Effectiveness of feature. To demonstrate how our features facilitate the detection, we compute the importance of our features. For the space limitation, we present the top-3 features that had the largest contributions (f_1^i: Day intervals, f_{10}^i: Average number of installs, f_{12}^i: Developer Entropy). We extracted these three features by using tree-based feature selection method [2], which uses forests of trees to evaluate the importance of features.

Figure 5 shows the CDF of the day intervals of promotional attackers and those of normal reviewers. We can see that promotional attackers usually have shorter day intervals than normal reviewers. It is likely that promotional attackers want to get revenue quickly or are required by their employers to do so. Figure 6 shows the CDF of the number of installs of promotional attackers and those of normal reviewers. We can figure out that promotional attackers tend to promote apps whose number of installs is not very large due to the prohibition of promotion activity by Google Play [1]. Figure 7 shows the CDF of the developer entropy of promotional attackers and those of normal reviewers. We can see that promotional attackers tend to promote apps produced by the same developer. Because promotional attackers are probably hired by the same developer.

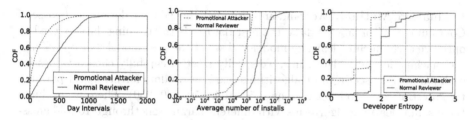

Fig. 5. f_1^i: Day intervals.   **Fig. 6.** f_{10}^i: Average number of installs.   **Fig. 7.** f_{12}^i: Developer Entropy

We note that these three features are informative for identifying promotional attackers from normal reviewers. We also found that the features extracted from metadata are more effective than those from UGC in PA detection, because it is not easy for attackers to manipulate the metadata such as developer and number of installs.

Description of detection model. We build our detection model using the library scikit-learn [6] because it is efficient, and implement several supervised learning algorithms, including support vector machine (SVM), k-nearest neighbor (KNN), random forest, decision tree, and adaBoost. To determine the best algorithm and parameters, we test the algorithms and parameters using our labeled dataset. The detailed model selection process and its results are presented in Sect. 4. Finally, we use the best detection model to perform a large-scale analysis of our real-world dataset.

4   Performance Evaluation

This section presents the evaluation result of PADetective. We first introduce how we prepare the labeled dataset (i.e., the *ground truth*), and then describe the evaluation method and the result, respectively.

Training Dataset. We first generate the training dataset with the ground truth. Since legitimate reviewers may comment bad apps and/or post reviews to malicious apps, we define a PA attacker as a reviewer who only posts reviews to malicious apps and comments at least three malicious apps. We determine whether an app was malicious by submitting the app to VirusTotal [8] and making the decision based on the results from a set of antivirus systems. Note that we did not verify all the apps in our dataset to generate the training dataset because of the limitation of time and computer resources. We also note that VirusTotal usually classifies malicious apps into two categories: malware and adware. We did not distinguish between these categories because PAs would likely be used to promote both malware and adware apps. With this approach and additional manual inspection, we identified 723 promotional attackers. Aside from this, we randomly selected 1,000 legitimate users to create the training dataset. The reason why we randomly sampled legitimate users was to achieve a good balance between the two classes when we trained our classifiers.

Evaluation Method. We randomly divided the labeled data into two sets. Containing 70% of labeled data, the first dataset is the training dataset used to optimize each machine learning model and select the best model. For optimizing the machine learning algorithms, we specify a set of carefully chosen values for each parameter used in those algorithms (e.g., for random forest, we set parameter "n_estimators" to a set of values: 50, 100, 150, 200, 250). Then, we evaluate the machine learning algorithms with different parameters through 10-fold cross-validation. Finally, we select the best result in consideration of accuracy, false positive and false negative. Having 30% of labeled data, the second dataset is the test dataset utilized to evaluate PADetective's performance after the best model is selected. To measure the accuracy of various supervised learning algorithms, we use three metrics: false positive rate (FPR), false negative rate (FNR) and accuracy (ACC), where $FPR = FP/(FP+TN)$, $FNR = FN/(TP+FN)$, and $ACC = (TP+TN)/(TP+TN+FP+FN)$, respectively. TP is true positive, FP is false positive, TN is true negative and FN is false negative. We also show the performance of the best detection model through the ROC curve, which can be used to determine the best combination of true and false positive rates.

Table 4. Classification accuracy. The means and standard deviations are calculated using 10-times 10-fold cross-validation tests for each machine learning algorithm.

Machine learning Algorithm	ACC		FPR		FNR	
	mean	std	mean	std	mean	std
SVM	0.661	0.041	0.059	0.072	0.372	0.048
RandomForest	**0.933**	**0.014**	**0.083**	**0.033**	**0.053**	**0.036**
KNN	0.894	0.020	0.162	0.027	0.050	0.022
DecisionTrees	0.902	0.020	0.091	0.035	0.100	0.033
AdaBoost	0.918	0.022	0.100	0.030	0.066	0.034

Evaluation Result. Table 4 lists the accuracy of different machine learning algorithms used by PADetective. Most of these algorithms discover the PA attackers with high accuracy and low false negative or false positive rate. Among the five machine learning algorithms we tested, RandomForest achieves the highest accuracy (i.e., 0.933) with the lowest false positive (i.e., 0.083) and false negative (i.e., 0.053) rates. Moreover, its standard deviations of the accuracy, false positive rate, and false negative rate of RandomForest are also low, indicating that RandomForest can identify promotional attackers effectively. We use the grid search to determine the best parameter for RandomForest, and find that 50 is the optimal number of trees. Based on these results, we select RandomForest as our detection model.

To better understand the root causes of false negative rate and false positive rate in our system, we conduct error analysis with manual inspection. It turns out that PADetective failed to detect the PA attackers who had posted reviews for a

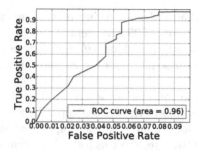

Fig. 8. Evaluation of detection model using test set.

period of two years or longer. On the other hand, PADetective wrongly flagged the legitimate reviewers whose behaviors were similar to a PA attacker (e.g., their reviews seemed to be fake, but the apps were not flagged as malware/adware by VirusTotal). Note that advanced malware may evade the online virus checkers. Finally, using the optimized RandomForest algorithm, we test PADetective's accuracy using the test dataset. Figure 8 shows that it can achieve 90% true positive rate with low false positive rate of 5.8%.

5 Promtional Attacks in the Wild

Using PADetective, we examined a large-scale data collected from the Google Play Store, and found 289,000 potential PA attackers from 2,605,068 reviewers. Table 5 summarizes the number of reviewers/apps detected by PADetective. The number of unique malicious apps reviewed by the potential PA attackers was 20,906, accounting for approximately 65% of the malicious apps reviewed by all observed reviewers. Many malicious apps having reviews were associated with the potential PA attackers. Moreover, the majority of malicious apps detected by VirusTotal had no user reviews. It may be due to the fact that the malicious apps were detected and deleted by mobile app stores in the early stage of distribution, and hence there are no comments on such apps. Another possibility is that mobile app stores deleted both malicious apps and their information including reviews simultaneously, and therefore we can not collect the reviews. We ranked

Table 5. Statistics of detected promotional attackers and apps. "–" indicates that we were not able to perform the evaluation due to the lack of resources.

	# reviewers	# apps	# malicious apps	# apps deleted by app store
All observed reviewers	2,605,068	234,139	32,367	–
Potential promotional attackers	289,000	135,989	20,906	–
Detected promotional attackers with high probability	1,000	2,904	486	148

the reviewers in descending order according to the probability of being a PA attacker, and investigated top 1,000 reviewers. The top 1,000 reviewers posted reviews for 2,904 of apps, which include 486 of malicious apps and 148 of apps deleted by the app store for some reasons, e.g., malware or potentially harmful apps.

Among the 1,000 promotional attackers, 136 reviewers (13.6%) posted reviews only for malicious apps or the deleted apps. We found that other detected reviewers posted reviews for not only malicious apps, but also for apps that were not regarded as malware/adware by VirusTotal. We acknowledge that using the online virus checkers might lead to false detection, and leave the checking of those undetected apps in future work.

Figure 9 shows the top 10 categories of the apps reviewed by PA attackers. Three categories (approximately 15% in total) are related to games, which was the primary target of the PAs. To study the impact of apps promoted by PA attackers, Fig. 10 illustrates the top 10 number of installs of the apps reviewed by PA attackers. It shows that the majority of such apps do not have many installs. This observation indicates that PAs are used when the app is not so popular. There may be other reasons that the data was captured when the PA was just launched (i.e., not yet finished).

We also investigate whether the detected PA attackers can be used to discover malicious apps. More precisely, we compare the time when the PA attackers posted reviews on malicious apps and the time when the malicious app was first submitted to VirusTotal. If all the posting times are earlier than the first submission time, then our PA detection scheme has the potential to identify malicious apps that have not been listed in Virustotal. We examine the top 241 detected PA attackers who only reviewed malicious apps, and find that 72 of them reviewed malicious apps before these malicious apps were detected by VirusTotal. Among all the apps reviewed by these 72 promotional attackers, 217 apps were labeled as malicious app by VirusTotal. It is worth noting that other apps reviewed by the PA attackers might also be suspicious.

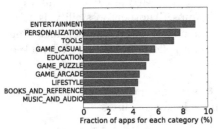

Fig. 9. Top 10 categories of apps reviewed by the detected promotional attackers.

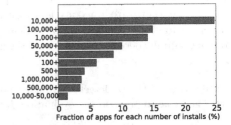

Fig. 10. Top 10 number of installs for apps reviewed by the detected promotional attackers.

6   Discussion

This section discusses some limitations of PADetective and future research directions.

Evasion. Advanced attackers may evade the PADetective system by employing lots of user accounts with different names and/or mimicking the reviewing behaviors of normal users. It is worth noting that such evasion strategies require much more resources and efforts. For example, attackers may acquire lots of fake user accounts and use each account to just post one comment in order to degrade the detection accuracy of PADetective. However, since mobile app stores (e.g., Google Play) usually adopt advanced techniques [10] to deter automated account registration, it will cost the attackers lots of resources and efforts to create many accounts and it does not benefit the attackers if these accounts are just used to post one comment. Note that the primary goal of the attackers is to increase the success rate of attacks with lower costs [16]. Even if an attacker affords to adopt such an expensive approach, the stakeholders of mobile app stores can enhance PADetective with additional information about each account, such as IP address which could be correlated with user accounts to detect malicious users [24]. The attackers may also mimic the reviewing behaviors of normal users by writing short/long reviews, reviewing both legitimate and malicious apps, adjusting the posting time, and etc. It will also significantly increase the cost of attacks. We leave the challenge of differentiating such advanced attacks and human reviewers in future work.

Number of apps reviewed by each reviewer. PADetective does not consider reviewers who posted comments for only one or two apps. This constraint originates from the fact that computing some features such as entropy or coefficient variants require more than two samples. In this work, we empirically set the number as 3 because increasing the number was not sensitive to the final outcomes. Since attackers usually employ the accounts to post a number of comments as we discussed above, we believe that this number is reasonable to capture promotional attackers. As the number of apps reviewed by a reviewer may exceed the threshold, 3, over time, PADetective could identify them by continuously collecting and analyzing the comments. We will construct a real-time detection system for fetching and examining UGC and the metadata continuously in future work.

7   Related Work

Review Analysis. Kong et al. [13] designed AutoREB to automatically identify users' concerns on the security and privacy of mobile apps. They applied the relevance feedback technique for the semantic analysis of user reviews and then associated the results of the user review analysis to the apps' behaviors by using the crowd-sourcing technique. Mukherjee et al. [17,18] proposed new approaches to detect fake reviewer groups from Amazon product reviews. They first used a frequent itemset mining method to identify a set of candidate groups, and then adopted several behavioral models based on the relationships among groups such as the review posting time and similarities. Fu et al. [11] proposed WisCom to provide important insights for end-users, developers, and potentially the entire mobile app ecosystem. They leveraged sentiment analysis, topic model analysis, and time-series analysis to examine over 13 M user reviews.

Rating Analysis. Xie et al. [22] proposed a new method for discovering colluded reviewers in app stores. They built a relation graph based on the ratings and the deviations of the ratings, and applied a graph cluster algorithm to detect collusion groups. Oh et al. [19] developed an algorithm that calculates the confidence score of each app. Market operators can replace the average rating of each app with the confidence score to defend against rating promotion/demotion attacks. Lim et al. [15] devised an approach to measure the degree of spam for each reviewer based on the rating behaviors, and evaluated them using an Amazon review dataset.

Among previous works mentioned above, [17,18,22] are closely related to our work. The major differences between PADetective and Xie et al. [22] is the scalability. More precisely, their system is not scalable because it is not possible to build a tie graph of large-scale dataset in physical memory. Moreover, they performed the evaluation on a small and local dataset (200 apps collected from the china apple store). In contrast, since our detection model uses static features, our system can conduct large-scale analysis. Moreover, we investigate the prevalence of PAs in the official Android app store by collecting information on more than 1 M apps. The method of review analysis is the main difference between PADetective and [17,18]. Since they aimed to identify copy reviews used by spammers, their method only extracts the similar reviews in keyword level, e.g., "good app" and "good apps". Since users can express the same opinion using different words and expressions, e.g., "nice app" and "good app", we leveraged the state-of-the-art NLP technique called Paragraph vector [14] to extract similar reviews at the semantic level for better accuracy.

8   Conclusion

In this study, we developed PADetective to detect PA attackers in mobile app stores using UGC and metadata as well as machine-learning techniques. The large-scale evaluation revealed that we can exploit the PA attackers identified by PADetective to discover potentially malicious apps effectively and efficiently. We believe that this research sheds a new light on the analysis of UGC and metadata of app stores as a complementary channel to find malicious apps for enhancing the widely used anti-malware tools or for market operators and malware analysts.

Acknowledgements. A part of this work was supported by JSPS Grant-in-Aid for Scientific Research (KAKENHI) B, Grant number JP16H02832. A part of this work was also supported by a Grant for Non-Japanese Researchers from the NEC C&C Foundation and a Waseda University Grant for Special Research Projects (Project number: 2016S-055).

References

1. Developer policy center. http://goo.gl/yA0qUb
2. Feature selection. http://scikit-learn.org/stable/modules/feature_selection.html
3. gensim:topic modelling for humans. https://radimrehurek.com/gensim/
4. Google play reviews collection service. https://play.google.com/store/getreviews
5. Natural language toolkit. http://www.nltk.org
6. scikit-learn:machine learning in python. http://scikit-learn.org/stable/
7. Textblob: Simplified text processing. http://textblob.readthedocs.io/en/dev/
8. Virustotal- free online virus, malware and url scanner. https://www.virustotal.com
9. The FTC's endorsement guides: What people are asking (2015). http://goo.gl/3875GT
10. El Ahmad, A.S., Yan, J., Ng, W.-Y.: Captcha design: color, usability, and security. IEEE Internet Comput. **16**(2), 44–51 (2012)
11. Fu, B., Lin, J., Li, L., Faloutsos, C., Hong, J.I., Sadeh, N.M.: Why people hate your app: making sense of user feedback in a mobile app store. In: Proceedings of the ACM KDD (2013)
12. Ganguly, R.: App. store optimization - a crucial piece of the mobile app marketing puzzle (2013). https://blog.kissmetrics.com/app-store-optimization/
13. Kong, D., Cen, L., Jin, H.: AUTOREB: automatically understanding the review-to-behavior fidelity in android applications. In: Proceedings of the ACM CCS (2015)
14. Le, Q.V., Mikolov, T.: Distributed representations of sentences and documents. In: Proceedings of the ICML (2014)
15. Lim, E., Nguyen, V., Jindal, N., Liu, B., Lauw, H.W.: Detecting product review spammers using rating behaviors. In: Proceedings of the ACM CIKM (2010)
16. Liu, B., Nath, S., Govindan, R., Liu, J.: DECAF: detecting and characterizing ad fraud in mobile apps. In: Proceedings of the NSDI (2014)
17. Mukherjee, A., Liu, B., Glance, N.S.: Spotting fake reviewer groups in consumer reviews. In: Proceedings of the WWW (2012)
18. Mukherjee, A., Liu, B., Wang, J., Glance, N.S., Jindal, N.: Detecting group review spam. In: Proceedings of the WWW (2011)
19. Oh, H., Kim, S., Park, S., Zhou, M.: Can you trust online ratings? A mutual reinforcement model for trustworthy online rating systems. IEEE Trans. Syst. Man Cybern. Syst. **45**(12), 1564–1576 (2015)
20. Statista Inc.: Number of apps available in leading app stores as of June 2016. http://goo.gl/JnBkmY
21. Viennot, N., Garcia, E., Nieh, J.: A measurement study of google play. In: Proceedings of the ACM SIGMETRICS (2014)
22. Xie, Z., Zhu, S.: Grouptie: toward hidden collusion group discovery in app stores. In: Proceedings of the ACM WiSec (2014)
23. Xie, Z., Zhu, S.: Appwatcher: unveiling the underground market of trading mobile app reviews. In: Proceedings of the ACM WiSec (2015)
24. Zhao, Y., Xie, Y., Yu, F., Ke, Q., Yu, Y., Chen, Y., Gillum, E.: Botgraph: large scale spamming botnet detection. In: Proceedings of the NSDI (2009)

Low-Data Complexity Attacks on Camellia

Takeru Koie[1(✉)], Takanori Isobe[2], Yosuke Todo[3], and Masakatu Morii[1]

[1] Graduate School of Engineering, Kobe University, Hyogo, Japan
koie@stu.kobe-u.ac.jp
[2] University of Hyogo, Hyogo, Japan
[3] NTT Secure Platform Laboratories, Tokyo, Japan

Abstract. In this paper, we propose low-data complexity attacks on reduced-round Camellia. Our attacks are based on deterministic truncated differential characteristics exploiting properties of binaries matrices and differential properties of S-boxes of Camellia. Combining these with the structure of Camellia, we obtain low data complexity attacks on 4 to 7 rounds of Camellia. Surprisingly, 4 to 6 rounds attacks are feasible with only two chosen plaintexts and the attacks complexity becomes very practical by increasing a small amount of data.

Keywords: Block cipher · Camellia · Truncated differential cryptanalysis

1 Introduction

Over the past 20 years, we have seen a significant progress in the field of blockciphers. Especially, knowledge and techniques for securely designing blockciphers are sufficiently accumulated. Nowadays, without strong constrains of implementations such as lightweight and low latency, it is relatively easy to develop secure blockciphers. As a practical evidence, there has not been any attack on the full AES-128 since it was published in 1998. Bogdanov, Khovratovich and Rechberger proposed full-round attacks on AES-128 [3]. However, time complexity of their attacks is slightly smaller than bruteforce attacks, and their attacks require large amounts of memory and data unlike brute force attacks. It is not sure that their attacks are more efficient than bruteforce attacks.

The security of blockciphers is evaluated on the basis of time complexity of the exhaustive key search. If there is an attack on certain numbers of rounds, which successfully recovers the key with time complexity less than that of bruteforce attack, the cipher with such a number of rounds is considered as insecure. On the other hand, it is important to evaluate the security of blockcipher from practical point of the view, i.e. we consider whether attacks are feasible in the practical setting. One of examples of such evaluations is *low-data complexity attack* where the number of available data is highly restricted. Considering practical attack scenarios, in order to collect pairs of plaintext/ciphertext, an adversary has to access a target blockcipher and execute it with known/chosen plaintexts or passively eavsdrop data in the network. Thus, data complexity

© Springer Nature Singapore Pte Ltd. 2017
L. Batten et al. (Eds.): ATIS 2017, CCIS 719, pp. 128–140, 2017.
DOI: 10.1007/978-981-10-5421-1_11

Table 1. Summary on our results on reduced round Camellia-128.

Attack type	Whitening	FL/FL^{-1}	Rounds	Data	Time
Tr.D(4.1)	✓		4	2CP	2^{23}
Tr.D(4.2)	✓		4	3CP	negl.
Tr.D(5.1)	✓		5	2CP	2^{58}
Tr.D(5.2)	✓		5	5CP	negl.
Tr.D(7.1)	✓	✓	5	9CP	2^{20}
Tr.D(6.2)	✓		6	2CP	2^{114}
Tr.D(6.2)	✓		6	5CP	2^{68}
Tr.D(6.1)	✓		6	24CP	2^{66}
Tr.D(6.1)	✓		6	93CP	2^{12}
Tr.D(7.2)	✓	✓	6	9CP	2^{84}
Tr.D(7.2)	✓	✓	6	129CP	$2^{64.3}$
Collision [12]			6	2^{10}CP	2^{15}
Tr.D(6.3)	✓		7	24CP	2^{122}
Tr.D(6.3)	✓		7	93CP	2^{76}
Collision [12]			7	2^{12}CP	$2^{54.5}$
MitM [10]	✓	✓	11	2^{117}CP	$2^{121.3}$
Imp.D [5]	✓	✓	11	$2^{118.4}$CP	$2^{118.43}$
ZC [2]	✓	✓	11	$2^{125.3}$KP	$2^{125.8}$

Tr.D: Truncated differential cryptanalysis, Collision: Collision attack,
MitM: Meet-in-the-Middle attack, Imp.D: impossible differential
cryptanalysis,
ZC: Zero correlation linear cryptanalysis.
CP: Chosen plaintext, KP: Known Plaintext.

heavily depends on attack scenarios, while time and memory requirements are estimated by computational resource of the adversary independently from attack scenarios. Therefore, data-complexity may be crucial in the practical setting. Several low-data complexity attack on AES were recently proposed [4,8,11].

In this paper, we propose low-data complexity attacks on 128-bit blockcipher Camellia [1], which was designed by NTT and Mitsubishi corporation, and is currently selected as ISO standard [9] and CRYPTREC recommended ciphers [7]. Under the assumption that available data is restricted, we are not able to mount statistic cryptanalysis such as differential, linear and impossible differential attacks. In the sense of the low data, one may consider that meet-in-the-middle attacks are promising candidates. However it basically requires a large amount of memory. Chen and Li studied low-data attacks on Camellia-256 by using the meet-in-the middle approach [6]. Their attack requires 2^{19} chosen plaintexts and around 2^{230} time and memory complexity. Recall one of our purposes is to minimize time and memory requirements as possible for practical estimations. Therefore, meet-in-the-middle attacks do not match with our purposes. Our attacks are based on deterministic truncated differential characteristics exploiting properties of binaries matrices and differential properties of S-boxes of Camellia. Combining these with the structure of Camellia and linearity of Matrices, we obtain low-complexity data attacks on 4 to 7 rounds of Camellia-128 with whitening keys. Table 1 shows the summary of our results. Surprisingly, 4 to 6 rounds attacks are feasible with only two chosen plaintexts. In addition, by increasing a small amount of data, time complexity becomes very practical, and the required memory is negligible. Compared to previous results, the amount of required data is dramatically reduced while keeping practical time complexity, even if our attacks include whitening keys and unlike previous attacks. Finally we show that our low-data complexity attacks are applicable to Camellia including FL functions.

2   Preliminaries

This section gives notations used in this paper and explains the description of Camellia blockcipher.

2.1   Notations

The following notations are used in this paper:

P_L, P_R : left and right 64-bit halves of the plaintext
C_L, C_R : left and right 64-bit halves of the ciphertext
L_r, R_r : left and right 64-bit halves of the r-th round input
k_r : subkey used in the r-th round
kl_i : 64-bit subkey used in the FL/FL^{-1} layer ($i = 1, 2, 3, 4$)
w_i : whitening key used in the beginning and the end of Camellia ($i = 1, 2, 3, 4$)
ΔX : XOR difference of X and X'
$0, ?$: '0' denotes the zero difference byte and '?' denotes the unknown byte
$\oplus, \cap, \cup$: bitwise exclusive OR(XOR), AND, OR
$\lll_1$: left rotation of a bit string
$\|$: bit string concatenation

2.2   Specification of Camellia

Camellia [1] is based on an SP-type Feistel structure with a 128-bit block length and variable key lengths of 128, 192 or 256 bits. The number of rounds depends on the key length: 18 rounds for 128-bit keys and 24 rounds for 192/256-bit keys. In this paper, we consider only Camellia-128 which is the one supporting a 128-bit key.

The 64-bit F function of Camellia, $F : \{0, 1\}^{64} \times \{0, 1\}^{64} \rightarrow \{0, 1\}^{64}$, consists of a key addition layer, a S-layer and a P-layer. In the key addition layer, a 64-bit subkey K_r is Xored to the input state. The S-layer $S: \{0, 1\}^{64} \rightarrow \{0, 1\}^{64}$ consists of four 8-bit Sboxes, S_1, S_2, S_3, S_4, and execute these in the parallel in the order of $S_1, S_2, S_3, S_4, S_2, S_3, S_4$ and S_1. In the P-layer, an 8×8 binary byte

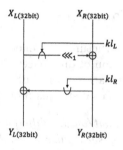

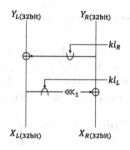

Fig. 1. FL layer   **Fig. 2.** FL^{-1} layer

matrix M: $\{0,1\}^{64} \to \{0,1\}^{64}$ is applied, where the matrix M and its reverse M^{-1} are given as follows:

$$M = \begin{pmatrix} 1 & 0 & 1 & 1 & 0 & 1 & 1 & 1 \\ 1 & 1 & 0 & 1 & 1 & 0 & 1 & 1 \\ 1 & 1 & 1 & 0 & 1 & 1 & 0 & 1 \\ 0 & 1 & 1 & 1 & 1 & 1 & 1 & 0 \\ 1 & 1 & 0 & 0 & 0 & 1 & 1 & 1 \\ 0 & 1 & 1 & 0 & 1 & 0 & 1 & 1 \\ 0 & 0 & 1 & 1 & 1 & 1 & 0 & 1 \\ 1 & 0 & 0 & 1 & 1 & 1 & 1 & 0 \end{pmatrix}, M^{-1} = \begin{pmatrix} 0 & 1 & 1 & 1 & 0 & 1 & 1 & 1 \\ 1 & 0 & 1 & 1 & 1 & 0 & 1 & 1 \\ 1 & 1 & 0 & 1 & 1 & 1 & 0 & 1 \\ 1 & 1 & 1 & 0 & 1 & 1 & 1 & 0 \\ 1 & 1 & 0 & 0 & 1 & 0 & 1 & 1 \\ 0 & 1 & 1 & 0 & 1 & 1 & 0 & 1 \\ 0 & 0 & 1 & 1 & 1 & 1 & 1 & 0 \\ 1 & 0 & 0 & 1 & 0 & 1 & 1 & 1 \end{pmatrix}$$

For $r = 6, 12$, key-dependent linear functions, FL/FL^{-1}: $\{0,1\}^{64} \times \{0,1\}^{64} \to \{0,1\}^{64}$, are applied. Let $X = (X_L \parallel X_R)$ and $K = (K_L \parallel K_R)$ be 64-bit blocks, where X_L, X_R, K_L, and K_R are 32-bit words, respectively. Then FL/FL^{-1} are defined as follows. Figures 1 and 2 illustrate the descriptions of FL and FL^{-1}, respectively.

$$FL(X, K) = ((((X_L \cap K_L) \lll_1 \oplus X_R) \cup K_R) \oplus X_L) \parallel ((X_L \cap K_L) \lll_1 \oplus X_R)$$
$$FL^{-1}(X, K) = (X_L \oplus (X_R \cup K_R)) \parallel (((X_L \oplus (X_R \cup K_R)) \cap K_L) \lll_1 \oplus X_R)$$

In this paper, we omit the description of the key scheduling function, because our attacks do not use any property of the key scheduling function. We refer to [1] about details of the key scheduling function.

The encryption procedures of Camellia-128 are given as follows.

1. $L_1 \parallel R_1 = (P_L \oplus w_1) \parallel (P_R \oplus w_2)$
2. For $i = 1$ to 18:
   if $i = 6$ or 12,
   $\qquad L_{i+1} = \text{FL}((\text{F}(L_i, k_i) \oplus R_i), kl_{\frac{i}{6}})$
   $\qquad R_{i+1} = \text{FL}^{-1}(L_i, kl_{\frac{i}{6}+1})$
   else
   $\qquad L_{i+1} = \text{F}(L_i, k_i) \oplus R_i$
   $\qquad R_{i+1} = L_i$

3. $C_L \parallel C_R = (R_{19} \oplus w_3) \parallel (L_{19} \oplus w_4)$

3 Observations on the Structure of Camellia

In this section we present two observations on the structure of Camellia. The first one is a well-known property regarding the relation of differences through S-boxes, and is also utilized for low-data complexity attacks on AES [4]. We experimentally confirmed that four S-boxes of Camellia satisfy this property.

Observation 1. *Consider pairs $(\Delta\alpha \neq 0, \Delta\beta)$ of input/output differences for one of a single S-box in the S-layer. For 129/256 of such pairs, the differential transition is impossible, i.e. there is no pair (x, y) such that $x \oplus y = \Delta\alpha$ and $S_i(x) \oplus S_i(y) = \Delta\beta$. For 126/256 of the pairs $(\Delta\alpha, \Delta\beta)$, there exist two ordered pairs (x, y) that satisfy the input/output differences. And for the remaining 1/256 of the pairs $(\Delta\alpha, \Delta\beta)$ there exist four ordered pairs (x, y) that satisfy the input/output differences.*

In the other word, once a pair of input/output *differences* of S-box $(\Delta\alpha, \Delta\beta)$ is given, corresponding pairs of input/output *values* (x, y) are immediately found by using the difference distribution table (DDT). Note that time complexity to construct DDT is estimated as 2^{16} evaluations of the S-box. Since Camellia uses four types of S-boxes, the total complexity for creating DDT tables of these S-boxes is estimated as $2^{18} (= 2^{16} \times 4)$ S-box evaluations, and the memory required to store the tables is about 2^{19} bytes.

The second one is obtained by the property of the balanced Feistel structure and linearity of Matrices.

Observation 2. *An output difference of the S layer in round n $(S(\Delta L_n))$ is expressed by left and right 64-bit inputs of round $n - 2$ $(\Delta L_{n-2}, \Delta R_{n-2})$, and a left 64-bit input of round $n + 1$ (L_{n+1}).*

$$S(\Delta L_n) = S(\Delta L_{n-2}) \oplus M^{-1}(\Delta L_{n+1} \oplus \Delta R_{n-2})$$

This relation is obtained using linearity of P layers as follow.

$$
\begin{aligned}
S(\Delta L_n) &= M^{-1}(M(S(\Delta L_{n-2})) \oplus \Delta L_{n+1} \oplus \Delta R_{n-2}) \\
&= M^{-1}(M(S(\Delta L_{n-2}))) \oplus M^{-1}(\Delta L_{n+1} \oplus \Delta R_{n-2}) \\
&= S(\Delta L_{n-2}) \oplus M^{-1}(\Delta L_{n+1} \oplus \Delta R_{n-2})
\end{aligned}
$$

4 Low-Data Complexity Attacks on 4-Round Camellia-128

In this section, we presents two types of low-data complexity attacks on 4-round Camellia-128 using some observations in the previous section. One is *data optimized attack* which aims to reduce the required data as possible. The other is *time-optimized attack* which tries to reduce time complexity by increasing a small amount of data compared to data-optimized attacks but the required data is still sufficiently small.

4.1 Data-Optimized Attack

We use only two chosen plaintexts in the difference form of $\Delta P_L = 0$ and $\Delta P_R = \Delta(a,0,0,0,0,0,0,0)$, where a is an arbitrary 1-byte value. Then, we can construct a truncated differential characteristic of 4-round Camellia as shown in Fig. 3. Importantly, this truncated differential characteristic holds with probability one thanks to the deterministic diffusion property of Matrices.

From Observation 2, an output of S-box in round 4, $S(\Delta L_4)$, is expressed as

$$S(\Delta L_4) = S(\Delta L_2) \oplus M^{-1}(\Delta L_5 \oplus \Delta R_2),$$

where ΔL_5 equals ΔC_R and ΔR_2 is zero. $S(\Delta L_2)$ is given as

$$S(\Delta L_2) = S(\Delta(a,0,0,0,0,0,0,0)) = \Delta(x,0,0,0,0,0,0,0).$$

From Observation 1, Δx has 127 candidates. Then, we obtain the following equation regarding an output of S-box in round 4.

$$S(\Delta L_4) = \Delta(x,0,0,0,0,0,0,0) \oplus M^{-1}(\Delta C_R)$$

Since an input differences of S-box of round 4, namely ΔL_4, is same as ΔC_L, we know values of input and output difference of S-boxes of round 4 by guessing the value of Δx. According to Observation 1, we obtain candidates of values of input/outputs pairs of each S-boxes by using DDTs. Here given the value of an input of S-box and C_L, the values of $k_4 \oplus w_3$ is determined. Thus, the number of candidates of each byte of $k_4 \oplus w_3$ is reduced to two. The total number of remaining candidates of $k_4 \oplus w_3$ is expected to be 2^8. Since Δx has 127 patterns, all possible $k_4 \oplus w_3$ values are estimated as $2^{15}(\approx 2^8 \times 127)$.

Once the value of $k_4 \oplus w_3$ is determined, a pairs of input and output differences of S-layer in round 3 is computable. Then, $k_3 \oplus w_4$ has 2^8 candidates by using DDT table in the same manner of the attack in round 4. Total space of $k_3 \oplus w_4$ and $k_4 \oplus w_3$ is reduced to 2^{23} ($\approx 2^{15} \times 2^8$) from 2^{128}. Thus, time complexity of the 4-round attack is estimated as 2^{23} encryptions, and the required data is only 2 chosen plaintexts.

4.2 Time-Optimized Attack

As with the data-optimized attack, we prepare two chosen plaintexts in the difference form of $\Delta P_L = 0$ and $\Delta P_R = \Delta(a,0,0,0,0,0,0,0)$, and utilize the same deterministic truncated differential characteristic. Unlike the data-optimized attack, the time-optimized attack does not guess the value Δx in the following equation to further reduce time complexity.

$$S(\Delta C_L) = \Delta(x,0,0,0,0,0,0,0) \oplus M^{-1}(\Delta C_R)$$

Since the S-layer is a byte-wise operation and bytes of ΔL_2 except the first byes are known as zero, we can obtain candidates of each byte of $k_4 \oplus w_3$ except a

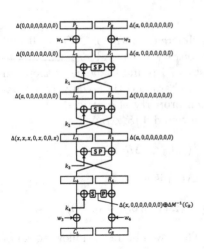

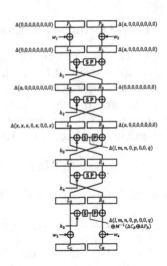

Fig. 3. Truncated differential of 4-round Camellia

Fig. 4. Truncated differential of 5-round Camellia

first byte without guessing Δx. The number of remaining candidates of 7 bytes of $k_4 \oplus w_3$ is 2^7.

Next, we prepare a new pair of chosen plaintexts in the difference form of $\Delta P_L = 0$ and $\Delta P_R = \Delta(0, a, 0, 0, 0, 0, 0, 0)$. Then we obtain the following equation.

$$S(\Delta C_L) = \Delta(0, x, 0, 0, 0, 0, 0, 0) \oplus M^{-1}(\Delta C_R).$$

In this case, we can obtain candidates of each byte of $k_4 \oplus w_3$ except a second byte. Now, 6 bytes except first and second bytes can be determined to one value by comparing candidates obtained by first and second results. The number of remaining candidates of first two bytes is 2^2. Once $k_4 \oplus w_3$ is determined, a pairs of input and output differences of S-layer in round 3 is also obtained. Using two pairs of plaintexts, all bytes of $k_4 \oplus w_3$ can be determined.

Time complexity is estimated as 2^2 encryptions and $2^7 \times 2 + 2^8 \times 2$ table access. It is less than that for creating DDT table (2^{16}), thus time complexity is negligible. Also, two pairs of our chosen plaintexts are created by only three plaintexts. Thus, the required data is 3 chosen plaintexts.

5   Low-Data Complexity Attacks on 5-Round Camellia-128

This section proposes low-data complexity attacks on the 5-round Camellia-128. Similar to attacks on the 4-round Camellia, we introduce two types of attacks, namely a data-optimized attack and a time-optimized attack.

5.1   Data-Optimized Attack

We use a deterministic truncated differential characteristic of the 5-round Camellia as shown in Fig. 4, which is obtained by the same pair of chosen plaintexts of the 4-round attack. From Observation 2, an output of S-box in round 5, $S(\Delta L_5)$, is expressed as

$$S(\Delta L_5) = S(\Delta L_3) \oplus M^{-1}(\Delta L_6 \oplus \Delta R_3),$$

where ΔL_6 and ΔR_3 are known as ΔC_R and ΔP_R, respectively. ΔL_3 is expressed as $\Delta L_3 = \Delta(x, x, x, 0, x, 0, 0, x)$, where the number of candidates of Δx is 127. Then, $S(\Delta L_3)$ is expressed as

$$S(\Delta L_3) = S(\Delta(x, x, x, 0, x, 0, 0, x)) = \Delta(l, m, n, 0, p, 0, 0, q),$$

where l, m, n, p, q are unknown five bytes, respectively. The number of candidates of l, m, n, p, q is estimated as $127 \times 127^5 = 127^6$, because each candidate of Δx takes 127 patterns, and each candidate changes to 127 patterns through each S-box. Now we obtain a pair of input and output differences of the S layer in round 5 by guessing five bytes of l, m, n, p, q. Since the number of candidates of each byte of $k_5 \oplus w_3$ is reduced to two (Observation 1), the number of remaining candidates of $k_5 \oplus w_3$ is expected to be 2^8. So all possible $k_5 \oplus w_3$ values are estimated as $2^8 \times 127^6 \approx 2^{50}$.

Once $k_5 \oplus w_3$ is determined, a pairs of input and output differences of S-layer in round 4 is also obtained. Then, $k_4 \oplus w_4$ has 2^8 candidate values. Thus, space of $k_4 \oplus w_4$ and $k_5 \oplus w_3$ is reduced to 2^{58} from 2^{128}. Time complexity is estimated as 2^{58} encryptions, and data complexity is 2 chosen plaintexts.

5.2   Time-Optimized Attack

We use the same truncated differential characteristic of the data-optimized attack on the 5-round Camellia as shown in Fig. 4. The time-optimized attack does not guess the five bytes of x, l, m, n, p, q in the following equation to reduce time complexity unlike the data-optimized attack.

$$S(\Delta L_3) = S(\Delta(x, x, x, 0, x, 0, 0, x)) = \Delta(l, m, n, 0, p, 0, 0, q)$$

Without guessing these values, we can obtain candidates of 3 bytes of $k_5 \oplus w_3$ where there is no zero difference in $\Delta(x, x, x, 0, x, 0, 0, x)$. The number of candidates of 3 bytes of $k_5 \oplus w_3$ is 2^3. Using another pair of chosen plaintexts in the form of $\Delta P_L = 0$ and $\Delta P_R = \Delta(0, a, 0, 0, 0, 0, 0, 0)$, we can obtain another set of candidates of 3 bytes of $k_5 \oplus w_3$.

Specifically we mount these procedures with four different pairs of chosen plaintexts such that $\Delta P_R = \Delta(a, 0, 0, 0, 0, 0, 0, 0)$ and $\Delta P_L = \{\Delta(a, 0, 0, 0, 0, 0, 0, 0),\ \Delta(0, a, 0, 0, 0, 0, 0, 0),\ \Delta(0, 0, a, 0, 0, 0, 0, 0),\ \Delta(0, 0, 0, a, 0, 0, 0, 0)\}$. Then we have following sets of $S(\Delta L_3)$

$$S(\Delta L_3) = \begin{cases} \Delta(?, ?, ?, 0, ?, 0, 0, ?), \\ \Delta(0, ?, ?, ?, ?, ?, 0, 0), \\ \Delta(?, 0, ?, ?, 0, ?, ?, 0), \\ \Delta(?, ?, 0, ?, 0, 0, ?, ?). \end{cases}$$

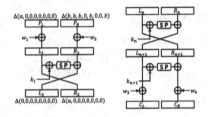

Fig. 5. Additional round of first and last

In this case, last 4 bytes of $k_5 \oplus w_3$ can be determined, and remaining 4 bytes has 2^4 candidate values. Once $k_5 \oplus w_3$ is determined, a pair of input and output differences of S-layer in round 4 is obtained. Two pairs of plaintexts is enough to determine the value of $k_4 \oplus w_4$.

Time complexity is estimated as 2^4 encryptions and $2^3 \times 4 + 2^8 \times 2$ table access. It is less than that for creating DDT table (2^{16}), thus time complexity is negligible. Our attack utilizes four differential characteristics. Such four pairs of plaintexts are created by only five chosen plaintexts.

6   More-Round Attacks

This section proposes methods to add more rounds on the begin and the end of 5-round attacks on Camellia-128, and describe low-data complexity attacks on the 7-round Camellia-128.

6.1   Adding First Round

Adding one more round on the begin of 5-round attacks on Camellia (Sect. 5) is achieved by using a pair of plaintexts in the difference form of

$$\Delta P_L = \Delta(a, 0, 0, 0, 0, 0, 0, 0), \Delta P_R = \Delta(b, b, b, 0, b, 0, 0, b),$$

where a and b are arbitrary 1-byte values, respectively. Let us consider the event where an output difference of the F function in round 1 is cancelled out by ΔP_R as follows.

$$M(S(\Delta(a, 0, 0, 0, 0, 0, 0, 0) \oplus (k_1 \oplus w_1)) = \Delta(b, b, b, 0, b, 0, 0, b).$$

In this case, the truncated characteristic from round 2 follows the same one used for the 5-round attacks as shown in the left of Fig. 5. Since the probability of this event is estimated as 2^{-8}, we should collect $2^8 (= 256)$ pairs of the chosen plaintexts. Given 24 plaintexts, the number of possible pairs is estimated as $\binom{24}{2} = 276$. Thus, the data-optimized attack on the 6-round Camellia is feasible with time complexity of $2^8 \times 2^{58} = 2^{66}$ and 24 chosen plaintexts.

The time-optimized attack on the 5-round Camellia utilizes four differential characteristics with different input differences. It seems to require $24 \times 4 = 96$ chosen plaintexts to add the first round. However, one pair of plaintexts which works for one differential characteristic can be reused for remaining three ones. Thus, the time-optimized attack on the 6-round Camellia is feasible with time complexity of $2^4 \times 2^8 = 2^{12}$ and 93 chosen plaintexts.

6.2   Adding Final Round

Guessing 64 bits of the sum of the whitening key and 6-th subkey, i.e., $w3 \oplus k6$, we can add one round in the end of 5-round attacks. Note that in this case, we do not need to guess the 4-round subkey, because once 5 and 6-round keys are determined, the other keys can be recovered by using relations of the key scheduling function. Therefore, the data-optimized attack requires $2^{114}(= 2^{50} \times 2^{64})$ time complexities and 2 chosen plaintexts, the time-optimized attack on the 6-round Camellia requires time complexitiy of $2^{68}(= 2^4 \times 2^{64})$ and 5 chosen plaintexts.

6.3   Attacks on 7-Round Camellia-128

Making use of both methods for adding the first and last rounds, we can achieve the low-data complexity attacks on 7-round Camellia-128.

Since the data-optimized attack on the 5-round Camellia exploits only one differential characteristic, the required data for adding the first round is 24 chosen plaintexts, and time complexity increases 2^8 times. If we add one round in the end of round, time complexity increases multiple of 2^{64}. Then, the 7-round attack is feasible with time complexity of 2^{122} and 24 chosen plaintexts.

Since the time-optimized attack on the 5-round Camellia uses four differential characteristics, the required data for adding the first round is 93 chosen plaintexts, and time complexity increases 2^8 times. Adding last one more round increase the multiple of 2^{64} time complexities. Then, the 7-round attack is feasible with time complexity of 2^{76} and 93 chosen plaintexts.

7   Attacks on Camellia-128 Including FL/FL^{-1} layers

In this section, we describe low-data complexity attacks on 5 and 6 round Camellia including FL/FL^{-1} layer between round 2 and round 3.

7.1   Attack on 5-Round Camellia with FL/FL^{-1}

We prepare a pairs of chosen plaintexts in the difference form of $P_L = 0, P_R = \Delta(0,0,0,0,a,0,0,0)$. In this attack, we considers a truncated differential characteristic of Fig. 6.

An output difference of FL^{-1} is $\Delta R_3 = \Delta(x,0,0,0,y,0,0,0)$, and an input difference of FL^{-1} is same as ΔP_R. The values of Δx and Δy are determined by

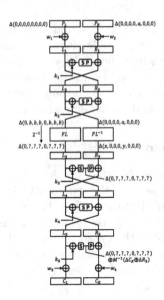

Fig. 6. Truncated differential of 5th round Camellia with FL layer Here, $0 \times 01 \leqq a \leqq 0 \times 7f$.

kl_2 in FL^{-1}. Here, we do not need to guess all the key bits of kl_2 to know values of Δx and Δy, and instead guess only bits having a difference thanks to the bit-based key AND/OR operations. If the number of the bit having difference is 1 (e.g. $\Delta a = 1, 2, 4, 8, 16, 32, 64$), only 2 bit of kl_2 are enough to guess.

Next, let us consider FL layer. Here an input difference of the FL layer is $\Delta(0, b, b, b, 0, b, b, b)$, where b is unknown one byte value. In the FL function, 1-bit rotation is executed as shown in Fig. 1. If the most significant bit of b has no difference, namely between 1 and 127, we can obtain an output of the FL layer of $\Delta(0, ?, ?, ?, 0, ?, ?, ?)$, The probability that Δb is between 1 and 127 is 2^{-1}.

Now we get the value of ΔR_3 and zero difference byte position at $S(\Delta L_3)$. Similar to the 5-round data-optimized attack, we can find 2 byte of $k_5 \oplus w_3$. Changing the place of input differences, we obtain other 2 bytes of $k_5 \oplus w_3$ as follows.

$$\Delta P_R = \begin{cases} \Delta(0, 0, 0, 0, a, 0, 0, 0), \\ \Delta(0, 0, 0, 0, 0, a, 0, 0), \\ \Delta(0, 0, 0, 0, 0, 0, a, 0), \\ \Delta(0, 0, 0, 0, 0, 0, 0, a). \end{cases} \Rightarrow S(\Delta L_3) = \begin{cases} \Delta(0, ?, ?, ?, 0, ?, ?, ?), \\ \Delta(?, 0, ?, ?, ?, 0, ?, ?), \\ \Delta(?, ?, 0, ?, ?, ?, 0, ?), \\ \Delta(?, ?, ?, 0, ?, ?, ?, 0). \end{cases}$$

By using four pairs, we can reduce candidates of $w_4 \oplus k_4$ to 2^8 from Observation 1. The probability that all four pairs follow the truncated differential characteristic of Fig. 6 is 2^{-4}, and we need to guess 8 bits of kl_2. Thus, time complexity for finding $w_4 \oplus k_4$ is estimated as $2^{20} (= 2^8 \times 2^4 \times 2^8)$. The data requirement is 9 chosen plaintexts (required differentials are 8).

7.2 Attack on 6-Round Camellia with FL/FL^{-1}

This part describes additional first round or last round and 6 round attack. If last round is added, time complexity increases 2^{64} and 6 round attack requires 2^{84} time complexities and 9 chosen plaintexts.

In additional first round, we collect $2^9 = 512$ differences because the 5 round attack needs 2 differentials between 1 and 127. 33 chosen plaintext yield $\binom{33}{2} = 528$ pairs, and that is enough. At FL^{-1}, the 2^9 differentials branch 17136 patterns. We calculated that. Results, additional the first round requires $33 \times 4 - 3 = 129$ chosen plaintext ('-3' is reworking plaintexts) and $2^8 \times 17136^4 \approx 2^{64.3}$ time complexities.

8 Conclusions

In this paper, we proposed low-data complexity attacks on reduced-round Camellia. Our attacks are based on deterministic truncated differential characteristics exploiting properties of binaries matrices and differential properties of S-boxes of Camellia. Combining these with the structure of Camellia, namely balanced Feistel, we obtain low data complexity attacks on 4 to 7 rounds of Camellia. Surprisingly, 4 to 6 rounds attacks are feasible with only two chosen plaintexts and the attack complexity becomes very practical by increasing a small amount of data.

References

1. Aoki, K., Ichikawa, T., Kanda, M., Matsui, M., Moriai, S., Nakajima, J., Tokita, T.: Camellia: a 128-bit block cipher suitable for multiple platforms—design and analysis. In: Stinson, D.R., Tavares, S. (eds.) SAC 2000. LNCS, vol. 2012, pp. 39–56. Springer, Heidelberg (2001). doi:10.1007/3-540-44983-3_4
2. Bogdanov, A., Geng, H., Wang, M., Wen, L., Collard, B.: Zero-correlation linear cryptanalysis with FFT and improved attacks on ISO standards camellia and CLEFIA. In: Lange, T., Lauter, K., Lisoněk, P. (eds.) SAC 2013. LNCS, vol. 8282, pp. 306–323. Springer, Heidelberg (2014). doi:10.1007/978-3-662-43414-7_16
3. Bogdanov, A., Khovratovich, D., Rechberger, C.: Biclique cryptanalysis of the full AES. In: Lee, D.H., Wang, X. (eds.) ASIACRYPT 2011. LNCS, vol. 7073, pp. 344–371. Springer, Heidelberg (2011). doi:10.1007/978-3-642-25385-0_19
4. Bouillaguet, C., Derbez, P., Dunkelman, O., Fouque, P.A., Keller, N., Rijmen, V.: Low-data complexity attacks on AES. IEEE Trans. Inf. Theory 58(11), 7002–7017 (2012)
5. Boura, C., Naya-Plasencia, M., Suder, V.: Scrutinizing and improving impossible differential attacks: applications to CLEFIA, Camellia, LBlock and SIMON. In: Sarkar, P., Iwata, T. (eds.) ASIACRYPT 2014. LNCS, vol. 8873, pp. 179–199. Springer, Heidelberg (2014). doi:10.1007/978-3-662-45611-8_10
6. Chen, J., Li, L.: Low data complexity attack on reduced Camellia-256. In: Susilo, W., Mu, Y., Seberry, J. (eds.) ACISP 2012. LNCS, vol. 7372, pp. 101–114. Springer, Heidelberg (2012). doi:10.1007/978-3-642-31448-3_8
7. CRYPTREC: Cryptrec ciphers list (2013)

8. Grassi, L., Rechberger, C., Rønjom, S.: Subspace Trail Cryptanalysis and its Applications to AES. IACR Trans. Symmetric Cryptol. 2016(2) (2016)
9. ISO/IEC 18033-3: Information technology - security techniques - encryption algorithms - part 3: Block ciphers (2005)
10. Li, L., Jia, K., Wang, X., Dong, X.: Meet-in-the-middle technique for truncated differential and its applications to CLEFIA and Camellia. In: Leander, G. (ed.) FSE 2015. LNCS, vol. 9054, pp. 48–70. Springer, Heidelberg (2015). doi:10.1007/978-3-662-48116-5_3
11. Tiessen, T.: Polytopic cryptanalysis. In: Fischlin, M., Coron, J.-S. (eds.) EUROCRYPT 2016. LNCS, vol. 9665, pp. 214–239. Springer, Heidelberg (2016). doi:10.1007/978-3-662-49890-3_9
12. Wu, W., Feng, D.: Collision attack on reduced-round Camellia. Sci. China Ser. F Inf. Sci. 48(1), 78–90 (2005)

RESTful Is Not Secure

Tetiana Yarygina[✉]

Department of Informatics, University of Bergen, Bergen, Norway
tetiana.yarygina@uib.no

Abstract. The shift in web service design towards the REST paradigm has spawned a series of security concerns. To date there has been no general agreement on how the REST paradigm addresses security and what web security mechanisms adhere to the REST style. This paper analyzes the REST paradigm from a security perspective and shows significant incompatibilities between the style constraints and typical security mechanisms. We conclude that the REST style was not designed with security properties in mind and does not fit the security requirements of modern web applications.

Keywords: Web services security · REST · Stateless · Token authentication

1 Introduction

Web services enable rapid design, development, and deployment of software solutions. They provide a unified web interface and hide complexity and heterogeneity of the underlying infrastructure, enabling simple integration of diverse clients and external components [1]. Unfortunately, the desirable simplicity does not extend to the security aspects of web services.

Representational State Transfer (REST) is an architectural style for web services that is widely adopted. As an architectural style, REST imposes six general design constraints [2]: *client-server, stateless resource, cacheable responses, uniform interface, layered,* and *code-on-demand* (optional constraint). These constraints enforce the original concept of the Web as a scalable distributed hypermedia system with loosely coupled components. Web services that strictly adhere to REST style constraints are commonly referred to as RESTful services, while those with loose adherence are often called REST-like services.

It was long believed [3] that RESTful services should be used for ad hoc integration over the Web, whereas Big Web services (see [1] for naming convention) were preferable in enterprise application integration scenarios with longer lifespans and advanced security requirements. However, today we find that more and more corporate solutions, even the most security demanding ones like financial systems and sensitive data operations, are based on RESTful or REST-like services. In contrast to Big Web services, no formal security framework exists for RESTful services.

© Springer Nature Singapore Pte Ltd. 2017
L. Batten et al. (Eds.): ATIS 2017, CCIS 719, pp. 141–153, 2017.
DOI: 10.1007/978-981-10-5421-1_12

There are relatively few studies of RESTful services security, herein we mention most of them. A recent study by Gorski et al. [4] compares the security stacks of Big Web services and RESTful services. A paper by Lo Iacono and Nguyen [5] compares RESTful authentication mechanisms with focus on message signing. In particular, the authors propose a signing mechanism not limited to HTTP. Finally, two papers describe approaches to message security for RESTful services [6] and secure communication between mobile clients and RESTful services [7]. Although all of these studies claim to deal with RESTful security, they do not discuss the REST architectural style from security perspective.

A much debated question among practitioners is what security mechanisms are truly RESTful. As an example, discussion threads on RESTful authentication[1] and best practices for securing REST APIs[2] are viewed more than 250,000 times each. The introduction of security components often changes system behavior, which can affect how a system adheres to the REST style constraints. To date there has been no general agreement on how the REST paradigm should address security. Apart from Inoue et al. [8], who argued that a session state is not against the REST architectural style, there is a lack of research in the area.

This paper aims to unravel some of the mysteries surrounding RESTful security. We analyze the REST paradigm from a security perspective and show significant incompatibilities between the style constraints and typical security mechanisms. To our knowledge, we are the first to conduct such a detailed security evaluation of the REST style and prove that RESTful security is impossible.

The rest of the paper is organized as follows. In Sect. 2, an overview of common web security mechanisms and a brief discussion of their security merits are given. Section 3 explores in detail how particular security decisions and especially authentication schemes relate to core principles of the REST style. Section 4 concludes the paper by summarizing the uncovered contradictions, discussing the implications of the findings, and providing insights for future research.

2   Overview of Security Mechanisms for the Modern Web

Adequate security mechanisms are needed to build secure RESTful services. This section focuses on common security mechanisms such as Transport Layer Security (TLS), cryptographic objects in JavaScript Object Notation (JSON), token-based authentication, client side request signing, and delegated authorization and shared authentication. The overview creates a background for a more advanced analysis of how common security mechanisms adhere to the REST style constraints.

TLS was originally designed to be independent of any application protocol and has became a de facto security protocol on the Web. Although the design of

---

[1] https://stackoverflow.com/questions/319530/restful-authentication.

[2] https://stackoverflow.com/questions/7551/best-practices-for-securing-a-rest-api-web-service.

TLS supports mutual authentication, HTTPS in its current form is largely used to authenticate the gateway, but not the client. Even though the idea of both parties maintaining digital certificates is simple and secure, embedding a unique certificate into each client is a serious implementation obstacle. Therefore, client authentication must be provided on the application (message) level.

To provide higher security, as well as client authentication, TLS can be and often is combined with encryption and signing on the message level. Standards for cryptographic objects in JSON and XML were created to address security needs on the message level and to facilitate interoperability. Cryptographic objects can be seen as containers incorporating secured data and the information necessary for its processing. The JSON Object Signing and Encryption (JOSE) suite of specifications offers powerful and flexible building blocks for message security in web services by providing a general approach to signing and encryption of JSON-formatted messages. The JOSE suite is essential for delegated authorization and shared authentication schemes, such as OAuth 2.0 and OpenID Connect (see Fig. 1).

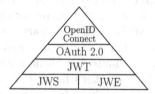

Fig. 1. The hierarchical relation between the JOSE suite, OAuth 2.0, and OpenID Connect. The JOSE suite incorporates JSON Web Signature (JWS), JSON Web Encryption (JWE), JSON Web Token (JWT) [9], and several other specifications.

HTTP is a stateless protocol, which implies that requests are treated independently of each other. Nevertheless, most web applications require sessions. Session management in HTTP is historically performed via HTTP cookies, URL parameters, HTTP body arguments in requests, or custom HTTP headers. A natural extension of session management is client authentication. In modern web applications, there exist two main approaches to authentication: *token-based authentication* and *client side request signing*. The following discussion focuses on the security aspects of these approaches.

Traditionally [10], message authentication methods include Message Authentication Codes (MACs), digital signature schemes, and appending a secret authenticator value before encrypting the whole text. In the context of modern web services, either JWS or XML Signature standards can be used for message authentication depending on the message format. For the sake of simplicity, the term signature is used to refer to both MACs and actual digital signatures.

2.1   Token-Based Authentication

Token-based authentication via HTTP cookies is the most widely adopted authentication mechanism in web applications. The mechanism is based on a notion of security tokens—cryptographic objects containing information relevant for authentication or authorization.

An authentication token is generated by a web service and sent to a client for future use. A service generates a token upon the successful validation of the client's credentials either during the initial user log in or a re-authentication. A token can be seen as a temporary replacement for the client's credentials: every request from a client must include a valid token to be fulfilled. A token-based authentication scheme was first analyzed by Fu et al. in 2001 [11].

Security considerations. Server-created security tokens ensure scalability of the solution and server statelessness by moving the maintenance responsibility for tokens to clients. Additionally, a limited lifetime of security tokens makes them superior to direct use of passwords such as in HTTP Basic/Digest Authentication. A server-side secret used to create tokens is the most important security asset of the server. If the secret is leaked, the damage is not limited to one user: an adversary can impersonate any user of his or her choice.

Hijacking of security tokens is another serious threat. Token-based mechanisms rely on channel confidentiality. If compromised, a security token can be used by an adversary to impersonate the client until the token expires or is revoked. Short expiration time of tokens limits the possible damage, but also reduces usability of a system by requiring frequent user re-authentication.

The severity of security token hijacking is rooted in the static nature of such tokens and their independence of particular requests. Dacosta et al. [12] proposed to switch from static cookies to dynamic ones (request-specific). Channel-binding cookies is another approach to strengthen cookie-based authentication by binding cookies to TLS channels using TLS origin-bound certificates [13]. However, no approach has gained wide adoption mostly due to increased complexity. The evidence presented herein suggests that token-based authentication requires minimal amount of data being stored on the server-side, i.e. contributes to server statelessness, but also has significant security limitations.

2.2   Client Side Request Signing

Many existing RESTful services implement client authentication and in-transit tampering protection by requiring a client to sign each request. Cryptographic keys are established between parties during or after the initial authentication step. Request signing implies signing of an actual message (HTTP payload) and, optionally, HTTP headers.

Request signing involving HTTP headers has been successfully deployed by several major web services such as Amazon Web Services (AWS) [14] and Microsoft Azure [15]. Both are cloud services intended only for programmatic use through REST APIs. An investigation shows that numerous newly developed systems borrow AWS' HMAC-SHA256-based approach to request signing [14].

A comparison of REST message authentication mechanisms based on request signing was performed by Lo Iacono and Nguyen [5]. The paper contributes a detailed HMAC-based scheme for authentication of all types of REST messages, including HTTP messages. A similar, but not as detailed approach to HTTP signing can be found in the IETF draft *Signing HTTP Messages* [16].

Security considerations. Client-signed requests provide stronger authentication than mere token-based schemes. Signing of each client request effectively mitigates session hijacking attacks by limiting damage only to a single request. A signing key never leaves a client which makes stealing the key much more difficult than stealing a token that is not only stored on the client, but also repeatedly sent over the channel. As often happens, higher security comes at a price of lower scalability and higher complexity since a server needs to maintain a separate key for each user.

2.3 Delegated Authorization and Shared Authentication

Delegated authorization and shared authentication have become an integral part of modern web security. The popular security protocols underlying delegated authorization and shared authentication mostly instantiate the token-based authentication introduced earlier. Therefore, they share both advantages and disadvantages of token-based authentication.

Delegated authorization. We consider a scenario where a user, or resource owner, has stored some sensitive information on a server. The desire to separate the login process on the server from the process of granting permissions to a client application on the behalf of the user has stimulated the emergence of OAuth [17]. OAuth is a delegated authorization protocol providing third-party applications (clients) with delegated access to protected resources on behalf of a user (resource owner). Client side request signing in OAuth 1.0 enables client authentication and message integrity, while OAuth 2.0 does not. Developers often fail to implement OAuth correctly due to its ambiguity and complexity [18–20].

Shared authentication. OAuth 2.0 is used as an underlying layer for shared authentication protocols and Single-Sign-On (SSO) systems. Prominent examples are OpenID Connect [21], Facebook Login, and Sign In With Twitter. In such schemes the user authenticates into a third party service (a Relying Party or RP) using a digital identity at an Identity Provider (IdP) of the user's choice. However, additional steps must be taken in order to use OAuth 2.0 for authentication. Security analyses of commercially deployed OAuth-based SSO solutions (i.e. popular social login providers) [20,22] have revealed various security and privacy issues.

3   REST Architectural Style and Security

So far this paper has focused on the security mechanisms commonly used to secure RESTful services. This section elaborates on why none of the systems using such mechanisms are strictly RESTful by analyzing the REST style and its constrains from a security perspective. It is worth mentioning that the majority of RESTful services actually fail to adhere to REST for reasons unrelated to security. Absence of custom media types support and use of verbs in URIs are common examples of such violations.

The REST architectural style was introduced by Fielding in his influential dissertation [2] and related paper [23] in 2000. The style is widely adopted and many popular web services, such as Twitter[3] and LinkedIn[4], have REST APIs. The dissertation remains the most fundamental source when talking about the core principles of REST.

3.1 Not Designed with Security in Mind

The REST style was proposed as an architectural standard for the Web and introduced only the properties that seemed necessary for the Web at that time. Fielding makes no attempt to address the question of security in REST. The words security, authentication, and authorization are rarely mentioned in Fielding's work. The words encryption and signing do not appear at all.

According to Fielding [2], "REST emphasizes scalability of component interactions, generality of interfaces, independent deployment of components, and intermediary components to reduce interaction latency, *enforce security*, and encapsulate legacy systems." The claim that REST enforces security is neither justified in the dissertation nor explained in any other literature related to REST.

When talking about scalability of the Web, Fielding writes [2, Sect. 4.1.4.1] "since authentication degrades scalability, the architecture's default operation should be limited to actions that do not need trusted data." In modern Web, and especially for REST APIs, the situation is reversed: some form of authentication is always present. TLS is only mentioned as a connector type [2, Sect. 5.2.2], no encryption on the message level is considered.

The REST architectural style does not incorporate security as one of its goals and leaves it up to the developer to decide how security fits the six core principles. The introduction of security components affects system behavior initially shaped by REST constraints. Most of the constraints, such as client-server, uniform interface, and layered system, are high-level and flexible enough to not interfere with adopted security mechanisms. At the same time, the stateless, cacheable, and code-on-demand constraints have several practical security implications. The security implications of the relevant REST constraints are discussed in the following sections.

3.2 Stateless Constraint

Revisiting the definition. The stateless resource constraint is particularly problematic from a security perspective. The constraint is often misunderstood

---

[3] https://dev.twitter.com/rest/public.

[4] https://developer.linkedin.com/docs/rest-api.

by practitioners and overlooked in the scientific literature. According to Fielding [2, Sect. 5.1.3], for a resource to be stateless "each request from client to server *must* contain all of the information necessary to understand the request, and cannot take advantage of *any stored context on the server*." Such a definition makes no exceptions and, when followed to the letter, leaves no room for security mechanisms.

Furthermore, [2] specifies that the "session state" (also referred to as "application state") should be stored exclusively on the client side; however, a definition of session state is never given. A commonly used interpretation of the stateless resource constraint introduced in [1] differentiates between *application state* and *resource state*. A resource state is defined as any information about the underlying resource [1].

While the resource state belongs to the server, it still can be changed in response to a client request. If we consider a user as a resource, then the balance of the user's bank account is a resource state that is changing with each performed transaction. Similarly, usernames and passwords are also resource states that change over time.

Security implications. Most security components introduce additional resource states. Stateless security protocols do not exist. It is very hard, if at all possible, to prevent replay attacks without maintaining at least some form of client state on the server side. Nonces (numbers used once), counters, and timestamps are examples of such a resource state. All authentication mechanisms described in Sect. 2 incorporate one or more such components. Thus, web services utilizing these mechanisms are not strictly RESTful.

Differentiating between application state and resource state can be difficult. For example, security tokens are stored by the client, but are issued exclusively by the server. The server must maintain the key(s) used to sign tokens, which introduces more resource states.

The demand of "taking no advantage of any stored context on the server" is impractical. For example, a common security practice of restricting the number of login attempts made per specific account relies on the login history being available.

As pointed out by Fielding [2, Sect. 6.3.4.2], HTTP cookies fail to fulfill the stateless constraint of REST. An example of such a violation is the use of cookies to identify a user's "shopping basket" stored on the server, while the basket can be stored on the client side and presented to the server only when the user checks out. This mismatch between REST and HTTP makes a huge part of the modern Web not RESTful and implicitly deprecates cookie-based authentication for RESTful web services.

When token-based mechanisms, such as JWT, OAuth 2.0, and OpenID Connect are used, a server needs $\mathcal{O}(1)$ resource states to authenticate N users [11]. With client request signing as in OAuth 1.0a and AWS, the server needs to maintain a separate key for each client, thus having $\mathcal{O}(N)$ resource states. Therefore, token-based mechanisms can be considered stateless in a sense that there is no per-user or per-session state when compared to client request signing given a substantial number of clients. Although token-based authentication fits the REST style better then the client side request signing, the latter is generally more secure as explained in Sect. 2.

Additionally, it is possible to classify application state into two classes, security insensitive and security sensitive, that must be treated differently. The server cannot prevent the client from tampering with the data given to it, nor can the server directly protect data stored on a client from malicious third parties. The latter puts user privacy at risk if the data stored is security sensitive.

Even though the definition of the stateless constraint dictates that a client's request must contain all of the information necessary to understand the request, sensitive information should not be transferred unless absolutely necessary. All security sensitive application states must belong to the server and be resource states.

Advantages and disadvantages. To evaluate immediate importance of stateless resource constraint for modern security-aware applications, the advantages and disadvantages of the constraint must be revisited. According to Fielding [2], stateless resource constraint induces the properties of visibility, reliability, and scalability.

The original argument for improved visibility [2] was that the server should process a client request without looking beyond this request. The argument is valid until security is involved. Let us consider an online store. If some items are added to the shopping basket, the only allowed step should be a payment step, and not goods delivery. To ensure this restriction, the user must have state within the system.

Additionally, intrusion detection systems (IDS), anti-denial-of-service, and anomaly detection mechanisms are more likely to mitigate attacks when they have knowledge of the state and the history of requests. If we consider security sensitive data such as authentication tokens, the server unavoidably needs to validate the token, which requires retrieval of the cryptographic key used to generate the token. The step of token verification can also be seen as one that decreases visibility. The aforementioned suggests that improvement of visibility can only be seen for security insensitive data.

The common belief is that maintaining client states on the server side can potentially create a high load of session management and degrade system performance. However, storing clients states on the server side does not cause significant performance problems for existing high load systems and Cloud services; a study of REST session state [8] showed that the impact of the stateless resource constraint on scalability and reliability of REST in the modern Web is insignificant.

Moreover, maintaining client states on the server side is a desired property in many cases, for example personalized services, targeted advertisement, smart suggestion systems, and IDS benefit from it. An alternative solution to scalability and reliability issues is adoption of special software architecture styles, such as microservices [24].

The stateless constraint puts significant limitations on handling session synchronization. In the example with the shopping basket, the problems occur when the user has initialized a session on a mobile device and wants to continue the session using the browser on a laptop. Storing session state exclusively on the client side and not on the server makes it impossible to keep persistent state in such situations. Hence, current demand for client state synchronization negates the stateless resource constraint of REST.

3.3 Other Constraints Affecting Security

Cache constraint. The cachebility constraint is affecting security much less than the stateless criteria, but the effect is still noteworthy. The definition of the constraint [2] states that the server responses must be explicitly marked as cacheable or noncacheable. Of course, only actual caching of responses improves scalability and network efficiency by eliminating identical repeating interactions. Caching of server responses can be performed by intermediates, i.e. proxies and gateways, or clients themselves.

Caching by intermediates has less value on the modern Web due to an increasing amount of encrypted traffic such as HTTPS traffic. As of February 2017, 52.8% of the most popular websites implemented HTTPS [25]. When encrypted either by TLS or on the message level, server responses are not cacheable by intermediate proxies. Encrypted content cannot be cached unless the intermediates are allowed to decrypt the traffic, which defeats the purpose of encryption in the first place.

Although caching by clients is not affected by encryption, it loses its importance due to different reasons. Modern websites include large amounts of dynamic personalized content that cannot and should not be cached. In case of online banking or online shopping the content (the bank account balance or availability of specific items in the shopping basket) is dynamic and gets outdated fast. Such content is not suitable for caching due to reliability reasons. Similarly, sensitive content should never be cached for security reasons.

Taken together, encryption and personalized content dramatically reduce the benefits of traditional web caching in general, and the importance of cache constraint of the REST style in particular. While the content marked as noncacheable does not contradict the definition of the cache constraint (since the constraint only requires proper labeling), it brings no actual benefit in terms of scalability or network efficiency.

Code-on-demand constraint. In the code-on-demand paradigm the code for a specific task is requested by the client, provided by a server, and executed in the client's context. As argued in [2], the code-on-demand constraint of REST improves system extensibility, but also reduces visibility. Therefore, it is only an optional constraint.

It should be noted that the code-on-demand constraint is relevant primarily within the browser environment. In semantic web with machine-to-machine communication and native clients consuming REST APIs, execution of external JavaScript code in the native applications is currently uncommon.

An important security implication of the code-on-demand paradigm is an increased attack surface on a client. Among the major security concerns are authenticity of the received code and the client's ability to limit the behavior of the code. These problems have been studied for a long time and mitigation techniques, such as sandboxing, Address Space Layout Randomisation (ASLR), and Data Execution Prevention (DEP), are implemented in modern browsers. However, the problems still persist.

4   The Way Forward

4.1   Security Failure of REST

The main goal of this paper was to asses how the REST style addresses security and whether security mechanisms adhere to the style constraints. The study has shown that the REST style fails to take security into account, or to explain security implications of the constraints. To fill the gap, we provided the missing security interpretation of the relevant style constraints and made the following observations:

- *Stateless resource constraint.* The more security critical a system is, the more resource states it is likely to have. Among authentication approaches, token-based authentication most closely fits the stateless resource constraint. However, it is not entirely stateless.
- *Cache constraint.* Although formally the cache constraint (labeling of responses) is not directly affected by security mechanisms, the constraint loses its meaning for security critical systems. Encrypted, dynamic, and personalized content is not suitable for caching.
- *Code-on-demand constraint.* The optional code-on-demand constraint reduces security of the system by increasing the attack surface on the client side.

To be strictly RESTful and follow all the constraints as they were originally defined, a system should neither deploy authentication nor store session identifiers in HTTP cookies or headers. Since only the absence of security mechanisms allows an entity to provide truly RESTful APIs, a bank claiming to have RESTful APIs either has serious security problems or the APIs do not satisfy all the RESTful requirements.

An important finding is that the concept of RESTful security is impossible. We conclude that the strict REST style on one side and security mechanisms and security best practices on the other side are incompatible. We suggest that secure applications trying to adhere to the REST style should never be called RESTful, but REST-like, i.e. partially adhering to the REST style constraints. Although the term REST-like does appear in some security specifications, such as OpenID Connect [21], it has never been justified from a security perspective.

4.2 What to Do

The right security approach is system-specific and heavily dependent on the context. In particular, the frameworks OAuth 2.0 and OpenID Connect rely on TLS for confidentiality, integrity, and server authentication. These frameworks prioritize scalability over security because they use server signed tokens for client authentication. The overall conclusion from the analysis is that systems with high security requirements should deploy client signatures, even though it comes with the cost of reduced performance when compared to token-based approaches. Social login solutions are both easy to support and convenient for users, but should be avoided if privacy is a serious concern. OAuth should not be relied on for authentication and needs to be combined with a component for authentication. Figure 2 contains a flow chart showing how to choose the correct security architecture.

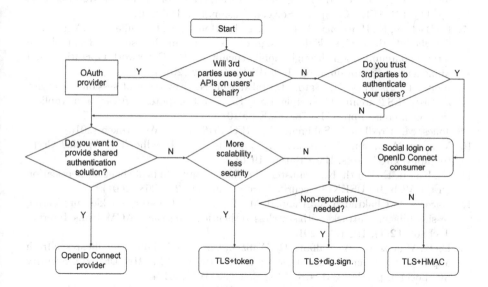

Fig. 2. Making the right security decision

4.3 Future Research

Inoue et al. [8] introduced an architectural style called RESTUS, which incorporates session state at the server-side as an additional constraint. RESTUS partially addresses the security issues of the stateless resource constraint, but not the issues related to the cache and code-on-demand constraints. Similarly to REST, it does not accommodate security. Future research should therefore concentrate on resolving the existing conflicts. A natural progression of this work is to propose an architectural style that incorporates basic security principles.

References

1. Richardson, L., Ruby, S.: RESTful Web Services. O'Reilly Media, Sebastopol (2007)
2. Fielding, R.T.: Architectural Styles and the Design of Network-based Software Architectures. Ph.D. thesis, University of California, Irvine (2000)
3. Pautasso, C., Zimmermann, O., Leymann, F.: RESTful web services vs. big web services: making the right architectural decision. In: 17th International World Wide Web Conference (WWW 2008), Beijing, China, pp. 805–814 (2008)
4. Gorski, P., Lo Iacono, L., Nguyen, H., Torkian, D.: Service security revisited. In: IEEE International Conference on Services Computing, pp. 464–471. IEEE Computer Society, Washington, DC (2014)
5. Lo Iacono, L., Nguyen, H.: Authentication scheme for REST. In: International Conference on Future Network Systems and Security, pp. 113–128 (2015)
6. Serme, G., de Oliveira, A., Massiera, J., Roudier, Y.: Enabling message security for RESTful services. In: IEEE 19th International Conference on Web Services, pp. 114–121. IEEE Computer Society, Washington, DC (2012)
7. De Backere, F., Hanssens, B., Heynssens, R., Houthooft, R., Zuliani, A., Verstichel, S., Dhoedt, B., De Turck, F.: Design of a security mechanism for RESTful web service communication through mobile clients. In: IEEE Network Operations and Management Symposium, pp. 1–6. IEEE, Krakow (2014)
8. Inoue, T., Asakura, H., Sato, H., Takahashi, N.: Key roles of session state: not against REST architectural style. In: IEEE 34th Computer Software and Applications Conference, pp. 171–178. IEEE (2010)
9. Jones, M., Bradley, J., Sakimura, N.: RFC 7519. JSON Web Token (2015)
10. Menezes, A.J., van Oorschot, P.C., Vanstone, S.A.: Handbook of Applied Cryptography. CRC Press, Boca Raton (1996)
11. Fu, K., Sit, E., Smith, K., Feamster, N.: The dos and don'ts of client authentication on the Web. In: USENIX Security Symposium, pp. 251–268 (2001)
12. Dacosta, I., Chakradeo, S., Ahamad, M., Traynor, P.: One-time cookies: preventing session hijacking attacks with stateless authentication tokens. ACM Trans. Internet Technol. 12(1), 1:1–1:24 (2012)
13. Dietz, M., Czeskis, A., Balfanz, D., Wallach, D.S.: Origin-bound certificates: a fresh approach to strong client authentication for the web. In: 21st USENIX Security Symposium, pp. 317–331. USENIX, Bellevue, WA (2012)
14. Amazon S3: Authenticating requests (AWS Signature v4). https://docs.aws.amazon.com/AmazonS3/latest/API/sig-v4-authenticating-requests.html
15. Microsoft Azure documentation: Authentication for the Azure Storage Services (2015). https://msdn.microsoft.com/en-us/library/dd179428.aspx
16. Cavage, M., Sporny, M.: IETF draft. Signing HTTP messages (2015)
17. Hammer-Lahav, E.: RFC 5849. The OAuth 1.0 protocol (2010)
18. Chen, E., Pei, Y., Chen, S., Tian, Y., Kotcher, R., Tague, P.: OAuth demystified for mobile application developers. In: ACM SIGSAC Conference on Computer and Communications Security, pp. 892–903. ACM, New York (2014)
19. Wang, R., Zhou, Y., Chen, S., Qadeer, S., Evans, D., Gurevich, Y.: Explicating SDKs: uncovering assumptions underlying secure authentication and authorization. In: 22nd USENIX Security Symposium, pp. 399–314. Washington, DC (2013)
20. Sun, S.T., Beznosov, K.: The devil is in the (implementation) details: an empirical analysis of OAuth SSO systems. In: ACM Conference on Computer and Communications Security, pp. 378–390. ACM, New York (2012)

21. Sakimura, N., Bradley, J., Jones, M., de Medeiros, B., Mortimore, C.: OpenID Connect Core 1.0 (2014)
22. Wang, R., Chen, S., Wang, X.: Signing me onto your accounts through Facebook and Google: a traffic-guided security study of commercially deployed single-sign-on web services. In: IEEE Symposium on Security and Privacy, pp. 365–379. IEEE Computer Society, Washington, DC (2012)
23. Fielding, R.T., Taylor, R.N.: Principled design of the modern web architecture, pp. 407–416, June 2000
24. Fetzer, C.: Building critical applications using microservices. IEEE Secur. Priv. 14(6), 86–89 (2016)
25. Trustworthy Internet Movement: SSL Pulse (2017). https://www.trustworthy internet.org/ssl-pulse/

Malware and Malicious Events Detection

UnitecDEAMP: Flow Feature Profiling
for Malicious Events Identification
in Darknet Space

Ruibin Zhang[✉], Chi Yang, Shaoning Pang, and Hossein Sarrafzadeh

Decentralized Machine Learning Intelligence Laboratory Department of Computing,
Unitec Institute of Technology, Auckland, New Zealand
{pzhang,cyang2,ppang,hsarrafzadeh}@unitec.ac.nz
http://www.unitec.ac.nz

Abstract. This paper proposes a traffic decomposition approach called
UnitecDEAMP based on flow feature profiling to distinct groups of
significant malicious events from background noise in massive historical darknet traffic. Specifically, we segment and extract traffic flows
from captured darknet data, categorize the flows according to sets of
criteria derived from our traffic behavior assessments. Those criteria
will be validated through the followed correlation analysis to guarantee that any redundant criteria be eliminated. Significant events are
appraised by combined criteria filtering, including significance regarding volume, significance in terms of time series occurrence and significance regarding variation. To demonstrate the effectiveness of our
UnitecDEAMP, real world darknet traffic data sets with twelve months
are used for conducting our empirical study. The experimental results
show that UnitecDEAMP can effectively select the most significant malicious events.

Keywords: Darknet traffic analysis · Cyber threats · Malicious event
detection · Flow feature profiling · Malicious traffic flow identification

1 Introduction

Observing traffic over darknet space (i.e., non-active IP addresses) has become
an increasingly important analyzing technique for detecting malicious activities
on the Internet. Since there are no legitimate hosts existing in darknet space,
any observed traffic could be the backscatter packets of Distributed Denial of
Service (DDoS) attacks that are using spoofed source addresses; Scanning from
worms and another network probing; or misconfiguration [13]. Regarding this
fact, the traffic observed on darknet is invaluable for monitoring and analyzing
cyber threats. Darknet traffic has been extensively used in observing a broad
range of activities which includes denial of service [5,10,13], worms and scanning
[7,13,19], misconfigured network traffic [6], and malware behaviour categorising
[10]. In practice, over 50% of cyber attacks are preceded by some form of network

© Springer Nature Singapore Pte Ltd. 2017
L. Batten et al. (Eds.): ATIS 2017, CCIS 719, pp. 157–168, 2017.
DOI: 10.1007/978-981-10-5421-1_13

scanning activity according to Panjwani et al. [16], and in most of the cases, it is the first stage of an intrusion attempt that enables an adversary to locate, target, or exploit vulnerable systems remotely.

For malicious network activity analysis, cyber security researchers have drawn attention to the utilization of darknet monitoring [13] and data collection. Such collected data will enable researchers to analysis and obtain practical insight into not only the operation of the Internet background but also particular global and local events including worms probing and distributed denial of service (DDoS) attacks. Moreover, the benefit of the darknet is that this allows cyber security researchers to perform analysis among traffic without concerning privacy issues over the captured data [15]. According to the works done by Shannon [18] and Moore [12], data collected from darknet telescope has made an impressive contribution towards worm analysis, especially Code Red; the first worm has been revealed on network telescope.

The fundamental proposition of our work is that by carefully examining the packets transmission and underlying features of the sources sending traffic to the darknet space, we can extract the most up-to-date details of such events for the next stage analysis. We conduct close observations on captured darknet traffic data, which contains the load of malicious activities. We show that it is possible to study the flow features that extracted from flow segmentation of packets data capture, which then allows us to recover a broad range of significant malicious events. Also, we propose that the combination of flow feature measurements is a powerful tool for the detection and classification of network anomalies. The intuition behind this work is that most kinds of malicious threats cause anomaly changes in the measures of addresses or ports observed in darknet traffic.

Please note that this work does not evaluate on the TCP protocol traffic and we have only applied the approach on selected protocols (UDP & ICMP). There are two reasons for this. First, the well-populated TCP traffic contains massive background noise, which will cost us huge computation regarding efficiency and second, since there is no ground truth for our dataset, such massive amount of background noise will interfere the understanding of traffic behavior and judgment. In Sect. 2, we discuss the status of darknet traffic analysis for cybersecurity. Section 3 we describe the proposed flow feature profiling approach for malicious darknet events identification and explains its differences to existing methods. Section 4 presents the experiment setup, results and discussion. In Sect. 5 we will conclude our work and its contribution to the field.

2   Background

Darknet points at a group of network security sensors deployed by cybersecurity researchers for observing events that take place on the internet [12,14]. The purpose of such darknet monitoring is to capture traffics to the unused IP address space of the network. Consider those unallocated IP addresses are not being engaged for active and legitimate services, there should be no traffics destined to those unused IP addresses. Therefore, any incoming traffics observed from the darknet space are suspicious, and can be considered as unsolicited or miscon-figured [8]. Visual representation of network data contributes alot as volume of network data generated and captured keep growing, which makes it increasingly difficult to detect sophisticated network threats, thus Alsaleh, Barrera & Van Oorschot [2] propose a network flow filtering mechanism that take advantage of exposure maps technique to reduce the traffic for the visualization process according to the network services being offered. There is a significant decrease in the volume of traffic according to their experiment, which results in visible patterns and insights not previously apparent. Three years later, apart from presenting a lightweight network scan detection algorithm (LQS) that detects scanners in the livenet network, Alsaleh, Barrera & Van Oorschot [3] also propose a novel method to obtain an estimated ground truth in terms of performence evaluation.

The definition of flow is introduced in [4], and it is essential in the passive network traffic measurement and analysis filed. In [9], Kim et al. use flow-based network traffic analysis technique to detect abnormal network traffic activities. They indicate that certain malicious activities are not going to be identified through time series data examination alone, and a flow-based anomaly network traffic detection method has been proposed and validated. Salem, Vaton and Gravey [17] propose a new flow-based approach for high-speed network traffic anomaly detection and classification. In their approach, they start with the data reduction phase through flow sampling by filtering the short-lived flows only, then perform random aggregation of some descriptors such as some packets per flow in two different data structures. After that, the sketch cell values are continuously monitored through a sequential change-point detection algorithm, and finally, any significant change in cell values will raise the alarm for the anomaly.

In signature-based approach, a general to a specific framework is proposed by Agarwal and Joshi, and in their model, the classifier learns from widely various class distributions in the dataset [1]. They trained their system with KDD Cups databased, and four groups of attacks were classified: Denial of Service (DoS): deny legitimate access and request to the server; Probing: information gathering; User to Root: unauthorized access to root and Remote to Local: unauthorized access from the remote server to local. Overall, while the traditional signature-based technique performed well in anomaly detection for darknet space malicious traffic analysis [11,17], it is rigid and not feasible to develop a comprehensive signature database for maximum coverage of malicious activity. Especially in practice, there are new variations of malicious activity unveil every day, which means theoretically, the size of the signature database will be infinite to cover every possible threat. Also, those zero-day malicious activities will still potential to cause great harm when it is not recorded.

3   The Proposed UnitecDEAMP

The Profiling module is part of our Unitec Darknet Event Analytic Model (UnitecDEAMP). Further to our previous study, the objective of this work, which is to identify the most significant malicious events from background noise for later regional analysis. As mentioned earlier in [20], the existing time series based anomaly detection techniques not satisfy our requirement, as they only cover the temporal feature of any suspicious activities from the presence of abnormal peaks in the time series data. To obtain additional knowledge for the better understanding of events' behavior, we now have to consider discovering the causes behind such anomaly and also the varieties of activity on the same host to produce multiple dimensional analysis regarding outcomes. Therefore we segment the traffic data into flows first so that each flow will be considered as an individual activity. Once the flow segmentation completes, we will end up with tons of malicious activities. Due to the nature of darknet, we should only consider the most significants to be the candidates for our investigation, and all the rest are redundant to our design. Also, it is not feasible to develop a comprehensive signature database that covers every piece of malicious activity. Thus we propose to introduce sets of criteria that summarized from our traffic behavior observation, utilize such combination of criteria to distinct the events. Such criteria including strength (significance regarding volume), frequency (significance in terms of time series occurrence) and degree of transmission order (significance regarding variation). In the end, correlation measurement is taking place to eliminate any redundant criteria, also unveil the intra-event connections embedded while providing sufficient illustration for the user to validate through visual analytics.

3.1   Flow Segmentation

To achieve a better understanding and interpretation of the event behavior, we pay very special attention to those captured event data that being transmitted pre, during and post the event. Given darknet data $\mathbf{X} = \{\mathbf{x}(1), \mathbf{x}(2), \ldots, \mathbf{x}(t), \ldots, \mathbf{x}(T)\}$ in L emission events, where $\mathbf{x(t)} = \{a_1(t), a_2(t), \ldots, a_M(t)\}$ denotes one network packet consists of M attributes, and T represents elapsed time. A single point is no sense for event detection, but a time series could be very long, sometimes containing millions of packets. For host behavior analyzing, it is desirable to apply a sliding window w to $\mathbf{X}$ and produce an observation of darknet traffic as a sequence of shorter time series. The observed variable can be any packet attribute a_i, or its statistical representation. In our case, we simply use the number of packets, the number of source IPs, the number of destination IPs, and the number of the (source and destination) IP combinations.

We conduct first flow segmentation using Maximum Packets Interval (MPI). Given a sequence of packets $x(1), x(2), \ldots, x(t)$ from the same host and the time stamp $ts(1), ts(2), \ldots, ts(t)$ for each packet, a new flow starts at a packet $x(i)$ that has a delay to its previous packet $Dly(i) = ts(i) - ts(i-1)$ greater than a predefined MPI. In other words, the delay between two sequential packets is smaller than MPI and that between two flows are greater than MPI. Figure 1 gives an example of flow segmentation. As seen, packets transmitted from two source hosts are plotted as two streams, and each stream represents a source

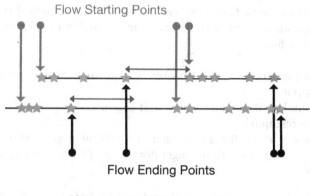

Fig. 1. Example of flow segmentation

host. Flow A is extracted from the first stream, in which the flow starts at the 1*st* packet and ends at the 4*th*. The 5*th* packet has a delay greater than MPI. Thus a new flow (i.e., flow B) creates. The same regulation applies to the other stream for flow segmentation.

We consider each flow as an activity, and apparently, such flow segmentation helps distinguish the events on the same host. For MPI, we calculate the cumulative distribution of packet delay over traffic data in the previous work [20], and observed that over 80% samples' packet delay is less than 10 s. Therefore, we adopt MPI as 15 s to ensure that our flow segmentation satisfies (1) small packet delay with good sample coverage; and (2) each flow covers the whole period of an event.

3.2   Flow Feature Profiling

At the completion of the above segmentation, we also have extracted the following eight flow features for conducting the profiling: number of packets ($nPkt$), number of destination IP addresses ($nDstIP$), number of destination port ($nDstPort$), average packets per second ($PktSec$), number of packets per destination IP ($nPktDstIP$), number of source port ($nSrcPort$), time length (TL) and number of packets per destination port ($nPktDstPort$)

Criteria for identifying events that are commonly understood (i.e. frequency, strength), the threshold will be adjusted later during the experiment stage:

– Frequency:
  • Type I: an event that has been energetic for a short period, but contributes a huge amount of traffic. i.e. a huge number of packets with only a few flows.

- Type II: an event that has been active for a long period to contribute an enormous amount of traffic. i.e. a huge number of packets plus a huge number of flows.
- Strength:
  - Packets per second: a lot of packets sent in short period generating huge throughput.
  - Total number of packets: a host that produces a lot of packets with constant throughput.
  - Flow power ratio: flows that share same/similar peak throughput provides weaker impacts from longer flow length (Peak Throughput per Flow Length).

Various flow features are selected and deployed to perform the feature profiling to distinguish the most significant malicious events from the background noise. The selection of flow features for each event categories is conducted through the traffic behavior observation. Once the candidate features are well defined, a threshold will be applied for the filtering process. The threshold for each flow features will be different, so to solve this problem, a threshold will be initialized at the first place which based on that particular flow feature data. The procedure of flow feature profiling is summarized in Algorithm 1.

Algorithm 1. Flow Feature Profiling

Input: Matrix F contains n flows with m dimensional features, and combination matrix R for various criteria setup. $\{F\}^m = F^m(1), F^m(2), \ldots, F^m(n)$.

Output: Indices $\{I\}_n^p$ for n varieties of malicious activities of protocol p

1: Obtaining
2: Compute significance index S_m^p by Filtering F_m^p by applying z
3: **if** $S_m^p < \alpha$ **or** $S_m^p < \beta$ **then**
4:     **repeat**
5:         *threshold z by $a\%$ increment* **or** *$b\%$ reduction*
6:     **until** fulfilment of S_m^p
7: **else**
8:     $S_m^p \in \{I\}_n^p$
9: **end if**

For the purpose of obtaining a crispy understanding of the nature of malicious activities and associated combination of criteria on various attributes that comprise a Transmission Control Protocol/Internet Protocol (TCP/IP) connection. We observed and analyzed hundreds of malicious activities in our previous work from similar dataset [20]. Looking at the traffic in various anomalous time window at the IP flow level, and trace back to its original packet data are strategies involved with our manual inspection (Fig. 2).

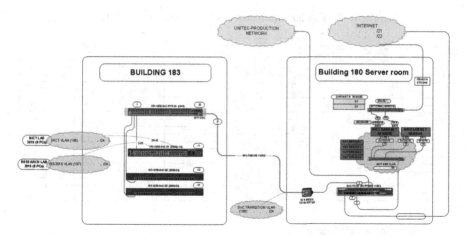

Fig. 2. The network configuration of Unitec darknet monitoring system

4 Experiment

The darknet monitoring system conducts real time monitoring within UNITEC's internal network infrastructure on total 2,014 (as of January 2014) public IP addresses. The dataset we used in this work is a selection of 12 months darknet traffic from 2013 January to December, and it was captured from the darknet monitoring system on a /22 network block, which incorporates 1,024 IP addresses. Table 1 gives the dataset category statistics in terms of network protocols applied. As seen from Table 1, TCP traffic is the leading portion of the whole set of data captured, and SYN packets contributes almost 90 percent of the TCP data. Despite the fact that the domination of TCP traffic could provide us well-population of data, we also need to take consideration of the background noise as it is one of the important characteristics of darknet traffic. Combating redundant data is a common practice to all darknet traffic analyst, and computational cost and interference are also the keys toward the model design. Therefore in our experiments, we adopt ICMP and UDP first to perform the proposed approach to provide the preliminary study efficiently, afterwards, a comprehensive study among the TCP dataset will be carried if the outcome from the preliminary study is positive.

Table 1. Overall breakdown of data in terms of network protocols

Protocol	Number of packets	Weight	Number of flows	TCP flag	Number of packets	Weight	Number of flows
TCP(6)	100,642,347	77.47%	28,808,419	SYN	85,988,605	86.08%	22,972,828
UDP(17)	24,809,348	19.10%	4,603,012	SYN/ACK	12,731,319	12.74%	4,858,380
ICMP(1)	4,458,033	3.43%	1,480,262	ACK/RST	1,183,628	1.18%	769,608

Table 2. Top 20 significant malicious events in ICMP

Events ID	Occurrence	Weight %	Power (Packets)	Signatures						
				nPkt	TL	PktSec	nDstIP	nPktDstIP	nDstPort	nSrcPort
I1	1,071	22.19	989,259	> 850 & < 1,000	> 200 & < 1,100	< 200	> 400 & < 500	< 5	n/a	n/a
I2	45	11.45	510,435	> 1,000 & < 72,975	> 1,100 & < 268,940	< 200	< 5	> 40 & < 72,975	n/a	n/a
I3	1,021	7.89	351,885	> 35 & < 850	> 200 & < 1,100	< 200	> 200 & < 400	< 5	n/a	n/a
I4	296	6.78	302,447	> 1,000 & < 72,975	< 20	> 1,200 & < 335,540	> 500 & < 1,023	< 5	n/a	n/a
I5	83	3.35	149,304	> 1,000 & < 72,975	> 20 & < 90	< 200	> 500 & < 1,023	< 5	n/a	n/a
I6	157	2.72	121,243	> 35 & < 850	> 200 & < 1,100	< 200	> 400 & < 500	< 5	n/a	n/a
I7	43	1.26	56,088	> 1,000 & < 72,975	> 90 & < 200	< 200	> 500 & < 1,023	< 5	n/a	n/a
I8	531	1.02	45,574	> 35 & < 850	> 90 & < 200	< 200	> 200 & < 400	< 5	n/a	n/a
I9	2,403	0.80	35,655	< 15	> 20 & < 90	< 200	< 5	> 5 & < 15	n/a	n/a
I10	2,343	0.79	35,167	> 15 & < 35	> 20 & < 90	< 200	< 5	> 15 & < 20	n/a	n/a
I11	2,333	0.78	34,995	< 15 & < 35	> 20 & < 90	< 200	< 5	> 15 & < 20	n/a	n/a
I12	2,333	0.78	34,995	> 15 & < 35	> 20 & < 90	< 200	< 5	> 15 & < 15	n/a	n/a
I13	23	0.69	30,887	> 1,000 & < 72,975	< 20 & < 90	< 200	> 500 & < 1,023	< 5	n/a	n/a
I14	31	0.69	28,328	> 850 & < 1,000	> 1,100 & < 1,100	< 200	> 400 & < 500	< 5	n/a	n/a
I15	5,105	0.57	25,591	< 15	< 20 & < 90	< 200	< 5	> 5 & < 15	n/a	n/a
I16	18	0.49	21,655	> 1,000 & < 72,975	> 1,100 & < 90	< 200	> 500 & < 1,023	< 5	n/a	n/a
I17	16	0.41	18,325	> 1,000 & < 72,975	> 200 & < 90	< 200	> 500 & < 1,023	< 5	n/a	n/a
I18	116	0.40	17,865	> 35 & < 850	< 20 & < 200	< 200	> 200 & < 400	< 5	n/a	n/a
I19	275	0.38	16,830	> 35 & < 850	> 20 & < 200	< 200	> 200 & < 400	< 5	n/a	n/a
I20	12	0.37	16,288	> 1,000 & < 72,975	< 20	> 200 & < 1,200	> 500 & < 1,023	< 5	n/a	n/a

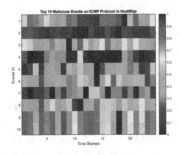

Fig. 3. Top 10 malicious events on ICMP protocol heatmap

Fig. 4. Correlation measurements within Top 10 malicious events on ICMP protocol (threshold 0.5)

4.1 Significant Malicious Events of ICMP

ICMP flood, also known as Ping flood is the most common malicious activity take place on the ICMP protocol. It is a variation of Denial of Service (DOS) attack by overwhelming the target host with the high amount of ICMP echo requests, to cause the degraded performance of the network or take down the service entirely in some instance. Despite the weight of total ICMP traffic less than 4% in the collected data, the practical consequences of such malicious activity is very harmful. By examining the characteristics of ICMP flood, which typically overloads the victim with a giant volume of requests, we summarized with two criteria. A massive amount of packets transmitted and high speed of packets transmission and the flow features associated with those criteria are $PktSec$, $nPktDstIP$, $nDstIP$, $nPkt$, TL. Table 2 gives the details of flow feature criteria for the top 20 events (Fig. 3).

In Fig. 3, we conduct an hourly behavior analysis over 24 h period, and present in the heat map format. As shown in the colormap beside, warmer color indicates the energic activity, and on the other hand, cooler color shows the inertia. We include all the traffic transmitted within the top ten events regarding strength;

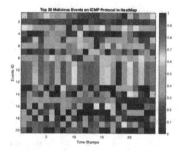
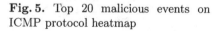

Fig. 5. Top 20 malicious events on ICMP protocol heatmap

Fig. 6. Correlation measurements within top 20 malicious events on ICMP protocol (threshold 0.5)

each block is representing the energy of specific event flow traffic during that hour. Thus we would obtain the multi-dimensional knowledge from both inter-event and intra-event analysis. The visualization of heat map positively provides us the better view and understanding of events along the time stamp. The heat map also outlines the previous mentioned two types of events. Type I events being very active and contribute a huge amount of packets during a short period (i.e. event ID 1, 2, 9 and 10), and Type II events provide a lot of packets with longer time duration, but less throughput (i.e. event ID 4, 5 and 7). This figure also shows that balanced distributions (sparsely distributed) are frequent in the traffic patterns. However, to avoid it lead us to the misjudgment (i.e. event ID 1 & 2), we measure the correlation coefficient of the above data and display in the circular graph Fig. 4, where each dot represents the even ID and connections between dots are the result of positive correlation. The circular correlation graph will truly unveil some intra-event connections embedded in the hourly activity heat map from our human eye (i.e. in Fig. 3, the positive correlation between event ID 3 & 8 is barely observable from the visualization) (Fig. 4).

4.2 Significant Malicious Events of UDP

One of well known malicious activity by using User Datagram Protocol (UDP) is UDP flood, and it is still one of the most common DoS attack today, since the UDP protocol is "connectionless" and does not have any type of handshake mechanism or session like TCP does. To saturate the bandwidth link id the main intention of a UDP flood. It works as, a targeted host receives huge number of UDP packets with spoofed source ip address on various ports, and the system checks for applications associated with these datagrams, replies back with a "Destination Unreachable" packet if the search is failed. Table 1 indicates that portion of UDP traffic is not major, but the impact of any successful UDP malicious activity is damaging, as by utilising the bandwidth and large capacity servers, attackers send more and more packets to flood the target host with unwanted traffic in order to make it no longer respond to legitimate services,

Table 3. Top 10 significant malicious events in UDP

Events ID	Occurrence	Weight %	Power (Packets)	Signatures					
				nPkt	PktSec	nDstIP	nPktDstIP	nDstPort	nSrcPort
U1	2,808	11.69	2,901,117	> 0 & < 170	< 1000	> 1.5 & < 3	> 30 & < 80	> 7 & < 20	> 29 & < 45
U2	203	10.53	2,613,471	> 0 & < 170	< 1000	> 1.5 & < 3	> 30 & < 80	> 7 & < 20	> 4 & < 7
U3	930	3.18	788,758	> 0 & < 170	< 1000	> 1.5 & < 3	> 10 & < 30	> 20 & < 396	> 15 & < 29
U4	28	2.92	724,860	> 0 & < 170	< 1000	> 1.5 & < 3	> 80 & < 160	> 0 & < 2	> 29 & < 45
U5	529	2.21	548,320	> 0 & < 170	< 1000	> 1.5 & < 3	> 80 & < 160	> 7 & < 20	> 29 & < 45
U6	15	1.98	491,328	> 0 & < 170	< 1000	> 1.5 & < 3	> 80 & < 160	> 2 & < 7	> 0 & < 4
U7	6	1.13	279,595	> 0 & < 170	< 1000	> 1.5 & < 3	> 80 & < 160	> 0 & < 2	> 45 & < 60463
U8	2256	1.08	269,123	> 0 & < 170	< 1000	> 0 & < 1.5	> 10 & < 30	> 2 & < 7	> 15 & < 29
U9	354	1.02	252,475	> 0 & < 170	< 1000	> 1.5 & < 3	> 30 & < 80	> 2 & < 7	> 4 & < 7
U10	85	0.93	230,222	> 0 & < 170	< 1000	> 1.5 & < 3	> 30 & < 80	> 20 & < 396	> 15 & < 29

Fig. 7. Top 50 malicious events on UDP protocol heatmap

Fig. 8. Correlation measurements within top 50 malicious events on UDP protocol (threshold 0.85)

including but not limited to DNS, SNMP, and DHCP. In the UDP flooding, the volume of packets transmitted is massive, this could also resulting in multiple source ports deployment, the duration of such activity is solely strategy dependent, and the target is clear. In the UDP port scanning, not only the volume of traffic is high, but also the number of destination ports involved with packets transmission. As shown in Table 3, by considering the above summaries, the flow features we make use of constructing the criteria for UDP malicious activities are $PktSec$, $nPktDstIP$, $nDstIP$, $nPkt$, $nDPort$, $nSrcPort$, and details of criteria indicate the diversity of flow feature profiling in this protocol (Fig. 8).

For UDP protocol, same as ICMP, we also generate the hourly activity heat map of packets that associated with the top 50 active events, and the same color map has been used. In Figs. 7 and 9, we could notice that, unlike ICMP, sparse distributions are less shown in the traffic patterns. This is due to the malicious activities such as UDP flood, and UDP port scan is often performed on the condition of either high volume of packets with small ranges of destination IP (due to multiple destination ports) or great packets transmission throughput (Fig. 10).

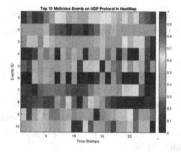

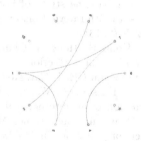

Fig. 9. Top 10 malicious events on UDP protocol heatmap

Fig. 10. Correlation measurements within top 10 malicious events on UDP protocol (threshold 0.85)

5   Conclusion

This work has made several contributions to deal with malicious events in darknet space for threats analytics. Firstly, in the UnitecDEAMP module, based on our previous work on event classification, we carried out traffic decomposition approach with the addition of proposed flow feature profiling for distinguishing groups of significant malicious events from massive historical darknet traffic data for further regional impact studies. At the same time, the background noise was also taken into consideration. To evaluate our approach, we have selected two IPv4 protocol datasets (UDP & ICMP). Then, we should integrated correlation analysis to guarantee that any redundant criteria be eliminated. The experiment results showed that our module can effectively select the most significant malicious events, and successfully unveil the embedded intra-event connections.

References

1. Agarwal, R., Joshi, M.V.: PNrule: a new framework for learning classifier models in data mining (a case-study in network intrusion detection). In: SIAM (2000)
2. Alsaleh, M., Barrera, D., van Oorschot, P.C.: Improving security visualization with exposure map filtering. In: Computer Security Applications Conference, ACSAC 2008, Annual, pp. 205–214. IEEE (2008)
3. Alsaleh, M., van Oorschot, P.C.: Network scan detection with LQS: a lightweight, quick and stateful algorithm. In: Proceedings of the 6th ACM Symposium on Information, Computer and Communications Security, pp. 102–113. ACM (2011)
4. Claffy, K.C., Braun, H.W., Polyzos, G.C.: A parameterizable methodology for internet traffic flow profiling. IEEE J. Sel. Areas Commun. **13**(8), 1481–1494 (1995)
5. Cooke, E., Jahanian, F., McPherson, D.: The zombie roundup: Understanding, detecting, and disrupting botnets. SRUTI **5**, 6 (2005)
6. Francois, J., Festor, O., et al.: Tracking global wide configuration errors. In: IEEE/IST Workshop on Monitoring, Attack Detection and Mitigation (2006)
7. Harder, U., Johnson, M.W., Bradley, J.T., Knottenbelt, W.J.: Observing internet worm and virus attacks with a small network telescope. Electron. Notes Theor. Comput. Sci. **151**(3), 47–59 (2006)

8. Irwin, B.: A baseline study of potentially malicious activity across five network telescopes. In: 5th International Conference on Cyber Conflict (CyCon), 2013, pp. 1–17. IEEE (2013)
9. Kim, M., Kong, H., Hong, S., Chung, S., Hong, J.: A flow-based method for abnormal network traffic detection. In: IEEE/IFIP Network Operations and Management Symposium (IEEE Cat. No.04CH37507), vol. 1 (2004)
10. Kumar, A., Paxson, V., Weaver, N.: Exploiting underlying structure for detailed reconstruction of an internet-scale event. In: Proceedings of the 5th ACM SIG-COMM Conference on Internet Measurement - IMC 2005, p. 1 (2005). http://portal.acm.org/citation.cfm?doid=1330107.1330150
11. Lakhina, A., Crovella, M., Diot, C.: Mining anomalies using traffic feature distributions. In: ACM SIGCOMM Computer Communication Review, vol. 35, pp. 217–228. ACM (2005)
12. Moore, D.: Network telescopes: observing small or distant security events. In: Proceedings of the 11th USENIX Security Symposium, pp. 167–174 (2002)
13. Moore, D., Shannon, C., Brown, D.J., Voelker, G.M., Savage, S.: Inferring Internet denial-of-service activity. ACM Trans. Comput. Syst. **24**, 115–139 (2006)
14. Moore, D., Shannon, C., Voelker, G.M., Savage, S.: Network telescopes: Technical report. Department of Computer Science and Engineering, University of California, San Diego (2004)
15. Pang, R., Yegneswaran, V., Barford, P., Paxson, V., Peterson, L.: Characteristics of internet background radiation. In: Proceedings of the 4th ACM SIGCOMM Conference on Internet Measurement, pp. 27–40. ACM (2004)
16. Panjwani, S., Tan, S., Jarrin, K.M., Cukier, M.: An experimental evaluation to determine if port scans are precursors to an attack. In: Proceedings of the International Conference on Dependable Systems and Networks, pp. 602–611 (2005)
17. Salem, O., Vaton, S., Gravey, A.: A scalable, efficient and informative approach for anomaly-based intrusion detection systems: theory and practice. Int. J. Network Manage. **20**(5), 271–293 (2010)
18. Shannon, C., Moore, D.: The spread of the Witty worm (2004)
19. Staniford, S., Moore, D., Paxson, V., Weaver, N.: The top speed of flash worms. In: Proceedings of the 2004 ACM Workshop on Rapid Malcode, pp. 33–42. ACM (2004)
20. Zhang, R., Zhu, L., Li, X., Pang, S., Sarrafzadeh, A., Komosny, D.: Behavior based darknet traffic decomposition for malicious events identification. In: Arik, S., Huang, T., Lai, W.K., Liu, Q. (eds.) ICONIP 2015. LNCS, vol. 9491, pp. 251–260. Springer, Cham (2015). doi:10.1007/978-3-319-26555-1_29

A Hybrid Approach for Malware Family Classification

Naqqash Aman[1(✉)], Yasir Saleem[1], Fahim H. Abbasi[2], and Farrukh Shahzad[2]

[1] University of Engineering and Technology, Lahore, Pakistan
naqqash.aman90@gmail.com, yasir@uet.edu.pk
[2] Lahore, Pakistan
f.abbasi@massey.ac.nz, farrukhshahzad0@yahoo.com

Abstract. One of the top most cyber security threats – in today's world – are malware applications. Traditional signature and static analysis based malware defenses are prune to obfuscation and polymorphism, so they fail to detect and classify malware variants and zero-day attacks, due to the exponential growth and ever increasing complexity of malware. Behavior-based malware detection provides better insight into malware execution behavior and hence can be used for family classification. This paper proposes a novel framework that can correctly classify known and in the wild malware samples into their families and can identify novel malware samples for analysis. Malware analysis environment is setup using an enhanced and scalable version of Cuckoo sandbox to generate behavior reports. These reports are used to extract a novel combination of features, used to train a machine learning classifier i.e., random forest to achieve a high predictive performance. The developed system can help in filtering novel (i.e., zero-day) malwares and can also help in dealing with the limitation of static analysis while classifying malware into their families.

Keywords: Malware · Family classification · Cuckoo sandbox · Dynamic analysis · Naive Bayes · J48 · Random forests · API call · Machine learning

1 Introduction

Internet surfing, using social media and information sharing is not as safe as it used to be. With the increased Internet usage, states, companies and private users have to secure themselves in order to protect sensitive information. Cyber-criminals employ malware to attack their targets in automated fashion. Malware is growing rapidly, it doubles every year and between years 2012 to 2014 it has actually tripled. As of 2015, 390 k new malware are registered everyday by AV-Test institute [4]. Malware exploit vulnerabilities in software to infect and control their victims. Therefore, security companies are required to detect malicious programs and protect their customers. A lot of human effort is required in

---

F.H. Abbasi and F. Shahzad—Security Researcher

L. Batten et al. (Eds.): ATIS 2017, CCIS 719, pp. 169–180, 2017.
DOI: 10.1007/978-981-10-5421-1_14

analyzing large number of malware samples manually and after malware detection an additional effort is required to classify malware into families depending upon their behavior and code similarities. Traditional static analysis based techniques are prune to sophisticated obfuscation, poly & metamorphic variations and encryption techniques; that make malware unidentifiable for security analysts. Therefore, researchers are now focusing on dynamic analysis of malware as compared to static analysis. Dynamic analysis techniques relies on logging malware behavior by executing it in a virtual sandbox environment and thus requires less human effort. Malware can be classified into families and types using machine learning. In this study we have made an effort to develop a framework which can be used as a filtering application to separate new malware samples from the already known malware families in order to provide fast and efficient coverage for new attacks. The known malware samples are than classified into their family based classes.

Major Contributions: We have made the following key contributions in this research:

- Developed a malware labeling mechanism which uses labels and information available from all AV vendors and assign label to malware samples based on a majority vote performed amongst AVs.
- In addition to API calls being used as features. Key family behaviors are extracted from arguments of the API calls. Regular expressions are used to identify distinct behavior patterns which cannot be represented using hard coded values for each malware family and these identified patterns are used as features.
- Developed a framework using machine learning techniques to classify known malware into their respective families and filter novel malware for detailed analysis.

The remaining paper is organized as follows. Section 2 provides an overview of related work, Sect. 3 covers the data set and method used for data collection. Section 4 covers methodology used for malware classification, In Sect. 5 we discuss results and evaluate performance and finally in Sect. 6 we conclude the paper.

2   Related Work

Various machine learning approaches have been used to detect and classify samples into their types and families to filter out malware for detailed analysis that show novel behavior. The literature related to these approaches is discussed in this section. In [10] they have used Honey clients and Amun to collect malware. Malware behavior is identified by executing it in two virtual platforms CWSandbox [5] and Anubis [3]. The behavior reports are customized using human analysis and are classified into two families Worms and Trojans. The customization using human analysis is not possible for large sample sets and this work don't cover all malware types. In [11] they have classified unpacked malware using edit distances and inverted indexes as features. The drawback of this method is that minor changes to malware result in a major difference in feature set, which reduces classification accuracy. [17] have proposed a multi-task learning system wchich can simultaneously separate malware from benign samples and also classify the malware based on its class using deep learning. [8] have used honeypots to collect malware samples. They collected 10000 malware samples belonging to 14 malware families. The sample set is labeled using Avira Anti Virus and executed in CW Sandbox [5] to generate behavior reports, which are used for classification. The limitation of this research is the use of non-uniform sample set for malware families which results in a biased classifier and in some cases they have very low number of samples for a family. For example only 4 samples are used to build beahvior profile of Worm.korgo. In [7] authors have proposed a solution to reduce noise and unnecessary text data from behavior reports by representing malware behavior using a special representation named Malware Instruction set (MIST). Each system call and its arguments are denoted using numeric identifiers which in turn reduces the run time of analysis algorithm. [18] used API names and their input arguments as features and built a binary classifier for the separation of malicious and clean files. They used a sample set of 826 malware and 385 clean files. Malware behavior is defined as non-transient state changes in [9] and hierarchical clustering algorithms are applied to identify malware classes. In [13] they have used Cuckoo sandbox [6] to generate behavior reports of around 42000 samples. Sequence and frequency representation of API calls are used as features. Random forest with 160 trees is used to build a classifier that is able to classify malware based on four types (Trojan, PUP, Adware and Rootkit) with an AUC value of 0.98 and F-measure of 0.898.

There are several weaknesses in the related work i.e., The use of smaller data sets for classifier building and very little contribution towards improving the labeling mechanism of malware samples as researchers tend to rely on a single AV vendor for labeling the data set. Our technique is different because: (a) We use a significantly large enough data set considering the total number samples available for each of these families on VirusTotal. (A minimum of 2000 samples for each family). (b) We have carefully selected high confidence features which commonly appear among malware families by ensuring selected features are based on activities performed by malware in the VM are not based on activities of other processes running in the VM. (c) Our technique has shown successful classification with 9 different malware families.

3   Dataset

In order to build an effective framework to accurately classify malware into their respective families it is essential to use a data set consisting of malware families which are active in the cyber-attacks and therefore, can be used to classify malware received by AV vendors every day. Due to the lack of standard data sets for malware classification, it is opted to collect our own sample set using VirusTotal [15]. During the first two quarters of 2016 malware binaries were collected on weekly basis. On average 0.5 million new binary samples are submitted on VirusTotal for analysis daily but a limited number of samples and their results can be retrieved using VirusTotal API. Malware samples were collected weekly for a period of 6 months, which we believe is a reasonable time to collect malware data set that represent the trend of cyber-attacks and the malware families which are most active in these attacks. From the collected sample set malware families with most number of samples are shown in Fig. 1.

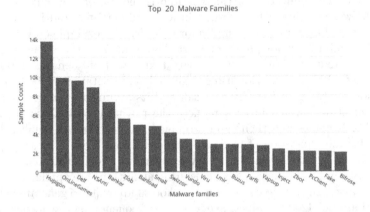

Fig. 1. Distribution of malware families

The graph has been cut off to show top 20 malware families. All those malware families having more than 2000 samples are considered for the classification framework. These families are than analyzed for the final selection. It is decided to use malware families having many variants as such families use obfuscation and polymorphism due to which they evade static analysis and as a result researchers have to repeatedly analyze them. Some malware families are analyzed and it is observed that they detect and evade virtual execution environment showing very little or no activity. One such case is Hupigon family, samples of this family detect VM environment and show no activity. Some of its variants are also able to crash the execution environment. Based on the matrices described above a data set of 32475 malware samples consisting of nine malware families is selected.

4   Methodology

We utilize a novel mechanism for malware family classification. This section describes the methodology used and will cover the four important parts, namely: data collection and report generation, label and feature extraction, feature representation, feature selection and classification.

4.1   Data Collection and Report Generation

Behavior reports of malware samples are obtained by using a secure and distributed setup for malware analysis based on Cuckoo sandbox [6]. The enhanced version has 11 new API hooked using HOOK_JMP_DIRECT technique. The implementation of hooking using HOOK_JMP_DIRECT is discussed in [12]. New API hooks are added because they are used by malware frequently and are helpful in generating a more clear behavioral profile of a malware. Table 1 shows the list of additional APIs hooked and the count of behavior reports in which these API calls are reported. The distributed virtual environment consists of 30 VMs and a controller which is responsible for the distribution of analysis and collection of reports. It is important to simulate real execution environment, therefore, Microsoft windows 7 without any service pack is installed in VMs along with exploitable and vulnerable version of some commonly used software [16]. Additionally scripts to emulate web activity and user interaction are also running in VMs. To ensure secure analysis environment malware samples are not provided Internet connectivity instead INetSim [14] is used to emulate Internet services. Malware samples are analyzed for 240 s and behavior reports are collected by controller in JSON format.

Table 1. Hooked APIs and number of reports in which API is reported

API	Number of reports
CreateWindow[ExA/ExW]	11486
ExitProcess	24473
ExitThread	8995
GetDiskFreeSpace[A/ExA]	12937
GetFileVersionInfoSizeW	2595
GetFileVersionInfoW	2375
NtCreateEvent	1600
NtOpenEvent	1581
NtResumeProcess	0
SetWindowLong[A/PtrA/PtrW/W]	7436
WaitForDebugEvent	813

4.2   Label Assignment and Feature Extraction

Malware family labels are extracted using VirusTotal [15]. Labels are extracted by using information available from all AVs rather than using label from any one of them due to problems of completeness, consistency, correctness and coverage raised by [1,2]. Signed binaries and other potential non malicious samples are filtered using Yara rules which are written after performing basic static analysis. In this research a labeling framework is developed by stripping malware type

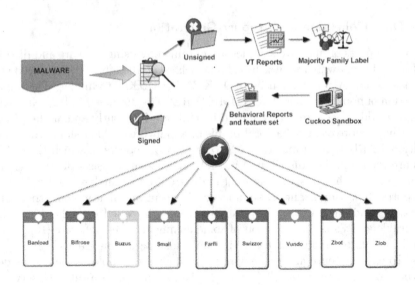

Fig. 2. Process flow diagram of framework

and other generic information from the labels assigned by AVs, remaining information is tokenized and label is selected based on a majority vote amongst the AV vendors. Features for malware classification are based on file, registry, network, process and system API calls that are invoked during the execution of the samples. In addition to API calls, signature based features are also used which denotes the unique behavior of the malware family. Signature based features are extracted from the arguments of API calls. The overall system is shown in the flow diagram in Fig. 2.

4.3 Feature Representation

API calls from file, registry, network, process and system activities observed during the execution of malware data set are used as primary features, whereas signatures based features which serve as complementary information for malware classification are extracted from arguments of the API calls. In total 287 features are used out of which 269 are primary and 18 are used as secondary features. Features are stored in a matrix where each column represents a fixed order of feature and each row represents a unique sample. For **Primary features**, API calls invoked during the execution of each malware sample are recorded. Based on the presence of API call in behavior report the corresponding entry in the feature matrix is set to '1' if feature is present and to '0' otherwise.

For **Secondary features**, binary representation is used to indicate if signature is present in API arguments or not. A total of 18 signature based features are used for the 9 malware families. These signatures are extracted by analyzing malware family reports and identifying unique activities that defines the key and trademark behavior of that particular malware family and hence can serve as

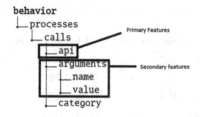

Fig. 3. Structure of JSON Behavior report

powerful features. For each malware family one static and one dynamic signature was identified. Figure 3 shows the structure outline of the behavior report section from the JSON report.

Static Signatures: Looks for a hard coded string or directory path or any other indicator in the arguments of API calls. We have analyzed and compared the behavioral reports of malware families and it is ensured that only those features are selected as signature features which represent the distinct behavior and are key indicators of a malware family.

Dynamic Signatures: By using regular expressions a more powerful set of signatures features can be generated. While analyzing behavior reports it was observed that malware families in addition to using hard coded names for activities performed (file, registry etc.) on target machine use pattern based names which are harder to identify and detect. E.g. Bifrose malware family samples create a mutex which starts with Bif followed by few decimal numbers. Decimal numbers are not fixed and may vary (Bif123, Bif1234, Bif345 etc.), therefore, a regular expression based signature is required to log this pattern based behavior. The regular expression 'Bif+' will provide coverage for mutex name variation in case of Bifrose family.

4.4   Feature Selection

The purpose of feature selection is to primarily avoid over fitting of the classification model. API calls that are pivotal in defining behavior of malware family are used as features, still feature set might have some irrelevant and redundant information. It is decided to use filters for feature selection as they are independent of classification algorithm as compared to wrappers and embedded methods which are not. Feature selection is performed using Information Entropy, which uses information gain ratio (IGR) as an important measure to rank a feature. Tests are executed with all (287), 200 and 100 features using both IG and IGR in conjunction with Ranker. Random Forest with 100 trees is used as classifier. The results of these tests are shown in Table 2.

It can be seen that best results both in case of IG and IGR are achieved when all (287) features are used for classification. It can be concluded from the

Table 2. Feature selection tests results (Weighted average)

FS Algorithm	Feature count	AUC	Precision	F-measure
IG + Ranker	287	0.99	0.928	0.927
IG + Ranker	200	0.97	0.84	0.83
IG + Ranker	100	0.95	0.82	0.81
IGR + Ranker	287	0.99	0.93	0.927
IGR + Ranker	200	0.974	0.85	0.84
IGR + Ranker	100	0.963	0.849	0.83

table that all features used in this study provide unique information and there is no redundancy or noise in the extracted features.

5   Results

From the data set, families with relatively uniform and large data set are selected. Based on this criteria 32475 samples from nine malware families are selected. The dataset is then split into a training set and test set, in such a way that both sets have coverage from all classes. 67% of the sample set is used for training and the remaining 33% is testing.

5.1   Model Selection and Training Set Evaluation

It is very important to analyze the feature set and machine learning algorithms in order to select a machine learning algorithm which is most suitable for malware classification problem. We are using API calls as features, The API calls are invoked in a sequential manner during the execution of a program and are dependent upon the each other. Therefore, it is essential to select machine learning algorithm which don't consider features separately and independently and can identify the relation between them. It is also important to consider the size of data set and select a machine learning algorithm which is low bias/high variance as they have a low asymptotic error and high bias algorithms are not powerful enough to provide accurate models.

Based on our analysis of feature set and machine learning algorithms it is decided to use J48 a decision tree algorithm, as decision tree classifiers are able to handle feature interactions and they are non-parametric due to which they can handle outliers. The only problem with decision tree classifiers is that they can sometimes over fit, this problem can be resolved using ensemble methods and therefore, Random forest is also selected to be used as classifier in the training phase. In order to support our study and to justify the decision of not using classifiers which consider each feature independently and are high bias/low variance, it is decided to use Naive Bayes classifier as well in the training phase in order to see if poor performance is observed.

In order to select the best model we shall rely on the classifier that yields the most correct results. Hence a simple 10-fold cross validation is used for evaluating the training set using three machine learning classifiers namely: J48, Naive Bayes and Random Forest. The weighted average results of 10-fold cross validation of each of these classifiers for the training phase are presented in Table 3.

Table 3. Training Results for the selected classifiers (Weighted Average).

Classification algorithm	TP rate	FP rate	Precision	F-measure	AUC
Naive Bayes	0.732	0.037	0.741	0.724	0.917
J48	0.908	0.012	0.911	0.908	0.97
Random Forest	0.927	0.009	0.93	0.927	0.99

From table it can be seen that Random forest is showing best results. J48 also has shown promising results with good classification accuracy and a very low FPR. Naive Bayes as expected has not performed well as it considers all features individually and independent of each other. Based on the 10-fold cross validation results on the training data it is decided to use Random Forest for classifying malware in the testing phase as it provides highest TP rate and Lowest FP rate amongst the classifiers used.

5.2   Test Set Evaluation

Random Forest was able to classify 93.0235% of the samples correctly with mean absolute error of 0.0292 and root mean square error of 0.1133. The classifier has a very low number of FPs and FNs, as it is indicated from high values of precision (0.933) and TP-rate (0.93). The classification results of the testing phase are described and evaluated using the following metrics: TP rate, FP rate, Precision, F-measure and Area under the curve. All these metrics are presented in the form of Table 4, these results are be followed by an overall summary in the form confusion matrix shown in Fig. 4.

If we look at the results presented in table for nine classes, it can be seen that the classifier has best results for "Swizzor" and "Vundo". This is due to the fact that these malware families have less number of variants as compared to other classes and most of the samples show distinct behavior represented by signature based features. "Small" on the other hand shows less promising results for TPR, FPR and F-measure as compared to other families. The predictions made by the framework for individual classes can be seen in the confusion matrix and are discussed in the next section.

5.3   Discussion and Analysis of Results

In this section we will try to analyze and asses the results and performance of proposed approach for malware classification. We will discuss if the results for

Table 4. Testing results for random forest using representation 2

Class	TP rate	FP rate	Precision	F-measure	AUC
Banload	0.93	0.007	0.962	0.946	0.99
Bifose	0.833	0.01	0.846	0.84	0.98
Buzus	0.887	0.01	0.891	0.889	0.98
Farfli	0.993	0.023	0.805	0.889	0.98
Small	0.862	0.023	0.866	0.864	0.98
Swizzor	0.993	0	0.999	0.996	0.99
Vundo	0.991	0	1	0.996	1
Zbot	0.92	0.001	0.985	0.951	0.99
Zlob	0.934	0.005	0.974	0.953	0.99
Weighted Avg.	0.93	0.009	0.933	0.931	0.99

a given malware class are useful enough to be used in the future system and opportunities that present themselves for future research.

Some of the "Banload" samples are classified as bifrose, buzus and small and vice versa. Banload is a family of Trojans used to download other malwares mostly responsible for stealing banking credentials. Buzus is also an information stealing family and bifrose is a combination of backdoor and trojan allowing remote access to the attacker which is also used for information stealing in most cases. This shows that banload has functional similarities with bifrose and buzus.

"Small" is another family which is showing some considerable number of FPs and FNs for all classes except for vundo and swizzor. This is due to the fact that small is a very generic malware family having a great number of variants. They are mainly used to download and execute malicious code and files on the affected computer, however its variants can be virtually use for any purpose. The result of generic behavior of small malware family is that it has less discriminative features and its functionality overlaps with that of other malware classes.

"Swizzor" and "Vundo" have shown best results in classification because they have some distinct functionality which as a result provide us with discriminative features. Swizzor are trojans which mostly inject code into web browser in order to display adware or sometimes to download additional threats and vundo is a multi-type family that is used to display irrelevant pop-up ads. They are mostly installed without user consent as helper object for browser.

A few number of instances from each malware family are classified as "Farfli". These FPs are observed because the activities of this family are limited, it drops a few files on infected machine and sometimes modifies start page of browser. It has capabilities to contact a remote attacker and wait for instructions. Samples from other malware families that contain limited number of events in the behavior report due to evasion, launching and arguments issues, communication errors between controller and guest VMs and incomplete analysis due to any other reason are classified as "Farfli".

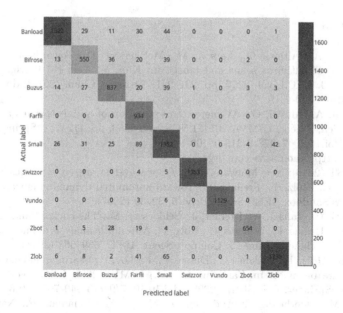

Fig. 4. Confusion matrix: Results of the testing phase

Overall the results of family classification are encouraging with very small number of miss predictions. In this study an effort is made to collect a large sample set but in order to enhance this system we intend to include more malware families and a larger sample set for new as well as existing malware families will be required.

6   Conclusion

This study proposes a malware family classification system based on malware behavior. High frequency malware samples comprising of 9 distinct classes are collected from VT and submitted to an enhanced version of Cuckoo sandbox to generate behavior reports. A novel labeling mechanism is employed to cope with AV's naming and coverage inconsistencies. Once labeled, novel features were studied and extracted into a multi-dimensional vector space, which include API calls, static and regular expression based signature features from APIs input arguments. 269 API calls based, 9 static and 9 regular expressions based features were used. The features set was represented in WEKA compatible format and submitted to three different machine learning classifiers namely: J48, Random Forest and Naive Bayes. In order to evaluate the training set we applied a 10 fold cross validation test which revealed that random forest performs the best classification compared to others. Random forest classifier with 100 trees was then used on test data set and it provided excellent results with a steep ROC, and an area under the curve of 0.9914. Precision, recall and F-measure of classifier are 0.933, 0.93 and 0.931 respectively.

References

1. Mohaisen, A., Alrawi, O., Larson, M., McPherson, D.: Towards a methodical evaluation of antivirus scans and labels. In: Kim, Y., Lee, H., Perrig, A. (eds.) WISA 2013. LNCS, vol. 8267, pp. 231–241. Springer, Cham (2014). doi:10.1007/978-3-319-05149-9_15
2. Mohaisen, A., Alrawi, O.: AV-meter: an evaluation of antivirus scans and labels. In: Dietrich, S. (ed.) DIMVA 2014. LNCS, vol. 8550, pp. 112–131. Springer, Cham (2014). doi:10.1007/978-3-319-08509-8_7
3. Anubis. http://anubis.iseclab.org/
4. AV-TEST (2016). New Malware, https://www.av-test.org/en/statistics/malware/
5. Willems, C., Holz, T., Freiling, F.: Toward automated dynamic malware analysis using CWSandbox. IEEE Secur. Priv. **5**, 32–39 (2007)
6. Guarnieri, C., Tanasi, A., Bremer, J., Schloesser, M.: The cuckoo sandbox (2012)
7. Rieck, K., Trinius, P., Willems, C., Holz, T.: Automatic analysis of malware behavior using machine learning. J. Comput. Secur. **19**(4), 639–668 (2011)
8. Rieck, K., Holz, T., Willems, C., Düssel, P., Laskov, P.: Learning and classification of malware behavior. In: Zamboni, D. (ed.) DIMVA 2008. LNCS, vol. 5137, pp. 108–125. Springer, Heidelberg (2008). doi:10.1007/978-3-540-70542-0_6
9. Bailey, M., Oberheide, J., Andersen, J., Mao, Z.M., Jahanian, F., Nazario, J.: Automated classification and analysis of internet malware. In: Kruegel, C., Lippmann, R., Clark, A. (eds.) RAID 2007. LNCS, vol. 4637, pp. 178–197. Springer, Heidelberg (2007). doi:10.1007/978-3-540-74320-0_10
10. Zolkipli, M.F., Jantan, A.: An approach for malware behavior identification and classification. In: 3rd International Conference on Computer Research and Development (ICCRD), pp. 191–194 (2011)
11. Gheorghescu, M.: An automated virus classification system. In: Virus Bulletin Conference, pp. 294–300 (2005)
12. Ferrand, O.: How to detect the cuckoo sandbox and to strengthen it? J. Comput. Virol. Hacking Tech. **11**, 51–58 (2015)
13. Pirscoveanu, R.S., Hansen, S.S., Larsen, T.M., Stevanovic, M., Pedersen, J.M., Czech, A.: Analysis of Malware behavior: type classification using machine learning. In: International Conference on Cyber Situational Awareness, Data Analytics and Assessment (CyberSA), pp. 1–7 (2015)
14. Hungenberg, T., Eckert, M.: INetSim: internet services simulation suite (2013). http://www.inetsim.org
15. VirusTotal. VT Community. https://www.virustotal.com/
16. Vulnerability & Exploit Database. https://www.rapid7.com/db/
17. Huang, W., Stokes, J.W.: MtNet: a multi-task neural network for dynamic malware classification. In: Caballero, J., Zurutuza, U., Rodríguez, R.J. (eds.) DIMVA 2016. LNCS, vol. 9721, pp. 399–418. Springer, Cham (2016). doi:10.1007/978-3-319-40667-1_20
18. Salehi, Z., Ghiasi, M., Sami, A.: A miner for malware detection based on API function calls and their arguments. In: 16th CSI International Symposium on Artificial Intelligence and Signal Processing (AISP), pp. 563–568 (2012)

Low-Complexity Signature-Based Malware Detection for IoT Devices

Muhamed Fauzi Bin Abbas[✉] and Thambipillai Srikanthan

Nanyang Technological University, Singapore, Singapore
{fauzi,astsrikan}@ntu.edu.sg

Abstract. The ominous threat from malware in critical systems has forced system designers to include detection techniques in their systems to ensure a timely response. However, the widely used signature-based techniques implemented to detect the multitude of potential malware in these systems also leads to a large non-functional overhead. Such methods do not lend well to the extremely resource constrained IoT devices. Hence, in this paper, we propose a low complexity signature-based method for IoT devices that only identifies and stores a subset of signatures to detect a group of malware instead of storing a separate signature for every potential malware, as done in the existing work. Experimental results show that the proposed approach can still achieve 100% detection rate while relying on a very low number of signatures for detection.

1 Introduction

The dramatic rise in the number of hacking attempts, often resulting in catastrophic losses, has made information security a critical concern for not only government agencies and large corporations but also the masses. Recently, with the sheer popularity of IoT devices that are typically ultra resource-constrained embedded systems, the number of malware [1] focusing on IoT has multiplied. The year 2015 saw the biggest jump in the number of malware targeted towards IoT devices [2,3]. [4,5] have shown that there is a rapid increase in the number of embedded malware that impacts every aspect of modern life. This could be attributed to the large number of embedded devices we use in our everyday lives - from smartphones to vehicles, kitchen appliances, and television sets - that all contain embedded systems and software. Hence, the impact of a malware attack can be very critical and potentially life threatening [6,7].

Additionally, malware has become more sophisticated, targeted and stealthier with time [8]. This makes it extremely challenging to detect them in a timely manner and take appropriate actions. Further, the computational effort required to be on a constant lookout and rapidly differentiate malicious application (malware) from non-malicious ones (benign) adds to the overhead in a system. This is especially troublesome for resource constrained embedded systems in general and considerably more so for ultra resource constrained IoT devices.

© Springer Nature Singapore Pte Ltd. 2017
L. Batten et al. (Eds.): ATIS 2017, CCIS 719, pp. 181–189, 2017.
DOI: 10.1007/978-981-10-5421-1_15

Existing techniques of detecting malware are either based on machine learning [9,10] or malware signatures [11,12]. Machine learning based techniques require meticulous selection of features that would best help classify the malware. In addition, machine learning based detector need careful training and long time for tuning [13]. Additionally, machine learning faces false alarms that can quickly erode users trust in the machine-learning-based solutions [14].

Currently, signature-based malware detection techniques are still the most widely used method for detecting malware [15,16]. However, in this method unique signatures need to be generated offline for every malware [17] and stored in the system for online detection. This puts additional pressure on the memory and computational resources of the already resource-constrained IoT devices.

Hence, in this paper we present an enhanced signature-based detection system that identifies and stores common signatures for a group of malware instead of storing unique signatures for every malware. An intelligent mechanism to fall back on the existing approach of generating and storing unique signature per malware is also used as a last resort to ensure close to 100% detection rate. This technique offers multiple advantages over existing solutions including high accuracy, no false alarm generation, and reduced memory resource requirement to store the signatures. These characteristics make our malware detection approach ideal for the ultra resource-constrained IoT devices.

The rest of the paper is organized as follows. Section 2 presents some of the recent and important work in this area. Section 3 discusses our proposed methodology while Sect. 4 presents the results. Section 5 concludes this paper.

2   Related Work

Currently, there are various malware classification techniques based on machine learning using features obtained from static and dynamic analysis of malware [18,19]. Static analysis is the technique to analyse malware without a need for executing it [20]. This is done by examining the malicious code and finding patterns such as strings and import functions etc. The drawback of this approach is that it is unable to detect complex and polymorphic malware. This problem can be solved by performing a dynamic analysis [21] which includes executing it in a controlled environment and monitoring various run-time activities like registry changes, system calls, performance counters etc. Combining both approach would improve the detection and classification of malware.

There are several research works that suggested monitoring the system calls of a program for the purposes of malware detection. Signature-based matching technique is one of the most popular approach for malware detection [15]. This technique has been applied in anti-virus products in the market. Forrest et al. [22] discovered that the short sequences of system calls made by a program during a normal executions are consistent but the sequences changes in an exploited application. Wagener et al. [23] proposed an automated approach to extract malware behavior by observing the system calls in a sandbox environment. Similarities and distances between malware behaviors are computed which allows classifying malware behaviors. The classification process uses phylogenetic tree which has limitation of wrongly classifying a few malware behavior.

In contrast, our approach is faster and computationally less intensive in generating the malware signatures while maintaining a high detection rate of known malware. Unlike existing signature-based approaches, our approach does not monitor specific byte-sequences or string that are unique for every malware. Instead, it strives to find common signatures across a group of malware to save on the computation and storage costs of these malware signatures and therefore is especially useful for extremely resource constrained IoT devices.

3   Proposed Malware Classification System

This section presents the proposed system for extracting a small set of malware signatures that are used to differentiate malware from benign applications. Figure 1 illustrates the design flow of the proposed malware signature extraction technique and its subsequent usage for malware detection. Our method works in two stages where the signatures are first extracted in an offline step and then subsequently used in an online malware detection step.

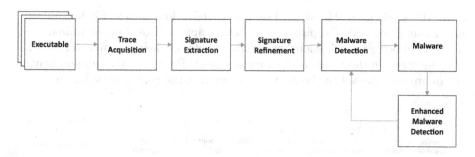

Fig. 1. Overview of the proposed technique

3.1   Offline Signature Extraction

As can be seen in Fig. 1, a system call trace is first obtained from the malware by executing it in a sandbox environment. The traces are then processed and analysed to extract *signatures*, which are essentially unique sequences of system calls that can be used to identify a particular malware executable. The minimal set of signatures are selected that can be used to identify a group of malware. In a similar fashion, signatures from benign executables were also obtained. Finally both the benign and malware signature list are analysed to select relevant signatures that can be used to accurately detect malware while eliminating the false positive. The description of various steps involved in the system is as follows:

Trace Acquisition: The executables are run in a Virtual Machine Linux sandbox environment as explained later in Sect. 4. This sandbox ensures that the system call trace can be obtained in a controlled and isolated environment. The execution step generates the real-time system call traces of the executable. Table 1 shows an excerpt of the system call trace before (Column 1) and after (Column 2) processing. This involves removing both the inputs and outputs.

Table 1. Processing system call trace

Raw trace	Processed trace
brk(NULL) = 0x892e000	brk
access("etc/ld.so.nohwcap",F OK) = −1 ENOENT	access
access("etc/ld.so.preload",R OK) = −1 ENOENT	access
open("etc/ld.so.cache",O RDONLY—O CLOEXEC) = 3	open
fstat64(3, fst mode = S IFREG—0644, st_size = 82832, ...g) = 0	fstat64
mmap2(NULL, 82832, PROT READ, MAP PRIVATE, 3, 0) = 0xf7719000	mmap2
close(3)	close

In this work, as in [24], we used common applications such as Firefox and various Linux commands (ls, pip, etc.) as benign applications. Similar to malware, we also use benign applications' executable to obtain their system call traces by running them on the same sandbox environment. Both the malware and benign traces are then passed to the next step to extract the respective signatures.

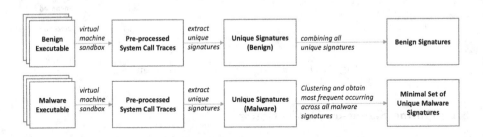

Fig. 2. Signature extraction

Signature Extraction: As shown in Fig. 2, signature is generated by extracting a sequence of 2 to 5 system calls for each system call, till the end of the trace. Here, *we define a signature as a list such sequential system calls.* All duplicate signatures are removed. This signature can be subsequently used to identify a particular executable. This procedure is then repeated for each of the malware and benign traces. Algorithm 1 shows a pseudo code for this procedure.

After obtaining the signatures for all malware, they are sorted based on their occurring frequency across all the malware. This procedure is repeated for benign

Algorithm 1. Extracting Unique Signatures

```
 1  for each Sₙ from 1 to n do
 2  |    add(SL, [Si, Si+1]);
 3  |    add(SL, [Si, Si+1, Si+2]]);
 4  |    add(SL, [Si, Si+1, Si+2, Si+3]);
 5  |    add(SL, [Si, Si+1, Si+2, Si+3, Si+4]);
 6  end
 7  for each i from 1 to i-1 do
 8  |    for each j from i+1 to n do
 9  |    |    if SL(i) == SL(j) then
10  |    |    |    remove(SL, SL[j]);
11  |    |    end
12  |    |    next j;
13  |    end
14  |    next i;
15  end
```

executables. However, rather than sorting the signatures, we chose to compile all the benign signatures in to a master list.

Signature Refinement: Finally, as shown in Fig. 3, the benign signature list and malware minimal set signature list are cross referenced. Any signature from the malware set that is found in the benign list is removed as a potential signature to uniquely identify a malware. This is to eliminate any false positive by ensuring that any signatures used for malware detection cannot be found in benign executables. The refined signature list can be further reduced while still maintaining the same detection rate. This is mainly due these signatures detecting the same set of malware. Thus removing either one of these signatures would yield the same detection rate. Algorithm 2 shows a pseudo code for this signature refinement step.

3.2 Online Malware Detection

As can be seen in Fig. 4, the application would be executed on the system while the system monitors keep tracks of any system call that is being executed [25]. If the system call matches with any of the system call in the first system call in refined malware signatures, the system would monitor and check if the subsequent system calls match. If so, then the application is a malware.

3.3 Enhanced Malware Detection Algorithm

In cases where the refined malware signatures fail to detect certain malware, the system can fall back on existing signature-based technique to extract system call signatures from each malware by cross-referencing the malware signatures with the benign signature list as shown in Fig. 5. These signatures were not included in the refined malware signatures as these malwares are unique (outliers) and do not share any similarities in system call signatures with other malwares.

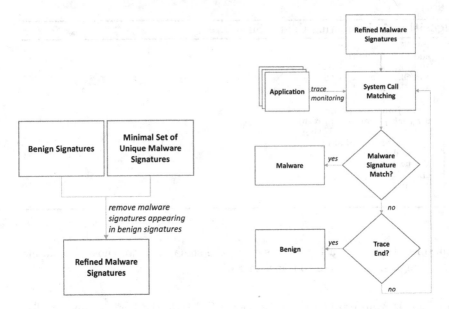

Fig. 3. Refining malware signature extraction

Fig. 4. Malware detection

Algorithm 2. Malware Signature Refinement

```
 1 for each Si from 1 to i do
 2 │   for each Si from 1 to i do
 3 │   │   add(SignatureList, Mj[Si]);
 4 │   end
 5 end
 6 for each i from 1 to i-1 do
 7 │   for each j from i+1 to n do
 8 │   │   if SignatureList(i) == SignatureList(j) then
 9 │   │   │   remove(SL, SL[j]);
10 │   │   end
11 │   │   next j;
12 │   end
13 │   next i;
14 end
```

Therefore, the overall purpose of the system is to find the balance between the minimal set of malware signatures and high detection accuracy. This would significantly reduce the iteration for enhanced malware detection algorithm.

4   Evaluation

We conducted our experiments on a Virtual Machine with 4-core CPU and 4GB RAM running Ubuntu 13.04 Linux OS with kernel version 3.8.0. We collected 70 malicious samples targeting Linux OS from Virusshare [26] database that is available in the public domain after free registration. These were scanned using

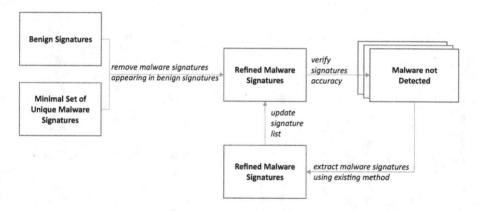

Fig. 5. Enhanced malware signature extraction

AVG anti-virus software to verify their maliciousness. As mentioned in Sect. 3, we used common applications such as Firefox and various Linux commands (ls, pip, etc.) as benign applications in this work. The system call trace was generated once and stored for all the malware and benign application executables.

4.1 Experiment Results

As discussed in Sect. 3, we identified the common system call based signatures from all the 70 malware samples' trace that do not appear in the benign applications' trace. Figure 6 plots the number of malware, in terms of percentage, that contain these identified signatures. The signatures, as plotted on the X-axis, are sorted in a descending order of their number of occurrences in the malware samples. For example, from Fig. 6, *Signature 1* appears in close to 48% of the malware samples, while *Signature n* appears in about 2% of the malware. We obtained an average of about 90% detection rate, as shown in the first column of Fig. 7, using only the top 3 most frequently occurring signatures.

In order to ensure a 100% detection rate, we identified additional signatures for the malware that cannot be detected using the top 3 most frequently occurring signatures, as described in Sect. 3.3. For the 70 malware samples, we identified 4 additional signatures that could be used to detect all the malware. The second column in Fig. 7 shows the detection rate after using the enhanced malware detection technique described in Sect. 3.3 after using the enriched set of signatures. Hence, it is evident that the proposed method only needs a total of 7 signatures to detect 70 malware samples. The small, but highly effective, set of signatures do not add a significant overhead to the malware detection mechanism and hence is useful for IoT devices.

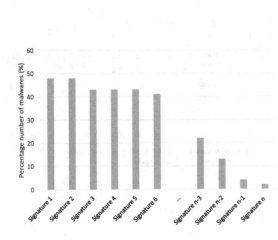

Fig. 6. Sorted malware signature by percentage (% found in malwares)

Fig. 7. Refined vs Enhanced technique (detection %)

5   Conclusion

In this paper, we presented an improved signature-based malware detection method. The system call based signatures provide a way to use a minimal set of signatures for detecting a group of malware instead of using unique signature per malware, as done in the existing methods. It was shown through experimental evaluation that only 7 signatures is enough to detect 70 malware taken from a popular malware dataset.

References

1. Moser, A., et al.: Exploring multiple execution paths for malware analysis. In: 2007 IEEE Symposium on Security and Privacy (SP 2007), May 2007
2. Symantec Security Response, IoT devices being increasingly used for DDoS attacks (2016). https://www.symantec.com/connect/blogs/iot-devices-being-increasingly-used-ddos-attacks. Accessed 28 Mar 2017
3. Snell, B.: Mobile threat report: whats on the horizon for 2016 (2016). https://www.mcafee.com/us/resources/reports/rp-mobile-threat-report-2016.pdf. Accessed 28 Mar 2017
4. Biswas, A.: Scary insights into the security of smart things: what the IoT startups dont pitch about (2016). http://electronicsofthings.com/expert-opinion/scary-insights-security-smart-things-what-the-iot-startups-dont-pitch-about/5/. Accessed 28 Mar 2017
5. Greenemeier, L.: IoT growing faster than the ability to defend it (2016). https://www.scientificamerican.com/article/iot-growing-faster-than-the-ability-to-defend-it/. Accessed 28 Mar 2017
6. Hasan, R., et al.: How secure is the healthcare network from insider attacks? An audit guideline for vulnerability analysis. In: IEEE Annual Computer Software and Applications Conference (COMPSAC), June 2016

7. Iqbal, M.S., et al.: SAM: a secure anti-malware framework for the smartphone operating systems. In: IEEE Wireless Communications and Networking Conference (2016)
8. Greengard, S.: Cybersecurity gets smart. Commun. ACM (2016). http://doi.acm.org/10.1145/2898969
9. Arslan, B., et al.: A review on mobile threats and machine learning based detection approaches. In: International Symposium on Digital Forensic and Security, April 2016
10. Kolosnjaji, B., et al.: Deep learning for classification of malware system call sequences. In: Australasian Joint Conference on Artificial Intelligence (2016)
11. Othman, Z.A., et al.: Improving signature detection classification model using features selection based on customized features. In: International Conference on Intelligent Systems Design and Applications, November 2010
12. Saracino, A., et al.: Madam: effective and efficient behavior-based android malware detection and prevention. IEEE Trans. Dependable Secure Comput. **PP**(99), 1 (2016)
13. Narayanan, B.N., et al.: Performance analysis of machine learning and pattern recognition algorithms for malware classification. In: IEEE National Aerospace and Electronics Conference (NAECON) and Ohio Innovation Summit (OIS), July 2016
14. Islam, N., et al.: On-device mobile phone security exploits machine learning. IEEE Pervasive Comput. **16**(2), 92–96 (2017)
15. Hellal, A., et al.: Maximal frequent sub-graph mining for malware detection. In: International Conference on Intelligent Systems Design and Applications (ISDA), December 2015
16. Sun, M., et al.: Monet: a user-oriented behavior-based malware variants detection system for android. IEEE Trans. Inform. Forensics Secur. **12**(5), 1103–1112 (2017)
17. Gandotra, E., et al.: Malware analysis and classification: a survey. J. Inform. Secur. **5**, 56–64 (2014)
18. Kong, D., et al.: Discriminant malware distance learning on structural information for automated malware classification. In: ACM SIGKDD International Conference on Knowledge Discovery and Data Mining (2013)
19. Nari, S., et al.: Automated malware classification based on network behavior. In: International Conference on Computing, Networking and Communications (ICNC) (2013)
20. Tian, R., et al.: Function length as a tool for malware classification. In: International Conference on Malicious and Unwanted Software, October 2008
21. Firdausi, I., et al.: Analysis of machine learning techniques used in behavior-based malware detection. In: International Conference on Advances in Computing, Control, and Telecommunication Technologies, December 2010
22. Forrest, S., et al.: A sense of self for unix processes. In: IEEE Symposium on Security and Privacy, May 1996
23. Wagener, G., et al.: Malware behaviour analysis. J. Comput. Virol. (2008). http://dx.doi.org/10.1007/s11416-007-0074-9
24. Kolosnjaji, B., et al.: Empowering convolutional networks for malware classification and analysis. In: International Joint Conference on Neural Networks (2017)
25. Rahmatian, M., et al.: Hardware-assisted detection of malicious software in embedded systems. IEEE Embedded Syst. Lett. **4**(4), 94–97 (2012)
26. VirusShare, VirusShare.com - Because Sharing is Caring (2017). https://virusshare.com/. Accessed 2 Apr 2017

System and Network Security

De-anonymous and Anonymous Technologies for Network Traffic Release

Xiang Tian[1,2,3], Yu Wang[4(✉)], Yujia Zhu[2,3], Yong Sun[2,3],
and Qingyun Liu[2,3]

[1] University of Chinese Academy of Sciences, Beijing, China
[2] National Engineering Laboratory for Information Security Technologies,
Beijing, China
{zhuyujia, sunyong, liuqingyun}@iie.ac.cn
[3] Institute of Information Engineering, Chinese Academy of Sciences, Beijing,
China
tianxiang@iie.ac.cn
[4] National Computer Network Emergency Response and Coordination Center,
Beijing, China
slimzczy@163.com

Abstract. With the rapid growth of data, the network traffic data is of great significance for the research and analysis. Through research and real events, anonymous network traffic is susceptible to de-anonymity attacks. Therefore, the release of network traffic need to consider the existence of de-anonymization attacks, and balance the privacy and utility of data. On the one hand, we summarize the anonymous technologies of network traffic, list some traffic anonymity methods. on the other hand, we analyze the anonymous strategy of network flow against de-anonymous attacks. Based on the research on de-anonymization attacks, this paper divides the de-anonymization method into three categories from the dimension of inferring attack object: restoring the network topology graph, inferring the host behavior, inferring the node and edge information. Specifically, we analyze the implementation methods of these three types of de-anonymization attacks respectively. In connection with the network traces anonymity method, we analyze the confrontation strategy of the above de-anonymity attacks.

Keywords: Network traffic · De-anonymous attack · Anonymization · Privacy · Data release

1 Introduction

The complexity of the modern network makes the use of real data in network research becomes critical, the authenticity of the data to a great extent affect the accuracy of the results. Real network data can be applied to the research and analysis of traffic characterization, the diagnosis of network events, and the assessment of network systems. Therefore, the network traffic data for the research and analysis of great significance. There are many de-anonymous attacks on anonymous network traffic, the maximum degree of anonymity of network traffic is a hot topic in the research.

© Springer Nature Singapore Pte Ltd. 2017
L. Batten et al. (Eds.): ATIS 2017, CCIS 719, pp. 193–200, 2017.
DOI: 10.1007/978-981-10-5421-1_16

1.1   Acquisition of Network Traffic Data

Real network data can be widely used in network analysis and research, but access to real packet traffic is challenging. The existing methods to obtain real network traffic mainly include obtaining the data traffic from the public library. The main public libraries are CAIDA [1], DeepSight [2], Dshield.org [3], Packetlife.net [4], Pcapr [5], ISCX [6], PCAPLib [7]. Most of the data traffic in the public library is disrupted the availability in the analysis.

1.2   Release of Network Traffic Data

Network traffic data is published in two ways: (1) simple release, release all the traffic data set, (2) incremental release, with a clear practical advantage, making the calculation of cost and the demand of storage of large data sets greatly reduce [8, 9]. There are some challenges in release of real network flow: (1) data traffic including privacy information, required anonymization before release. (2) Anonymous methods have been limited to a small number of protocols. (3) Most importantly, the existing traffic anonymity method can not completely confront the de-anonymity attack.

This paper studies anonymous network traffic trajectories for data releasing system based on de-anonymous network traffic, and mainly completes the following work:

(1)   First, we summarize the anonymous technologies, list six anonymous methods for traffic trajectories.
(2)   With the development of anonymous technology, de-anonymity attacks are generated and continuously derived. Based on the existing research on traffic anonymity, we classified the de-anonymity attack of anonymous network traffic from the dimension of the object to be inferred. Then, this paper analyzes the implementation of these three types of de-anonymous attacks.
(3)   Finally, we analyze the strategies to combat de-anonymous attacks from the perspective of the classification method proposed in this paper.

2   Traffic Anonymity Method

There are a large number of information that can not be released, which can directly or indirectly obtain privacy information in the network traffic. Even if the payload is deleted in all the packets, the attacker can infer the privacy information by analyzing the IP address. Therefore, it is significant to anonymize traffic data.

Anonymity is changing the network traffic data to protect its privacy. The goal of anonymity is remove the identifiable relationships between the two endpoints while ensuring data availability. By applying the anonymity algorithm to a specific field, it can provide privacy protection for the network data. The anonymization method can be subdivided into different levels of anonymous algorithms.

Anonymous method of address prefix preservation means that the value of an IP address is replaced by a synthetic value [10]. If the prefix value is preserved, the original structure of the IP address can be maintained. The address prefix preservation can be applied in whole or in part to the IP address. According to this feature, the anonymous method can be divided into full prefix preservation and partial prefix preservation [11]. The Tcpdpriv tool first applied the prefix to keep anonymous [12]. The encryption prefix preserves anonymous methods has been applied in the anonymous traffic tool Crypto-Pan [10].

Enumeration usually acts on an ordered data set. First sort the discrete data, and then select the first value from the record. The algorithm can not be used for all fields.

The hash algorithm replaces the data with a fixed byte-sized string, and any data transformation changes the hash value, which in some cases is shorter than the original value [13]. Truncation is usually used for anonymous IP addresses and MAC addresses, which delete some of the data while keeping the remaining data unchanged. The truncation method removes the n least significant bits of the field value and replaces them with 0. The elimination time unit is a partitioning algorithm for an anonymous timestamp. Which eliminates some of the timestamps with the value of 0 to replace these removed parts. The method deletes or replaces all the information in the field with a fixed value that can be applied to all fields in the traffic [7].

Before applying the anonymous algorithm, you must select the appropriate fields. Table 1 shows the commonly used anonymous fields and their application anonymous algorithm. There are many tools for anonymization of network traffic release [14–19].

Table 1. Common anonymous fields and corresponding algorithms.

Field	Algorithm
IP address	Prefix-preserving. replacement, truncation, black block mark
MAC address	Replacement, truncation, black block mark
Port number	Enumeration, black block mark
Timestamp	Replacement, eliminate the time unit, black block mark
Counter	Replacement, black block mark

3 De-anonymous Attacks

With the development of anonymous technology, de-anonymous attacks are generated and continue to be derived. The classification of attacks that are anonymous to network traffic is the basis for a comprehensive study of the security of anonymous policies.

Combined with Gattani, Daniels and King and others in the de-anonymous attack classification, we classify de-anonymous attack from the dimension of inferring attack object: (1) infer topology structure: the attack restore the network topology structure from the anonymous trajectory; (2) infer the host behavior: the attack can determine the host's characteristic behavior, in order to obtain the behavior of the host which can identify the characteristics; (3) infer the node information: the attack attempts to de-anonymize the nodes in the network and the edges representing the nodes connected and routed. It is concluded that the topology structure inference is a global de-anonymity attack method, and it is inferred the host behavior and the node information are local attack methods. The main difference between the latter two is that the host behavior is a dynamic interaction process, and it emphasizes that the dynamic information of the host can be recognized. Node information is a relatively static attribute. In de-anonymous attacks, the attributes of anonymous data are used to compare with known network structures to discover the relationship between anonymous and non-anonymous data (Table 2).

Table 2. De-anonymity attack multiple categories.

	Gattani [20]	King [21]	This paper
De-anonymous attack categories	Dynamic data injection	Fingerprint recognition	Infer topology structure
	Known mapping	Injection	Infer host behavior
	Network topology inference	Decryption IP address	Infer node information
	Encryption		

3.1 Infer the Topology Structure

Xu et al. proposed the use of subnet clustering to obtain summary information about backbone router traffic [22]. Coull et al. applied the sub-network clustering technique based on k-means [23]. For each cluster clustered by k-means, calculated the longest common prefix of the subnet address of all IP addresses as the subnet address (Fig. 1).

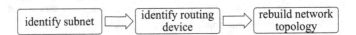

Fig. 1. Inference of the network topology implementation method.

3.2 Infer the Host Behavior

The main threat to traffic releasing is the host de-anonymity. If the behavior of the anonymous host can uniquely map to the real object, the attacker can localize the topology to de-anonymous attack, that is, infer the host behavior.

Dominant State Analysis. Xu et al. proposed a new method for determining the most characteristic behavior of a given host, called the dominant state analysis. The dominant state analysis algorithm can discover the behavior of each anonymous IP address.

Dynamic Data Injection Attack Data injection attack refers to the attacker in the network to inject information, the information in the anonymous track data can still be identified, as shown in Fig. 2 [24].

Fig. 2. Dynamic data injection attack implementation method.

K-vulnerable. In 2008, Ribeiro et al. pointed out that in the prefix-preserving anonymous network traffic, the attacker could achieve a systematic attack, that is, a k-vulnerable [25]. First, the attacker gets the traffic fingerprint of each host in the anonymous traffic. Then, he collects information from the external public sources, dig the network host fingerprint. Eventually, he uses the acquired fingerprints to find partial or completely anonymous mapping relationships.

3.3 Infer the Node Information

The node information refers to the static attribute information, which represented the node at the vertex at the top of the network topology and the edge between the nodes connecting and routing.

Frequency Analysis Injection Attack. Frequency analysis injection attack is a type of traffic analysis based on the assumption that the opponent has a priori knowledge of the traffic distribution of the observed network [26].

Web Server Fingerprint Attack. Web server fingerprints match an overview of the content of the URL in the anonymous traffic, identify the common URL. Bypass the anonymous identifiers of the known web server to achieve the de-anonymous site server's attack, which can be connected to an anonymous client IP [27]. The steps in this type of attack is shown in Fig. 3.

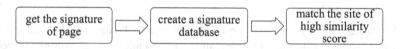

Fig. 3. Web server fingerprint attack implementation method.

Remote Physical Device Fingerprint Attack. The attacker gets the legitimate site traffic of the acquisition machine. Then anonymizing the IP address by comparing the clock offset in the probe with the clock offset in the TCP timestamp option [28].

K-edge Attack. The k-edge attack assumes that the attacker can inject enough information to identify the k edges in the anonymous traffic. In the graph structure, the node represents the IP address in the traffic, and the edge represents the connection between the two nodes. If the topology is not distorted, the degree remains the same, it is possible to infer the k edge associated node [29].

4 Anonymous Methods Against Attacks

Applying a specific anonymity method is critical to the implementation of traffic anonymization for attacks against different attack targets.

4.1 Against Topology Inference Attack

Publish the anonymous NetFlow log or remove the link layer header from the packet flow can against the network topology attack. In addition, by deleting the ARP (address resolution protocol) traffic information, we can make the attacker unable to obtain the link layer topology information.

4.2 Against Host Behavior Inference Attack

By re-mapping the port number, the attacker will not be able to directly infer the behavior information. Restricting the publication of anonymous data based on short intervals can counter the injection of dynamic data.

Qardaji et al. proposed an improved method for the full prefix anonymity, k-entity anonymity [30], which can against k-vulnerable. It is based on temporal consistency, and only the flow data that appears in the same time block remains anonymous consistent, ensuring that the anonymous entities have at least corresponding k different entities in anonymous traffic.

4.3 Against Node Information Inference Attack

The method of preventing fingerprint attacks from remote physical devices includes: ignoring the ICMP timestamp request and not enabling the TCP timestamp option in the output TCP packet.

Graph Confusion. Confusion of the graph can against k-edge attacks, and the core idea is to produce a side that combines all the communication relationships. Specific implementation: generate a bipartite graph, one side is a collection of special nodes, and all nodes on the other side can be merged into a single pass through traffic.

Netshuffle. Valgenti et al. proposed Netshuffle, by reassembling the attacker on behalf of the communication relationship in the traffic trajectory [31]. Netshuffle relies on edge properties, and an attacker would be misled or forced to guess the target entity from several possible candidates.

(k, j)-obfuscation. (k, j)–obfuscation method is proposed by Riboni et al. in 2012 [8, 9]. IP address and pseudo-random group ID achieve multi-to-mapping. In anonymous traffic, pseudo-random group ID replaces the real IP address, each IP address in the published traffic is hidden at least k possible IP addresses.

5   Summary and Future Work

Today, the information society is in the era of big data, the rapid growth of data has brought the serious challenges and valuable opportunities of the whole society. Accessing to real traffic data has been a major challenge. Published data were processed and anonymous, limiting their research value. Through research and real events, it is easy for anonymous data to be inferred sensitive information. Therefore, the release of network traffic data needs to balance the privacy and usability of data. This paper studies anonymous network traffic trajectories for data releasing system based on de-anonymous network traffic. We summarize the six anonymous methods for traffic trajectories, classify the de-anonymity attack of anonymous network traffic from the dimension of the object to be inferred, and divide into three categories. And then we conclude that the specific implementation methods. Finally, we analyze the strategies to against de-anonymous methods.

With the change of de-anonymous attack technology, a higher demand for traffic anonymity is proposed. It makes research related traffic anonymous more challenging, traffic anonymous methods need to innovate, based on attacks, continuous improving anonymous method. There is a trade-off between the privacy and the utility. Existing network traffic data anonymity methods mostly emphasize privacy, and how to maximize the availability of data relative to the expected network traffic is still a challenge. Differential privacy protection can be used to anonymize network traffic data. More research need to be applied to the use of differential privacy in network traffic data.

Acknowledgments. This work was supported by National Key R&D Program 2016 (Grant No. 2016YFB081304).

References

1. CAIDA traces dataset. http://www.caida.org/home
2. DeepSight. http://enterprisesecurity.symantec.com/products/products.cfm?ProductID= 158&EID=0
3. DShield.org. http://www.dshield.org
4. Packetlife repository. http://www.packetlife.net/captures
5. PCAPR collaborative network forensics. http://www.pcapr.net/forensics
6. Shiravi, A., Shiravi, H., Tavallaee, M., et al.: Toward developing a systematic approach to generate benchmark datasets for intrusion detection. Comput. Secur. **31**(3), 357–374 (2012)
7. Lin, Y.D., Lin, P.C., Wang, S.H., et al.: PCAPLib: a system of extracting, classifying, and anonymizing real packet traces. IEEE Syst. J. 1–12 (2014)
8. Riboni, D., Villani, A., Vitali, D., et al.: Obfuscation of sensitive data in network flows. In: IEEE INFOCOM, pp. 2372–2380. IEEE (2012)
9. Riboni, D., Villani, A., Vitali, D., et al.: Obfuscation of sensitive data for incremental release of network flows. IEEE/ACM Trans. Netw. **23**(2), 672–686 (2015)
10. Xu, J., Fan, J., Ammar, M., et al.: On the design and performance of prefix-preserving IP traffic trace anonymization. In: Proceedings of the 1st ACM SIGCOMM Workshop on Internet Measurement, pp. 263–266. ACM (2001)
11. Xu, J., Fan, J., Ammar, M.H., et al.: Prefix-preserving IP address anonymization: measurement-based security evaluation and a new cryptography-based scheme. In: IEEE International Conference on Network Protocols, Proceedings, pp. 280–289. IEEE (2002)
12. Minshall, G.: Tcpdpriv: program for eliminating confidential information from traces (2005)
13. Pang, R., Paxson, V.: A high-level programming environment for packet trace anonymization and transformation, pp. 339–351 (2003)

14. Sperotto, A., Schaffrath, G., Sadre, R., et al.: An overview of IP flow-based intrusion detection. IEEE Commun. Surv. Tutor. **12**(3), 343–356 (2010)
15. Mendonca, M., Seetharaman, S., Obraczka, K.: A flexible in-network IP anonymization service. In: IEEE International Conference on Communications. IEEE (2012)
16. Jeon, S., Yun, J.H., Kim, W.N.: Obfuscation of critical infrastructure network traffic using fake communication. In: International Conference on Critical Information Infrastructures Security (2014)
17. Lin, T.: Anonym: a tool for anonymization of the internet traffic. In: IEEE International Conference on Cybernetics, pp. 261–266 (2013)
18. Yurcik, W., Woolam, C., Hellings, G., et al.: SCRUB-tcpdump: a multi-level packet anonymizer demonstrating privacy/analysis tradeoffs. In: International Conference on Security and Privacy in Communications Networks and the Workshops (SECURECOMM 2007), pp. 49–56. IEEE (2007)
19. Stanek, J., Kencl, L., Kuthan, J.: Analyzing anomalies in anonymized SIP traffic. In: Networking Conference, pp. 1–9. IEEE (2014)
20. Gattani, S., Daniels, T.E.: Reference models for network data anonymization. In: ACM Conference on Computer and Communications Security, pp. 41–48 (2008)
21. King, J., Lakkaraju, K., Slagell, A.: A taxonomy and adversarial model for attacks against network log anonymization. In: Proceedings of ACM SAC, pp. 1286–1293. ACM (2009)
22. Xu, K., Zhang, Z.L., Bhattacharyya, S.: Profiling internet backbone traffic: behavior models and applications. ACM SIGCOMM Comput. Commun. Rev. **35**(4), 169–180 (2005)
23. Coull, S.E., Wright, C.V., Monrose, F., et al.: Playing devil's advocate: inferring sensitive information from anonymized network traces. In: Network and Distributed System Security Symposium (NDSS 2007), San Diego, California, USA, pp. 35–47, March 2007
24. Burkhart, M., Schatzmann, D., Trammell, B., et al.: The role of network trace anonymization under attack. ACM SIGCOMM Comput. Commun. Rev. **40**(1), 5–11 (2010)
25. Ribeiro, B.F., Chen, W., Miklau, G., et al.: Analyzing privacy in enterprise packet trace anonymization. In: Network and Distributed System Security Symposium (NDSS 2008), San Diego, California, USA, February 2008
26. Foukarakis, M., Antoniades, D., Polychronakis, M.: Deep packet anonymization, pp. 16–21 (2009)
27. Koukis, D., Antonatos, S., Antoniades, D., et al.: A generic anonymization framework for network traffic, vol. 5, pp. 2302–2309 (2006)
28. Kohno, T., Broido, A., Claffy, K.C.: Remote physical device fingerprinting. In: IEEE Symposium on Security and Privacy, pp. 211–225. IEEE Computer Society (2005)
29. Paul, R.R., Valgenti, V.C., Min, S.K.: Real-time netshuffle: graph distortion for on-line anonymization. In: IEEE International Conference on Network Protocols (ICNP 2011), Vancouver, BC, Canada, pp. 133–134 (2011)
30. Qardaji, W., Li, N.: Anonymizing network traces with temporal pseudonym consistency, pp. 622–633 (2012)
31. Valgenti, V.C., Paul, R.R., Min, S.K.: Netshuffle: improving traffic trace anonymization through graph distortion. In: IEEE International Conference on Communications, pp. 1–6. IEEE (2011)

Privacy-Aware Authentication for Wi-Fi Based Indoor Positioning Systems

Sang Guun Yoo[1,2(✉)] and Jhonattan J. Barriga[2]

[1] Departamento de Ciencias de la Computación, Universidad de las Fuerzas Armadas ESPE, Sangolquí, Ecuador
yysang@espe.edu.ec
[2] Facultad de Ingeniería de Sistemas, Escuela Politécnica Nacional, Quito, Ecuador
{sang.yoo,jhonattan.barriga}@epn.edu.ec

Abstract. Indoor location-based application and services have drawn businesses attention as they have shown advances in conjunction with a growing importance of ubiquitous computing and context-dependent information. However, current systems have serious problems in terms of privacy since attackers can track users by analyzing information captured from the network such as MAC addresses. In this situation, this work provides a practical solution to the privacy issue in indoor positioning systems. We propose the usage of pseudo-certificates issued by third-party authorities for anonymous auhentication of mobile devices. The proposed scheme provides privacy to users while providing governmental authorities the possibility to analyze the historical position of users when they are required. The proposed anonymous authentication system offers highest level of security while maintain minimal cryptographic overhead.

Keywords: Privacy · Anonymous authentication · Indoor positioning system · IPS · WLAN

1 Introduction

Indoor location techniques have captured the attention of research and industrial institutions, particularly in fields such as healthcare, national defense, social life, and Internet of things [1–3]. According to [1], people spend more than 80% of their time living indoors, which means that there is a need on having an adequate indoor location based services. The widely known positioning services based on Global Navigation Satellite Systems (GNSSs) is not recommended for indoor usage since they have signal loss and/or position accuracy problems because of the interference of Non Line Sight (NLOS) [1, 4]. In this situation, several technologies have been proposed for Indoor positioning systems. Among those, Wi-Fi technology has been considered important by the scientific community as it is widely used in private and public organizations [5].

To improve the accuracy of Wi-Fi based location systems, several algorithms have been proposed to improve its precision level while reducing the number of antennas. RADAR [6], RADAR with VL (Viterbi-like) [7], FBCM (Friis Based Calibrated

© Springer Nature Singapore Pte Ltd. 2017
L. Batten et al. (Eds.): ATIS 2017, CCIS 719, pp. 201–213, 2017.
DOI: 10.1007/978-981-10-5421-1_17

Model) [8] are some examples of such position computation algorithms which are based on Signal Strength (SS) cartography or propagation models [4]. However, even though Indoor Positioning Systems (IPSs) have denoted significant advances for improving accuracy, there are still issues in regarding to privacy of users, since some information can be directly acquired from protocol headers without consent of users [5, 9–11]. Because of this situation, several works such as [12] indicated the need for addressing the privacy issue when implementing IPSs since the position of users can deliver important and confidential information about them.

In this situation, we propose an privacy-aware authentication system for Wi-Fi based IPSs. The proposed system makes use of the pseudo-certificates issued by third-party authorities for anonymous authentication of mobile devices. The proposed scheme provides privacy to users while providing governmental authorities the possibility to analyze the historical position of users when they are required (e.g. for legal investigation).

The rest of the paper is structured as follows, Sect. 2 comprises a brief revision on indoor positioning algorithms based on WLAN; besides, privacy issues are discussed. Then, the proposed solution is explained with details in Sect. 3. Later, Sect. 4 analizes the proposed solution in terms of security and performance. Finally, the paper is concluded in Sect. 5.

2 State of the Art

2.1 Wi-Fi Based Indoor Positioning Systems

We can categorize the positioning systems in indoor, outdoor and mixed one. The most popular positioning system for the outdoor environment is the Global Positioning System (GPS) which is widely used for tracking and management of assets. Although GPS performs well in outdoor positioning, it has problems for indoors environments (buildings, underground) since it has a weak signal which cannot pass the walls easily. For this reason, other technologies have been used for IPSs such as Wi-Fi [3], RFID [13], Bluetooth [14], and Ultra Wide Band (UWB) [14]. Among the mentioned technologies, this paper focuses on the Wi-Fi based systems, since they are widley deployed in the real world.

The advanced Wi-Fi positioning systems use the signal strength fingerprinting methods which observe the Wi-Fi signal strengths from several Access Points (APs) within a determined environment. Those observations are registered in a database so a user, with the aid of smartphone Wi-Fi sensor, can perform positioning activities later inside an interest area. When a user wants to determine his/her location, he/she matches his/her Wi-Fi signal strength observation with Received Signal Strenght (RSS) values residing in the database to obtain the closest value which represents an estimated location.

2.2 Security Limitations of IPS Based on Wi-Fi

Some researchers have tried to solve the privacy and security issue in differents works. Reference [5] discusses several of those proposals, such as obfuscation of sensitive data and usage of random MAC addresses. However, those solutions do not solve the whole problem since they produce delays affecting the quality of service and since they can generate collisions because of duplicate MAC addresses on the same network. On the other hand, an architecture for disclosing information based on the sensitivity of an area was proposed in [9]; however, it also has several limitations since a malicious user can obtain other information that might lead to infer future location of a victim [9]. Additionally, other proposals were developed in [5, 9, 10]; however, those initiatives need to be supported by legal regulations to become stronger.

3 Proposed Protocol

3.1 Overview of the System

The proposed system is composed of three main entities (see Fig. 1):

(1) User environment, which is composed of the (a) user who wants to access to the IPS service and his/her (b) mobile device(s).
(2) Certificate authority (*CA*): this is a third party entity, responsible of managing users' accounts and the data of their mobile devices. This entity also issues the pseudo-certificates and private keys used by users to authenticate to the IPS server.
(3) IPS Server: this is the server that provides the indoor positioning service. The IPS Server that wants to be part of the proposed solution must be registered to the *CA*.

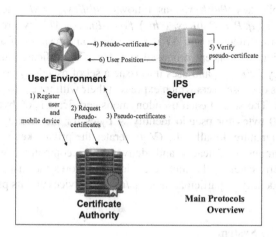

Fig. 1. Overview of proposed solution

The aforementioned entities interact each other executing the following steps.

The user who wants to access to the indoor positioning service must authenticate to the IPS server. The technological mechanism chosen in the proposed solution to allow users to authenticate anonymously to the IPS Server is the pseudonymous authentication scheme [15]. This means that users must get pseudo-certificates before accessing to the IPS service. For this, the user communicates with the Certificate Authority to register his/her data and his/her mobile device(s). Once created the user account in the Certificate Authority, the user requests the issue of a set of pseudo-certificates. The Certificate Authority, once verified the user's credentials, generates a set of pseudo-certificates for the connected mobile device and delivers it to the user.

The user, once with the pseudo-certificates, can authenticate to the IPS Server. Each time a user wants to know his/her position, a single pseudo-certificate is delivered to the IPS server. If the pseudo-certificate is valid, the IPS Server responds to user's request by providing the position of the user.

It is important to notice that each pseudo-certificate has an expiration time and it is valid only a single time. This means that the user must request for a new set of pseudo-certificates when his/her pseudo-certificates have been used.

3.2 Pseudonymous Authentication Scheme

As mentioned before, the proposed solution makes use of pseudo-certificates for authentication. This papers suggests the usage of PASS (pseudonymous authentication scheme with strong privacy preservation) [15] to authenticate participating mobile devices of users when accessing to IPS Servers.

Let $(\mathbb{G}_1, +)$ and $(\mathbb{G}_2, \cdot)$ be two cyclic groups of prime order q and $e : \mathbb{G}_1 \times \mathbb{G}_1 \rightarrow \mathbb{G}_2$ be an efficient admissible bilinear map. The CA selects a random generator $P \in \mathbb{G}_1$, two hash functions $h(\bullet)$ and $f(\cdot) : \{0,1\}^* \rightarrow \mathbb{G}_1$ and a random key $s \in \mathbb{Z}_q^*$. Then, the CA calculates its public key $PubKey_{CA}$ as follows $PubKey_{CA} = sP$ and distributes the parameters $(\mathbb{G}_1, \mathbb{G}_2, q, P, e, PubKey_{CA}, h(\cdot), f(\cdot), SEnc(\cdot), \Delta T)$ where $SEnc(\bullet)$ is a symmetric encryption function and ΔT is the expiration threshold of a pseudonymous certificate. Applying the concept proposed in [15], the Certificate Authority CA generates a private key $PriKey_{CA}$ and uses it to issue a set of pseudonymous certificates to the mobile devices of those users which expressed their willingness to participate in the proposed solution. The size of each pseudonymous certificate is 66 bytes: 21 bytes for the public key, 20 bytes for pseudo identity, 4 bytes for the validity period, and 21 bytes for digital signature. Finally, the CA generates the private key set corresponding to the pseudonymous certificates and delivers it accompanied with the set of pseudonymous certificates to the mobile device, and stores the mapping relationship between the real identity of participating users/mobile devices and its pseudo identities.

3.3 Details of the System

In the previous subsection, we described briefly the flow of the proposed system. The intention of this subsection is to describe the proposed system with more details.

The proposed solution is composed of a (1) system initialization phase and four main protocols. These main protocols are: (2) user registration protocol, (3) mobile device registration protocol, (4) pseudo-certificate issue protocol, and (5) IPS access protocol. The notation used to describe the protocols is detailed in Table 1.

System Initialization. In the proposed system, each CA manages a certain geographic/administrative regional area (e.g. a state, city, or district). All the CAs share the same ΔT, which indicates the validity period threshold of a pseudonymous certificate issued to a mobile device of a user. It is important to remember that each pseudonymous certificate is usable only once and it has an expiration time which is equal to $LastPCertTime_{MDj\_Ui} + \Delta T$, where $LastPCertTime_{MDj\_Ui}$ is the last time where a pseudonymous certificate of a specific mobile device of a user was used.

Since each pseudonymous certificate has an expiration time, the CA must estimate the number of certificates to be issued to each mobile device. We think it is a good idea to issue enough pseudonymous certificates for a year. For example, if $\Delta T = 1$ h, the number of pseudonymous certificates required for a mobile device during a year will be $24 \times 365 = 8760$. Considering that the certificate size is 66 bytes (as indicated in previous subsection), the total amount of space required will be approximately 565 KB, which is a reasonable overhead in term of storage. We recommend the usage of a tamper proof device for storage and management of confidential data (e.g. keys and pseudonymous certificates) in each mobile device. Security technologies such as TrustZone by ARM [16] and Secure RAM by Freescale [17] could be possible solutions for the mentioned tamper proof devices.

User Registration Protocol. This protocol is executed as follows (see Fig. 2). First, the user U_i inputs his/her identity ID_{Ui} and password PW_{Ui} to his/her mobile device MD_{j_Ui}. Then, MD_{j_Ui} communicates with the third-party CA and asks for user registration. After receiving the request message, CA generates a random number $RN1$ and sends it to MD_{j_Ui}. Once received the response from CA, MD_{i_Ui} generates a random nonce $RN2$, a random symmetric key $RK1$, and calculates $M1 = AEnc(Pubkey_{CA}, RK1)$ and $M2 = SEnc(RK1, RN1||RN2||ID_{Ui}||h(PW_{Ui}))$, where $AEnc(x,y)$ is an asymmetric encryption of message y using the key x, $Pubkey_{CA}$ is CA's public key, $SEnc(x,y)$ is a symmetric encryption of message y using the key x, $||$ is a concatenation operation, and $h(.)$ is a one-way hash function. Once calculated $M1$ and $M2$, MD_{j_Ui} sends those values to CA.

Table 1. Notations used in the proposed solution

Notation	Description
U_i	i^{th} user
MD_{j_Ui}	U_i's j^{th} mobile device
$RN1, RN2, ..., RNn$	Random nonces
$RK1, RK2... RKn, RK_{CA}, RK_{IPS}$	Random symmetric keys
CA	Certificate Authority
$Pubkey_{CA}, Prikey_{CA}$	CA's asymmetric key pair

(continued)

Table 1. (*continued*)

Notation	Description
$Pubkey_{IPS}$, $Prikey_{IPS}$	*IPS Server*'s asymmetric key pair
ID_{Ui}	Identification of U_i
PW_{Ui}	Password of U_i
$NAME_{MDj\_Ui}$	Name of MD_{j_Ui}
MAC_{MDj_Ui}	MAC address of MD_{j_Ui}
$\{PCert_{(CA,MDj\_Ui)1},\ldots, PCert_{(CA, MDj\_Ui)n}\}$	Pseudo-certificates of MD_{j_Ui}
$\{Prikey_{(CA,MDj\_Ui)1},\ldots, Prikey_{(CA, MDj\_Ui)n}\}$	Private keys of pseudo-certificates of MD_{j_Ui}
IP_{IPS}	*IPS Server*'s IP address
$ID\_ALREADY\_TAKEN$	Flag indicating if ID_{Ui} is already taken
SS_{APS}	Signal Strength of Access Points
$PCert_{(CA,MDj\_Ui)k}$	k^{th} (unused) pseudo-certificate
Pos_{MDj_Ui}	Current position of MD_{j_Ui}
$\|$	String concatenation
$h(.)$	One-way hash function
$AEnc(x,y)$	Asymmetric encryption of message y using the key x
$ADec(x,y)$	Asymmetric decryption of message y using the key x
$SEnc(x,y)$	Symmetric encryption of message y using the key x
$SDec(x,y)$	Symmetric decryption of message y using the key x
$Sign(x, y)$	Digital signature of message y using the private key x
$VerifySign(x,y)$	Digital signature verification of signature y using public key x

On the other side, *CA* gets *RK1* by executing $ADec(Prikey_{CA}, M1)$ where $ADec(x,y)$ is an asymmetric decryption of an encrypted message y using the key x, and uses *RK1* to get *RN1′*, *RN2′*, ID_{Ui}, and $h(PW_{Ui})$ by executing $SDec(RK1, M2)$, where $SDec(x,y)$ is a symmetric decryption of an encrypted message y using the key x. Once gotten *RN1′*, *CA* verifies the freshness of the message by comparing the decrypted *RN1′* with the random nonce created previously by itself i.e. *RN1*. This step allows *CA* to protect against replay attacks. After verifying the validity of the message, *CA* verifies if ID_{Ui} is available. If ID_{Ui} is already taken by another user, *CA* calculates $M3 = SEnc(RK1, RN2′\|ID\_ALREADY\_TAKEN)$ and sends *M3* to MD_{j_Ui}. If ID_{Ui} is available, *CA* stores the $\{ID_{Ui}, h(PW_U)\}$ tuple in its *DB*, calculates $M3 = SEnc(RK1, RN2′)$, and sends *M3* to MD_{j_Ui}. It is important to mention that $ID\_ALREADY\_TAKEN$ is a flag indicating that the user must select another identification.

Finally, MD_{j_Ui} gets *RN2′* by executing $SDec(RK1,M3)$ and compares *RN2′* with the random nonce generated previously i.e. *RN2*. If such values are the same, MD_{j_Ui} verifies if the flag $ID\_ALREADY\_TAKEN$ is included in *M3*; if such flag is present, MD_{j_Ui} informs to the user to select another identification, otherwise MD_{j_Ui} confirms the successful registration of the user.

Mobile Device Registration. Once U_i is registered in CA, he/she can register his/her mobile device MD_{j_Ui} (see Fig. 2). For this, U_i delivers his/her ID_{Ui}, PW_{Ui} and a recognizable name of MD_{j_Ui} i.e. $NAME_{MDj\_Ui}$ to MD_{j_Ui}. Then, MD_{j_Ui} communicates with CA and asks for mobile device registration. After receiving the request message, CA generates a random number $RN3$ and sends it to MD_{j_Ui}. Once received the response from CA, MD_{i_Ui} generates a random nonce $RN4$, a random symmetric key $RK2$, and calculates $M5 = AEnc(Pubkey_{CA}, RK2)$ and $M6 = SEnc(RK2, RN3||RN4||$ $ID_{Ui}||h(PW_{Ui})||NAME_{MDj\_Ui}||MAC_{MDj\_Ui})$, where MAC_{MDj_Ui} is the MAC address of the mobile device. Then, MD_{j_Ui} sends $M5$ and $M6$ to CA.

On the other side, CA gets $RK2$ by executing $ADec(Prikey_{CA}, M5)$ and uses it to get $RN3'$, $RN4'$, ID_{Ui}, $h(PW_{Ui})$, $NAME_{MDj\_Ui}$, and MAC_{MDj_Ui} by executing $SDec(RK2, M6)$.

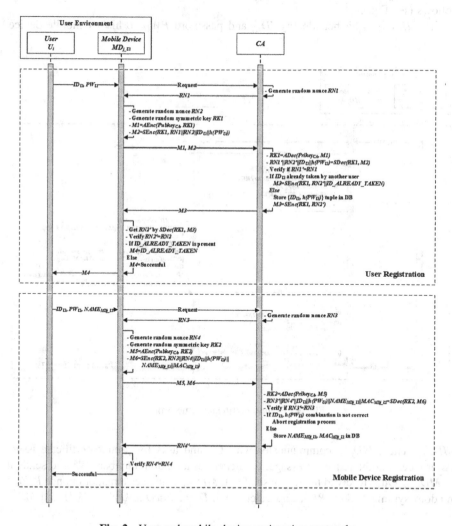

Fig. 2. User and mobile device registration protocols

Once gotten $RN3'$, CA verifies the freshness of the message by comparing the decrypted $RN3'$ with the random nonce created previously by itself i.e. $RN3$. After verifying the validity of the message, CA verifies the authenticity of the user by comparing the received tuple $\{ID_{Ui},\ h(PW_U)\}$ with the one stored in its DB. If the user is non-authentic, the registration process is aborted; otherwise CA stores $NAME_{MDj\_Ui}$, and MAC_{MDj_Ui} to U_i's record. Once registered the mobile device in CA, it sends the $RN4'$ to MD_{j_Ui}.

Finally, MD_{j_Ui}, once received $RN4'$ from CA, compares such value with the random nonce generated previously by itself i.e. $RN4$. If such values are the same MD_{j_Ui} confirms to U_i the successful execution of the protocol.

Pseudo-Certificate Issue Protocol. This protocol is executed for downloading a set of pseudo-certificates with their private keys and the information of the IPS Server (i.e. IP address IP_{IPS} and Public Key $Publickey_{IPS}$ of IPS Server). This protocol is executed as follows (see Fig. 3).

The U_i inputs his/her identity ID_{Ui} and password PW_{Ui} to his/her mobile device

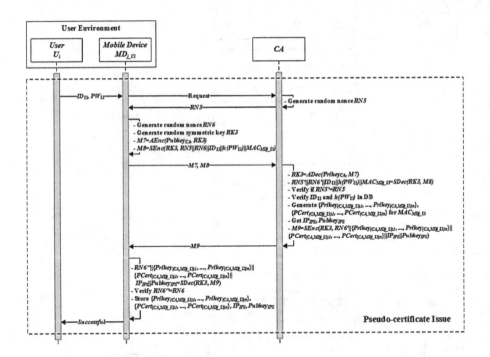

Fig. 3. Pseudo-certificate issue protocol

MD_{j_Ui}. Then, MD_{j_Ui} communicates with CA and asks for pseudo-certificate issue. After receiving the request message, CA generates a random number $RN5$ and sends it to MD_{j_Ui}. Once received the response of CA, MD_{i_Ui} generates a random nonce $RN6$, a random symmetric key $RK3$, and calculates $M7 = AEnc(Pubkey_{CA},\ RK3)$ and $M8 =$

$SEnc(RK3, RN5\|RN6\|ID_{Ui}\|h(PW_{Ui})\|MAC_{MDj\_Ui})$. Once calculated *M7* and *M8*, MD_{j_Ui} sends those values to *CA*.

On the other side, *CA* gets *RK3* by executing $ADec(Prikey_{CA}, M7)$ and uses it to get $RN5'$, $RN6'$, ID_{Ui}, $h(PW_{Ui})$, and MAC_{MDj_Ui} by executing $SDec(RK3, M8)$. Once gotten $RN5'$, *CA* verifies the freshness of the message by comparing the decrypted $RN5'$ with the random nonce created previously by itself i.e. *RN5*. After verifying the validity of the message, *CA* verifies the authenticity of the user by comparing the received tuple $\{ID_{Ui}, h(PW_U)\}$ with the one stored in its *DB*. If the user is non-authentic, the pseudo-certificate issue is aborted; otherwise *CA* generates a new set of pseudo-certificates $\{PCert_{(CA, MDj\_Ui)1}, ..., PCert_{(CA,MDj\_Ui)n}\}$ and the private keys corresponding to each pseudo-certificate $\{Prikey_{(CA,MDj\_Ui)1}, ..., Prikey_{(CA,MDj\_Ui)n}\}$ for MD_{j_Ui} with MAC_{MDj_Ui}. Additionally, *CA* gets the IP address of the IPS server its public key i.e. IP_{IPS}, $Pubkey_{IPS}$, calculates $M9 = SEnc(RK3, RN6'\|\{Prikey_{(CA,MDj\_Ui)1},..., Prikey_{(CA,MDj\_Ui)n}\}.\|\{PCert_{(CA,MDj\_Ui)1},...,PCert_{(CA,MDj\_Ui)n}\}\|IP_{IPS}\|Pubkey_{IPS})$ and send *M9* to MD_{j_Ui}. Meanwhile, MD_{j_Ui} gets $RN6''$, $\{Prikey_{(CA,MDj\_Ui)1}, ..., Prikey_{(CA,MDj\_Ui)n}\}$, $\{PCert_{(CA,MDj\_Ui)1}, ..., PCert_{(CA,MDj\_Ui)n}\}$, IP_{IPS}, and $Pubkey_{IPS}$ by executing $SDec(RK4, M9)$. After, MD_{j_Ui} compares the decrypted $RN6''$ with the random nonce generated previously by itself i.e. *RN6*. If such values are the same, MD_{j_Ui} stores the decrypted data to its DB and confirms the successful execution of the protocol to the user.

IPS Access Protocol. This protocol is executed when the user wants to access to the IPS service and it is executed as follows (see Fig. 4).

The MD_{j_Ui} generates a random nonce *RN7*, measures the signal strength of Access Points nearby i.e. SS_{APs}, and sends such values to the *IPS Server* accompanied with an valid pseudo-certificate $PCert_{(CA,MDj\_Ui)k}$. Once received the message, the *IPS Server*

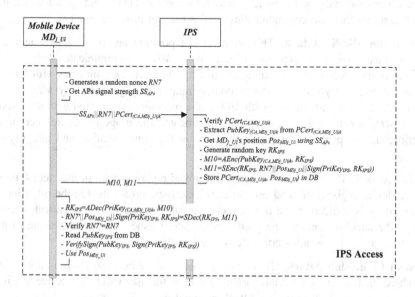

Fig. 4. IPS access protocol

verifies the validity of the $PCert_{(CA,MDj\_Ui)k}$ by using the public key of CA $Pubkey_{CA}$ and verifying the expiration time of the pseudo-certificate. The IPS $Server$ also registers the received certificate to make it invalid for further authentications.

After validating the pseudo-certificate, the IPS $Server$ extracts the public key $Pubkey_{(CA,MDj\_Ui)k}$ from $PCert_{(CA,MDj\_Ui)k}$, gets the current position of the mobile device Pos_{MDj_Ui}, generates a random key RK_{IPS}, and calculates $M10$ and $M11$, where $M10 = AEnc(PubKey_{(CA,MDj\_Ui)k}, RK_{IPS})$. $M11 = SEnc(RK_{IPS}, RN7||Pos_{MDj\_Ui}||Sign$ $(PriKey_{IPS}, RK_{IPS}))$, and $Sign(x,y)$ is the signing function of a message y using the private key x. Once calculated $M10$ and $M11$, the IPS $Server$ stores the $\{PCert_{(CA,}$ $_{MDj\_Ui)k}, Pos_{MDj\_Ui}\}$ combination in DB and sends $\{M10, M11\}$ to MD_{j_Ui}.

On the other side, the MD_{j_Ui} gets RK_{IPS} by executing $ADec(PriKey_{(CA,MDj\_Ui)k},$ $M10)$ and uses it to extract $RN7'$, Pos_{MDj_Ui}, and $Sign(PriKey_{IPS}, RK_{IPS})$ by executing $SDec(RK_{IPS}, M11)$. Then, MD_{j_Ui} verifies the freshness of the message by comparing the extracted $RN7'$ with $RN7$. After MD_{j_Ui} gets $PubKey_{IPS}$ and verifies the digital signature of the message by executing $VerifySign(PubKey_{IPS}, Sign(PriKey_{IPS}, RK_{IPS}))$ to ensure the authenticity of the message. Finally, once verified the authenticity of the message, the mobile device can use the Pos_{MDj_Ui} information.

4 Analysis of the Proposed Protocol

This section analyzes the proposed protocol in terms of security and performance.

4.1 Security Analysis

This part analyzes the security of the proposed protocol in terms of analysis of possible attacks. For this analysis, the widely known Dolev-Yao [18] threat model was used, which assumes that two communicating parties uses an insecure channel.

Man in the Middle Attack. This attack is not possible because the messages are encrypted using secure encryption functions. When MD_{j_Ui} communicates with CA, the message is encrypted using the public key of CA; when CA communicates with MD_{j_Ui} the message is encrypted with the random symmetric key generated by MD_{j_U}; and when IPS $Server$ communicates with MD_{j_Ui} the message is encrypted with the public key of MD_{j_Ui} extracted from the pseudo-certificate. The usage of secure encryption functions allows proposed protocols to maintain the confidentiality and integrity of messages.

Replay Attack. Random nonces are used to avoid replay attacks in user registration, mobile device registration, and pseudo-certificate issue protocols. On the other hand, replay attack is avoided in the IPS access protocol by using pseudo-certificates; even though the attacker captures the pseudo-certificate, he/she cannot authenticate to the IPS server since the pseudo-certificate is usable only once.

Password Guessing Attack. This attack is not possible because PW_{Ui} is not stored anywhere. Instead, a variant value $h(PW_{Ui})$ is used for user validation. Since $h(.)$ is a secure one-way hash function, the attacker cannot guess the PW_{Ui} from $h(PW_{Ui})$.

Privileged-Insider Attack. In the proposed solution, MD_{j_Ui} never transmits the password of the user PW_{Ui} in plaintext. Instead, a variant value $h(PW_{Ui})$ is sent to the CA. Even a privileged-insider of CA cannot guess the PW_{Ui} because $h(PW_{Ui})$ is calculated using a secure one-way hash function.

Many Logged-In Users with the Same Pseudo-Certificate. Since a pseudo-certificate is usable only once, it is not possible two users to login using the same pseudo-certificate.

Brute Force Attack. The attacker can attempt to authenticate by sending random or sequential messages to *IPS Server*. However, as well as explained in the replay attack, this attack becomes infeasible because each pseudo-certificate is usable once.

Anonymous Authentication. The proposed protocol makes use of a random pseudo-certificates to authenticate to the *IPS Server*. Since pseudo-certificates are random and since it was issued by a third party entity (*CA*), the *IPS Server* cannot guess the user being authenticated. This means that the *IPS Server* cannot track the position of the user.

Separation of Responsibilities. *CA* manages only the information of the users/mobile devices while *IPS Server* manages only the information about the relation between a pseudo-certificate and position. Therefore, the entities cannot determinate the position of users by themselves. The historical position of users can be obtained only with the permission of a governmental authority by assembling the information of both entities i.e. *CA* and *IPS Server*, for example, for crime scene investigation.

4.2   Performance Analysis

Table 2 indicates the overhead of cryptographic steps of each protocols. It important to mention that the cryptographic overhead in each protocol is minimal; therefore, it does not affect to the real implementation of the proposed solution.

Table 2. Cryptographic Overhead (i.e. number of operations)

Phase	Entity	Proposed
User registration	MD_{j_Ui}	1 AEnc + 1 SEnc + 1H + 1SDec
	CA	1 ADec + 1 SDec + 1 SEnc
Mobile device registration	MD_{j_Ui}	1 AEnc + 1 SEnc + 1 H
	CA	1 ADec + 1 SDec
Pseudo-certificate issue	MD_{j_Ui}	1 AEnc + 1 SEnc + 1 H
	CA	1 ADec + 1 SDec + Pseudo-certificate and private keys generation
IPS access	MD_{j_Ui}	1 ADec + 1 SDec + 1 VerifySign
	IPS Server	1 AEnc + 1 SEnc + 1 Sign

AEnc: Asymmetric encryption, *ADec*: Asymetric decryption, *H*: hash, *SEnc*: Symmetric encryption, *SDec*: Symmetric decryption, *Sign*: Creation of digital signature, *VerifySign*: Verification of digital signature

5 Conclusions and Future Direction

This paper has proposed a novel authentication system for Indoor Positioning Systems that delivers privacy to users. The proposed solution allows tracking the position of users when required by the governmental authorities (e.g. police, department of justice) for legal investigation procedures. Separation of responsibilities between CA and IPS Servers allows maintaining the privacy of users even if a malicious user compromises one of them. The proposed solution provides a secure authentication system for IPS while maintaining a minimal performance overhead. In the near future, we will continue our research in adding new features to the proposed authentication system such as pseudo-certificate revocation and mobile device revocation protocols.

References

1. Deng, Z., Yu, Y., Yuan, X., Wan, N., Yang, L.: Situation and development tendency of indoor positioning. China Commun. **10**(3), 42–55 (2013)
2. Mainetti, L., Patrono, L., Sergi, I.: A survey on indoor positioning systems. In: 2014 22nd International Conference on Software, Telecommunications and Computer Networks (SoftCOM), pp. 111–120 (2014)
3. Yang, C., Shao, H.: WiFi-based indoor positioning. IEEE Commun. Magaz. **53**(3), 150–157 (2015)
4. Cypriani, M., Lassabe, F., Canalda, P., Spies, F.: Open wireless positioning system: a Wi-Fi-based indoor positioning system. In: IEEE Vehicular Technology Conference, pp. 1–5 (2009)
5. Shokouhifard, M.: User privacy risks and protection in WLAN-based indoor positioning. Master of Science thesis, Tampere University of Technology, Tampere, Finland (2016)
6. Bahl, P., Padmanabhan, V.N.: RADAR: an in-building RF-based user location and tracking system. INFOCOM **2**, 775–784 (2000)
7. Lassabe, F.: Geolocalisation et prediction dans les reseaux Wi-Fi en iterieur. Ph.D. dissertation. Ecole doctorale SPIM (2009)
8. Lassabe, F., Baala, O., Canalda, P., Chatonnay, P., Spies, F.: A friis-based calibrated model for wifi terminals positioning. In: Proceedings of IEEE International Symposium on a World of Wireless, Mobile and Multimedia Networks, pp. 382–387 (2005)
9. Gruteser, M., Liu, X.: Protecting privacy in continuous location tracking applications. IEEE Secur. Priv. Magaz. **2**(2), 28–34 (2004)
10. Konstantinidis, A., Chatzimilioudis, G., Zeinalipour-Yazti, D., Mpeis, P., Pelekis, N., Theodoridis, Y.: Privacy-preserving indoor localization on smartphones. IEEE Trans. Knowl. Data Eng. **27**(11), 3042–3055 (2015)
11. Takeda, K.: User identification and tracking with online device fingerprints fusion. In: Proceedings - International Carnahan Conference on Security Technology, pp. 163–167 (2012)
12. Kjærgaard, M.B., Krarup, M.V., Stisen, A., Prentow, T., Blunck, H., Gronbaek, K., Jensen, C.S.: Indoor positioning using wi-fi: how well is the problem understood? In: International Conference on Indoor Positioning and Indoor Navigation (2013)

13. Al-Ammar, M., Alhadhrami, S., Al-Salman, A., Alarifi, A.: Comparative survey of indoor positioning technologies, techniques, and algorithms. In: Proceedings of the 2014 International Conference on Cyberworlds (CW), pp. 1–8 (2014)
14. Alarifi, A., Al-Salman, A., Alsaleh, M., Alnafessah, A., Al-Hadhrami, S., Al-Ammar, M., Al-Khalifa, H.: Ultra wideband indoor positioning technologies: analysis and recent advances. Sensors **16**, 707 (2016)
15. Sun, Y., Lu, R., Lin, X., Shen, X., Su, J.: An efficient pseudonymous authentication scheme with strong privacy preservation for vehicular communications. IEEE Trans. Veh. Technol. **59**(7), 3589–3603 (2010)
16. Alvez, A., Felton, D.: TrustZone: integrated hardware and software security. enabling trusted computing in embedded systems. ARM, White Paper (2004)
17. Freescale Semiconductors. Security features in the i.MX31 and i.MX31L multimedia application processors. Freescale Semiconductors, White Paper (2005)
18. Dolev, D., Yao, A.: On the security of public key protocols. IEEE Trans. Inf. Theory **29**(2), 198–208 (1983)

On the Effectiveness of Non-readable Executable Memory Against BROP

Christian Otterstad[✉]

Department of Informatics, University of Bergen, Bergen, Norway
christian.otterstad@uib.no

Abstract. With the advent of the low-level exploitation mitigation techniques W⊕X, ASLR, and stack canaries, the attacker has in most cases been forced to use ROP (Return-Oriented Programming) to enable successful arbitrary code execution. Strong, fine-grained ASLR has further raised the bar, requiring the attacker to possess an information leak or primitive to read memory. As a further mitigation technique to this attack scenario, XnR (Execute-no-Read) and similar protections have been suggested, which prevent an attacker from reading executable memory. This paper shows that BROP (Blind Return Oriented Programming) can in certain cases be used to exploit mitigation techniques similar to XnR on Linux x86-64. We examine some important aspects of BROP and its First Principles counterpart in the context of defeating XnR, and present and discuss extensions and complications. An exploit implementation is also presented and discussed, showing that XnR by itself—without sufficiently strong ASLR—offers no protection against BROP-type reading of memory.

Keywords: XnR · Low-level · Exploitation · Stack overflow · BROP

1 Introduction

Traditionally on x86, an attacker could inject and execute machine code on the stack and heap. W⊕X enabled the defender to flag pages as writable but not executable, hence stopping such attacks. However, with this scheme, the attacker is still able to execute arbitrary code, namely by code reuse. This technique was first established with the ret2libc (Return-to-libc) attack and was later generalized in a Turing complete form called ROP (Return-oriented Programming) utilizing short return-terminated snippets of machine code—gadgets. ASLR (Address Space Layout Randomization) makes the address of certain code segments unknown at runtime, thus preventing the attacker from reusing known code snippets. Academia has seen a number of ASLR techniques with different granularity and entropy [3,5,6,10,13]. However, the JIT-ROP paper [11] has shown that in some cases, when the attacker has an iterable read primitive, even arbitrarily strong ASLR can be defeated by reading the memory in situ.

XnR (Execute-no-Read) introduces the notion of executable but non-readable memory. This can be seen as a similar type of mitigation as the NX-bit

© Springer Nature Singapore Pte Ltd. 2017
L. Batten et al. (Eds.): ATIS 2017, CCIS 719, pp. 214–221, 2017.
DOI: 10.1007/978-981-10-5421-1_18

to prevent an executable and readable stack or heap. Effectively, it grows the attribute set which can be used by the kernel to define and enforce memory constraints. XnR prevents the attacker from obtaining a reliable read primitive causing techniques such as JIT-ROP to fail. There are also similar mitigation efforts, e.g. [4,12,14]. In this paper such systems will for simplicity collectively be referred to as XnR or XnR-like techniques.

The rest of the paper is structured as follows. Section 2 presents earlier relevant work and outlines the contributions of this paper. Section 3 presents and discusses an exploit capable of bypassing XnR in a particular environment based on the first principles technique. This section also considers complications and alternative ways to optimize the XnR exploit. Section 4 discusses the overall effectiveness of XnR. Finally, a conclusion is given in Sect. 5.

2   Earlier Work and New Contributions

The most relevant paper about indirectly reading memory, which this paper builds directly upon, is "Hacking blind" [2], where the BROP (Blind Return Oriented Programming) technique is presented. BROP relies on blind and guided execution of remote memory. However, the final step in the BROP variant of the attack relies on reading memory directly, which is specifically prevented by XnR [1]. The authors of the paper [2] also present the "first principles" technique which does not rely on direct reading, but with no implementation provided. Hacking Blind briefly discusses how exploitation may be optimized if the attacker has a copy of the target binary, but have only provided an example for a specific case, not generic spatial information obtained whilst probing. Another related technique is JIT-ROP, which enables defeating arbitrarily strong ASLR given a read primitive in a scripting environment [11].

BROP has been examined previously by Keener Lawrence [8] who found that not all programs contain the required gadgets. Furthermore, the thesis states that the first principles technique is not a reliable method to fall back on when BROP based attacks fail. Other research has found weaknesses in XnR in scripting environments and with gadget injection through a JIT compiler [9,14]. A completely different exploitation approach may also be taken in some cases, namely that of a data-oriented exploit [7].

This paper evaluates the feasibility of attacking XnR and similar mitigation techniques under special circumstances—a forking server with no scripting environment. In particular, it examines if the BROP and the "first principles" techniques [2] can be applied to attack XnR, and what extensions are useful. Furthermore, an extension to the first principles technique, relying on a priori information available when not attacking blindly, is presented and discussed in the context of defeating XnR. In particular, the notion of using a multi-threaded attack and exploiting spatial information gleaned from a copy of the target binary is discussed. Finally, to the knowledge of the author, the first principles technique has been implemented in C for the first time with some extensions. Although first principles was suggested in [2], the actual implementation is not straightforward as some of the gadget detection techniques required different approaches, care must also be taken to avoid false positives, as described later in this paper. The BROP technique previously implemented in Braille [2] has also been reimplemented in C and can be used as an attack method in the same exploit.

3   Exploitation Overview

This section discusses some important aspects related to detecting gadgets and avoiding false positives. It also outlines how the performance of gadget detection can be improved.

3.1   Exploitation Technique

Exploitation is achieved by finding gadgets to control `rax`, `rdi`, `rsi`, `rdx`, and `syscall`. This is due to the calling convention of x86-64 on Linux. Pop gadgets are not the only way to achieve such control, but it is the most straightforward.

There already exist [2] basic primitives to find the BROP gadget, the PLT, `pop` gadgets, `syscall` gadgets, and generic gadgets. However, pop gadget detection is not clearly described in [2] and differentiation of pop gadgets was also found during this research to be incorrectly described in the same paper.

A generic gadget is a gadget that executes some unknown code and returns safely, which is identifiable behavior. Useful gadgets such as `inc rdx` may be possible to locate by chaining together generic gadgets and then an identifying gadget. Since a true generic gadget is safe to execute, multiple such gadgets may be concatenated without the remote process crashing. Assume the attacker already has the ability to control `rax`, `rdi`, and `rsi` but cannot find a `pop rdx` gadget. If it is possible to set `rdx` to a non-zero value, the attacker has some control over it and can start attempts to read non-executable memory pages directly to confirm the behavior of the candidate gadget affecting `rdx`. Blind execution of generic gadgets may be combined with efforts to map regions of memory with known local memory, depending on the granularity of the ASLR in place.

The BROP gadget is useful in the original BROP attack, which involves reading the remote binary directly. It is useful since it offers control over both `rdi` and `rsi` with a single gadget. Nevertheless, after finding the BROP gadget it would still be necessary to scan for and identify all stack popping gadgets when using first principles, hence limiting its usefulness. However, it would be useful if `rdi` and `rsi` cannot be controlled with normal stack popping gadgets.

Care must be exerted when attempting to probe for popping gadgets as false positives can occur. This can happen for multiple reasons, e.g. probing at an offset into the procedure prologue of a function which skips a push opcode making the epilogue perform an additional pop on the stack, thus acting like a single pop gadget. Furthermore, a probed gadget that also is a stop gadget will result in a false positive, as may a leave and instructions manipulating rsp.

To correctly detect pop gadgets, the following probes should be used:

- probe $\Longrightarrow$ crash $\Longrightarrow$ stop $\Longrightarrow$ crash $\Longrightarrow$ crash
- probe+1 $\Longrightarrow$ stop $\Longrightarrow$ crash $\Longrightarrow$ crash
- probe $\Longrightarrow$ crash $\Longrightarrow$ crash $\Longrightarrow$ crash

To actually identify gadgets in first principles, Hacking Blind [2] suggests setting all identified pop gadgets to pause and check if the probe hangs. This procedure works. The exploit records known hang addresses while scanning for pop gadgets. These addresses can then be skipped when scanning for syscall. False positives can be identified by testing the functionality of the syscall gadget. If it does hang, then it should not hang on other syscall arguments.

To find rdi, Hacking Blind suggests using the nanosleep system call, stating it takes arguments of the form nanosleep(len,rem), where len is the nanoseconds to sleep. The argument is actually a pointer to a struct timespec, but it requires being filled with a set of specific values (at least on Linux 4.4.6), limiting its use. Such a structure in memory with these particular values is unknown at this point for the attacker. The attacker could possibly use the leaked stack frame pointer to determine where the stack is and use values written to the stack as a timespec structure. However, an alternative not mentioned in Hacking Blind is to use close and simply guess, or brute force the FD (File Descriptor). When the source target is available, the attacker can also in some cases simply determine the FD a priori.

To find rsi, Hacking Blind suggests using kill. However, kill(pid, sig) with pid = 0 and sig set to a terminating signal such as SIGTERM or SIGKILL will kill the whole group, including the parent. This causes the whole server to terminate and therefore stops the attack. A possible solution is to call setsid() first to create a new group, s.t. the parent process is not killed as well. It does not seem the setsid() call can be ignored. Even with a server that gets restarted by some other process, e.g. inetd or equivalent would have its entropy reissued by the system. Therefore, it cannot be relied on even with a server of this nature.

To find rdx, Hacking Blind suggests using clock_nanosleep. However, clock_nanosleep has the same issue as regular nanosleep. In the exploit it was decided to use write instead.

3.2   Performance

We shall now examine additional ways to improve the performance of the exploit. There are basically two ways the overall performance can be improved: By reducing the number of probes, and by improving the rate at which probes are evaluated. In general, the execution rate of the exploit is bounded by the attacker's timing, the defender's total CPU performance, defender side RAM (if applicable), the network connection, and the number of workers (if applicable) available to the defender.

The new exploit is able to take advantage of a priori spatial knowledge in the general case whenever the ASLR implementation allows for it. The exploit is supplied with an argument of a binary copy of the target program being attacked and uses it to locate spatially adjacent gadgets within the assumed size of the minimum basic block the target ASLR implementation works with. If assuming a unique gadget A is found remotely, e.g. a `pop rax` gadget residing at address x, and the local offset from gadget A to gadget B, has a difference less than the minimum basic block size, then the attacker will immediately know a possible remote address of gadget B as well, based on its location in the copy of the binary. This reduces the entropy of the remote machine memory. The ability of an exploit to variably adjust its minimum basic block size based on probes— whilst still able to fall back on first principles probes—is as far as the author is aware not previously published. The basic algorithm for such spatial inference is given in Algorithm 1.

Algorithm 1. Find gadgets by spatial inference

1: **procedure** FINDSPATIALGADGETS
2:     **for all gadgets** G **not spatially examined in** the list of gadgets **do**
3:         **for all adjacent gadgets in local memory** G_l **to** G **do**
4:             $\alpha \leftarrow$ remote address of G
5:             $\delta \leftarrow$ local offset to G_l from G
6:             **if** $\delta <$ minimum basic block size **then**
7:                 $G_r \leftarrow G + \delta$
8:                 **if** there exists a remote gadget of type G_l at G_r **then**
9:                     *Add G_r to the list of gadgets*
10:                    *Adjust the minimum basic block size*
       return

1: **procedure** FINDGADGETSCAN
2:     **for all remote memory offsets** i **do**
3:         *probe i*
4:         **if** a gadget G is found **then**
5:             *add G to the list of gadgets*
6:             FINDSPATIALGADGETS
7:             **if** all gadgets required have been found **then**
8:                 **return**

The Hacking Blind paper [2] already points out multiple ways to improve performance. However, it is also possible to do a binary search to eliminate popping gadgets. When searching for `pop` gadgets, at least one byte can be skipped once it has been found. The next instruction cannot be another true `pop` gadget.

Hacking Blind appears to get at most around 33 probes per second when attacking a remote host [2]. Based on testing, it is possible to get at least 77 probes per second against a local server with Braille, on average for a full exploit. However, multithreading as used in the new exploit can dramatically improve this figure in some cases when compared to the new exploit developed.

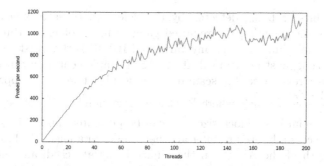

Fig. 1. Performance improvement as a result of multithreaded scanning on a system under load, scanning the non-executable region 0×0 to 0×10000 against the toy server on an Intel Core i7-3720QM, full load on all cores. Average of 8 runs per observation.

The performance gain becomes even more apparent as the system is put under load, as shown in Fig. 1. If there is no load on the server (which happens earlier in the exploit process), the same type of gain can be achieved with much fewer threads, but as the load increases more threads are required to compete with stray children spawned based on previous probes.

4   Effectiveness of XnR

XnR by itself offers no protection against BROP. The ASLR strength is critical for making XnR effective and directly dictates the required time budget of the attacker. Different defender systems may allow for a varying attack window due to different IDSes (Intrusion Detection System) and different levels of supervision. These factors make it hard to quantify the overall effectiveness of an attack, especially when the ASLR strength may be variable. Hacking Blind assumes eight hours in their longest example [2], however it is fair to assume some systems can be attacked for even longer.

High entropy but very coarse granularity ASLR—at a granularity similar to standard Linux ASLR where only an offset is moved—coupled with XnR has no effect against BROP due to Offset2lib type attacks. This is true even if the code itself is highly permuted and rewritten as the attacker is given a base address to scan. Furthermore, arbitrarily fine coarse granularity ASLR and high entropy ASLR that does not move any permuted code region away from the base offset also has no effectiveness against BROP. In both of these cases the base address can be obtained from the `rip`, just as in Offset2lib. It can then be scanned, and since all the code is found in the same region, the scanning process would be fast, on the order of what was pointed out in Sect. 3.2. However, strong ASLR that uses a large address space *and* places code blocks throughout the whole address space would be effective as it would require a larger address space to be scanned.

The running time of the attack is $\mathcal{O}(a)$, where a is the total number of possible addresses. If the attacker is unable to scan all the addresses due to time constraints or being detected by the defender, the attack *may* fail. As previously pointed out [8], the required gadgets may not exist. But assuming they do, the main limitation of any variant of BROP is the worst case number of addresses that must be scanned. If the ASLR implementation can place code at an n bit address space, the scanning time would at worst be approximately $\dfrac{2^n - ((B-1) \cdot G)}{P}$ seconds, where P is the average number of probes per second, B is the minimum basic block size that can be permuted, and G is the number of gadgets successfully used to infer another gadget in a basic block. Depending on the strength of the ASLR, on the binary being attacked, and on the time budget, it can then be decided if extended first principles is a feasible mode of attack in that particular case.

5   Conclusion

The first working implementation for an extended first principles attack, initially described in Hacking Blind [2], was presented. The improved exploit was then used to attack XnR and the result was analyzed. The first principles attack has been extended using the spatial locality of detected gadgets to reduce the number of required probes, as well as enhanced in terms of throughput with multithreading to demonstrate significant gains in scanning performance.

It has been shown that XnR by itself has no effect against BROP-like techniques, even when coupled with certain high entropy ASLR systems with an insufficient address space range. It was also argued that BROP-attacks are impractical when XnR is coupled with sufficiently strong ASLR/ASLP. However, given the performance cost of various strong ASLR implementations, it also seems fair to assume that not all targets will employ the strongest ASLR available. To that effect, an attacker facing ASLR of intermediate or weaker strength may find practical use of the extended first principles technique for indirect reading of memory.

References

1. Backes, M., Holz, T., Kollenda, B., Koppe, P., Nürnberger, S., Pewny, J.: You can run but you can't read: preventing disclosure exploits in executable code. In: Proceedings of the 2014 ACM SIGSAC Conference on Computer and Communications Security (CCS 2014), pp. 1342–1353, NY, USA (2014). http://doi.acm.org/10.1145/2660267.2660378
2. Bittau, A., Belay, A., Mashtizadeh, A., Maziéres, D., Boneh, D.: Hacking blind. In: Proceedings of the 2014 IEEE Symposium on Security and Privacy (SP 2014), pp. 227–242 (2014). http://dx.doi.org/10.1109/SP.2014.22
3. Conti, M., Crane, S., Frassetto, T., Homescu, A., Koppen, G., Larsen, P., Liebchen, C., Perry, M., Sadeghi, A.R.: Selfrando: securing the tor browser against de-anonymization exploits. In: The Annual Privacy Enhancing Technologies Symposium (PETS), July 2016

4. Crane, S., Liebchen, C., Homescu, A., Davi, L., Larsen, P., Sadeghi, A.R., Brunthaler, S., Franz, M.: Readactor: practical code randomization resilient to memory disclosure. In: 36th IEEE Symposium on Security and Privacy (Oakland), May 2015
5. Davi, L.V., Dmitrienko, A., Nürnberger, S., Sadeghi, A.R.: Gadge me if you can: secure and efficient ad-hoc instruction-level randomization for x86 and arm. In: Proceedings of the 8th ACM SIGSAC Symposium on Information, Computer and Communications Security (ASIA CCS 2013), pp. 299–310, NY, USA (2013). http://doi.acm.org/10.1145/2484313.2484351
6. Hiser, J., Nguyen-Tuong, A., Co, M., Hall, M., Davidson, J.: ILR: where'd my gadgets go? In: 2012 IEEE Symposium on Security and Privacy (SP), pp. 571–585, May 2012
7. Hu, H., Chua, Z.L., Adrian, S., Saxena, P., Liang, Z.: Automatic generation of data-oriented exploits. In: Proceedings of the 24th USENIX Conference on Security Symposium (SEC 2015), pp. 177–192. USENIX Association, Berkeley, CA, USA (2015). http://dl.acm.org/citation.cfm?id=2831143.2831155
8. Keener, L.: Evaluating the generality and limits of blind return-oriented programming attacks. Ph.D. thesis, Naval Postgraduate School, Monterey, California (2015). http://calhoun.nps.edu/handle/10945/47979
9. Maisuradze, G., Backes, M., Rossow, C.: What cannot be read, cannot be leveraged? revisiting assumptions of JIT-ROP defenses. In: 25th USENIX Security Symposium (USENIX Security 2016), pp. 139–156. USENIX Association, Austin, TX (2016). https://www.usenix.org/conference/usenixsecurity16/technical-sessions/presentation/maisuradze
10. Marco, H., Ripoll, I.: ASLR-NG: ASLR Next Generation. http://cybersecurity.upv.es/solutions/aslr-ng/aslr-ng.html. Accessed 06 July 2016
11. Snow, K.Z., Monrose, F., Davi, L., Dmitrienko, A., Liebchen, C., Sadeghi, A.R.: Just-in-time code reuse: on the effectiveness of fine-grained address space layout randomization. In: Proceedings of the 2013 IEEE Symposium on Security and Privacy (SP 2013), pp. 574–588 (2013). http://dx.doi.org/10.1109/SP.2013.45
12. Tang, A., Sethumadhavan, S., Stolfo, S.: Heisenbyte: thwarting memory disclosure attacks using destructive code reads. In: Proceedings of the 22nd ACM SIGSAC Conference on Computer and Communications Security (CCS 2015), pp. 256–267, NY, USA (2015). http://doi.acm.org/10.1145/2810103.2813685
13. Wartell, R., Mohan, V., Hamlen, K.W., Lin, Z.: Binary stirring: self-randomizing instruction addresses of legacy x86 binary code. In: Proceedings of the 2012 ACM Conference on Computer and Communications Security (CCS 2012), pp. 157–168, NY, USA (2012). http://doi.acm.org/10.1145/2382196.2382216
14. Werner, J., Baltas, G., Dallara, R., Otterness, N., Snow, K.Z., Monrose, F., Polychronakis, M.: No-execute-after-read: preventing code disclosure in commodity software. In: Proceedings of the 11th ACM on Asia Conference on Computer and Communications Security (ASIA CCS 2016), pp. 35–46, NY, USA (2016). http://doi.acm.org/10.1145/2897845.2897891

Author Index

Printed in the United States
By Bookmasters